This book is an incredible tool that, through a sound scriptural base, teaches God's heart for His people in sowing, giving and stewardship. This is a must-read if you want to know what God's Word has to say about prosperity and how to be freed from misconceptions that are holding you back from reaching your full potential.

Jerry Anderson
President, La Red Business Network International

Throughout the years, Ché has stepped out in faith to expand the Kingdom in his own heart and to those around the world. In *The Grace of Giving*, he shares some of these personal stories and the breakthroughs that have happened as a result. This book will equip you to break free from a poverty spirit to live the abundant life Jesus died for you to have. As God is our Great Provider, Ché demonstrates that a prosperous soul has much more to do with our perspective of God than it does with money. May *The Grace of Giving* inspire new levels of generosity and deepen your understanding of God's great love for you.

Heidi Baker
Founding Director, Iris Global

The Grace of Giving will help everyone who struggles with and wants to enjoy the benefits of giving. Wherever Pastor Ché ministers, the entire atmosphere shifts toward prosperity, and people begin to believe and act out of a prosperous spirit. As members of the apostolic team of H.I.M., we have been direct recipients of this grace of giving, and we have watched this blessing multiply in the lives of countless others. If you want to learn to give in biblical proportions and reap the results, this book is for you.

Wesley and Stacey Campbell
Senior Pastors, New Life Church, Kelowna, British Columbia (www.newlife.bc.ca)
Founders, Be a Hero (www.beahero.org)

The Grace of Giving, is a seminal work and a life-long learning manual on discovering how to live in the Father's love, share the Father's heart, and go on a giving journey with Him that will transform your life and everyone with whom you come into contact. Digest every word and take time to work through every area where the culture of the twenty-first century may have robbed you of living in the culture of the Father's house. Thank you, Pastor Ché, for being the voice you are to the Body of Christ and for teachin᠁ s about how amazingly good the Father is to us!

Mark Chironna
Founder, Church On The Living Edge and Ma᠁
Presiding Bishop, The Legacy Alliance, Orlando

The Grace of Giving is an anointed work on the subject of prosperity. This book should be required reading for every young person entering adulthood. I have spent much of my life trying to reconcile my calling into the marketplace with my desire to serve the Lord, and this book brought incredible insight to God's blueprints for how to do exactly that.

Sam Caster
Founder, Mannatech and MannaRelief Ministries

The Grace of Giving is the best book I have ever read on the subject of giving. Ché Ahn deals with the truth of God's promises about giving (especially sowing and reaping) while at the same time avoiding the mechanical approach of the prosperity gospel. Ché's own example of giving is powerful and his discussion of graduated giving was exemplary. This is the best book to read on this subject.

Randy Clark
Founder, Global Awakening, Mechanicsburg, Pennsylvania

Giving is a command from God because it is a powerful force that will free Him to release His unlimited resources of power, favor, finance and blessing in the lives of His givers. *The Grace of Giving* is timely, and its revelation will empower the Church of Jesus Christ to rise up as a mighty army anointed by the Spirit of the Lord to bring good news to the poor, overthrow the power of poverty, and advance the kingdom of God on earth as the blueprint of heaven.

Pat Francis
Founder, Pat Francis Ministries

This is a greatly needed book for the Body of Christ on the grace of giving. The teachings contained herein are not theories—they are eternal truths that work! I have watched as Ché Ahn lives this message in his own life and ministry. I perceive this is his most strategic work and is needed at such a pivotal time as this. May this grace gift flourish and cause a fresh people movement to occur of hilarious, effective and gracious Kingdom economics for Jesus Christ's sake.

James W. Goll
Founder, Encounters Network, Prayer Storm, GET E-School
Bestselling Author, *The Seer* and many others

As you read this book, you will gain knowledge that will enable you to prosper beyond your wildest imagination! Its truths concerning the principles of giving and receiving will enable you to obtain the prosperity that God desires for you. Ché Ahn gives a balanced and positive presentation of God's divine plan for prosperity. Every Christian needs to read this book, especially those who want to prosper, be able to bless others, and advance God's kingdom on earth.

Bill Hamon
Bishop, Christian International Ministries Network (CIMN), Christian International Apostolic Network (CIAN), and Christian International Global Network (CIGN)
Author, *The Day of the Saints, The Third and Final Church Reformation,* and others

Pastor Ché has written a powerful book that challenges a Christian's understanding of prosperity. This book is a must-read for anyone desiring to operate under God's grace to give. Pastor Ché has received a unique revelation of living on a higher level of Christlike giving.

Garland R. Hunt, Sr.
President, Prison Fellowship

The Grace of Giving is one of the must-read books for today. It is compassionate, compelling and challenging. Ché Ahn lives the message of this book. Read it! It will change your life forever!

Cindy Jacobs
Founder, Generals International

The Grace of Giving is one of the most balanced, faith-building and truth-filled books I have read on the doctrine of biblical prosperity. Ché Ahn shares with openness and vulnerability some of his own personal struggles and his journey to revealed truth on this subject. I am convinced that those who read this book will be empowered with hope and faith and will step into the realms of abundance offered by their loving heavenly Father. It is my personal desire to see *every* Christian read this book—it is that good!

Patricia King
Founder, XPministries and XPmedia.com Inc.

In *The Grace of Giving*, Ché Ahn helps us understand the true meaning of prosperity. He first lays a foundation, characterizing God as a loving father and a generous giver. Then, through biblical and historical references and stories from his own life, he shows us that God's definition of prosperity doesn't lie in personal wealth or money but in pursuing our Father's heart. If you catch Ché's timely message, it will change your life.

Robert Morris
Senior Pastor, Gateway Church
Bestselling author, *The Blessed Life, From Dream to Destiny* and *The God I Never Knew*

In *The Grace of Giving*, Ché Ahn has given us a powerful weapon to destroy the strongholds of warped philosophies that infiltrate our minds regarding the stewardship of the finances entrusted to our care. In this wonderful book, we hear echoes of the apostle Paul's advice to his protégé, Timothy: "Charge them that are rich in this world, that they be not high-minded, nor trust in uncertain riches, but in the living God, who giveth us richly all things to enjoy" (1 Tim. 6:17, *KJV*). I pray this book will prove to be a valuable GPS (God-Positioning-System) to align you with God's kingdom purposes for the stewardship of the funds He places in your care.

Peter Roselle
Tentmaker, Certified Financial Planner
Founder, King of Kings Worship Center, Basking Ridge, New Jersey

Ché Ahn is the most qualified man I know to write on the grace of giving! The love-foundation of giving is clearly unveiled in this personal and encouraging treatise. Wait until you read what Ché unveils about the Father's love as the basis of giving! This book will impact your life. Buy it for your church leadership team, for your friends and for yourself! A new grace is about to come upon your life to taste the miracles of the loving, giving heart of God. Enjoy!

Brian Simmons
The Apostolic Resource Center, New England
Translator, *The Passion* Translation Project

It's been a privilege to spend time with Ché and Sue Ahn for more than 15 years, and during that time my life has been transformed by the simple obedience and massive faith that I see in the way they live. Ché is one of the most generous men I've ever known! In almost 40 years of ministry, I've read many books on giving and finances, but this book may be the best I've ever read! *The Grace of Giving* presents a comprehensive theology for generosity. Beyond that, Ché shares his own story and his heart after God in an absolutely contagious manner. Read this book from cover to cover, and you will never be the same!

Charles Stock
Senior Pastor, Life Center Ministries, Harrisburg, Pennsylvania

The Grace of Giving is a radical departure from the culture of greed that is so prevalent in our society. In this powerful book, Ché Ahn takes us on a journey straight to the heart of our generous Father, unearths the lie of our orphan identity, and reveals the foundational truth of our position as heirs of the King. This book is a must-read for every Christian who longs to be transformed into the image of Christ in order to change the world. I highly recommend it!

Kris Vallotton
Senior Associate Leader, Bethel Church, Redding, California
Co-founder, Bethel School of Supernatural Ministry
Author, *The Supernatural Ways of Royalty, Spirit Wars,* and many more

A generation ago, we saw waves of serious criticism against the "prosperity gospel." However, *The Grace of Giving* is a different kind of book on prosperity for this new generation and for generations to come. Ché Ahn is able to explain prosperity as God's will for His people in such a clear and gentle way that I can assure you it will not provoke a fresh wave of criticism. It will help lift the whole Body of Christ to a new and more fruitful level!

C. Peter Wagner
Vice-President, Global Spheres, Inc.

The GRACE *of* GIVING

Unleashing the Power of a Generous Heart

CHÉ AHN

Chosen

a division of Baker Publishing Group
Minneapolis, Minnesota

© 2013 by Ché Ahn

Published by Chosen Books
11400 Hampshire Avenue South
Bloomington, Minnesota 55438
www.chosenbooks.com

Chosen Books is a division of
Baker Publishing Group, Grand Rapids, Michigan

Chosen Books edition published 2014
ISBN 978-0-8007-9629-7

Previously published by Regal Books

Printed in the United States of America

The Library of Congress has cataloged the original edition as follows:
Ahn, Ché, 1956-
    The grace of giving : unleashing the power of a generous heart / Ché Ahn.
        p. cm.
    ISBN 978-0-8307-6549-2 (trade paper : alk. paper)
    1. Generosity—Religious aspects—Christianity. 2. Wealth—Religious aspects—
Christianity. 3. Christian life. I. Title.
    BV4647.G45A56 2013
    241'.4—dc23   2012043439

Unless otherwise indicated, Scripture quotations are from the Holy Bible, New International Version®. NIV®. Copyright © 1973, 1978, 1984 by Biblica, Inc.™ Used by permission of Zondervan. All rights reserved worldwide. www.zondervan.com

Scripture quotations labeled AMP are from the Amplified® Bible, copyright © 1954, 1958, 1962, 1964, 1965, 1987 by The Lockman Foundation. Used by permission.

Scripture quotations labeled KJV are from the King James Version of the Bible.

Scripture quotations labeled THE MESSAGE are from The Message by Eugene H. Peterson, copyright © 1993, 1994, 1995, 2000, 2001, 2002. Used by permission of NavPress Publishing Group. All rights reserved.

Scripture quotations labeled NASB are from the New American Standard Bible®, copyright © 1960, 1962, 1963, 1968, 1971, 1972, 1973, 1975, 1977, 1995 by The Lockman Foundation. Used by permission.

Scripture quotations labeled NKJV are from the New King James Version. Copyright © 1982 by Thomas Nelson, Inc. Used by permission. All rights reserved.

Scripture quotations labeled NLT are from the Holy Bible, New Living Translation, copyright © 1996, 2004, 2007 by Tyndale House Foundation. Used by permission of Tyndale House Publishers, Inc., Carol Stream, Illinois 60188. All rights reserved.

Scripture quotations labeled Weymouth—Also known as The New Testament in Modern Speech or The Modern Speech New Testament, a translation into "modern" English as used in the nineteenth century from the text of The Resultant Greek Testament by Richard Francis Weymouth (1903).

Scripture quotations labeled YLT—The Bible text designated YLT is from Young's Literal Translation by Robert Young, © 1898 by Baker Book House, Grand Rapids, Michigan.

14   15   16   17   18   19   20   7   6   5   4   3   2   1

This book is dedicated to my first two grandchildren: Justice Daniel Baik and Annabelle Joy Ngu. May you both come to know Jesus at a young age and walk with Him all the days of your life. May each of you fulfill God's destiny and purpose in your life. And may God bless you with a Christlike spouse and give you godly children and grandchildren who will bring joy to your life, as you have brought joy to mine.

CONTENTS

Section 5: The Universal Laws of Prosperity

Section 6: Becoming a Christlike Giver

Section 7: The Transforming Power of Grace

ACKNOWLEDGMENTS

I want to thank my family and my church family, HRock Church, and the apostolic network that I lead, Harvest International Ministry, for releasing me to go on my first sabbatical in 2011 to work on a good portion of this book. A special thanks to my best friend and bride (my BB), Sue Ahn, for releasing me again, even though I am on the road most days.

Many thanks to those at Gospel Light and to my good friend Bill Greig III, president and CEO. It is always a joy to work with this outstanding Christian publishing company.

I also want to thank Linda Radford for the demonstration of her Christlike love and service as the primary editor of this book. Linda has been fighting and contending for her healing of a chronic disease and had a good excuse not to work on this book project. Nonetheless, she edited and reorganized my chapters into shorter entries with a practical application at the end of each. Beyond her dedicated service, she is a gifted writer who has collaborated with me on a number of my recent books; and for that, I am deeply grateful. It is an honor to be her pastor.

Finally, I want to thank my Lord and Savior, Jesus Christ, who has demonstrated His love and generosity throughout my walk with Him since day one of my conversion back in 1973. I give Him all the praise and glory for this book.

FOREWORD

Ché Ahn and I have been friends and covenant partners in ministry for many years. It all started in the late '90s when someone joined our hands together and prophesied about a partnership for the healing of the state of California. We both felt that this was a God moment and said yes. Ché lives in Pasadena, representing southern California, and I live in Redding, representing northern California. Historically, our state has been divided between north and south because of water issues that occurred many years ago. We have given ourselves to model God's plan of unity to the best of our ability.

Our friendship has proven to be a strategic Kingdom connection, as we visit each other's churches often and minister together in schools and conferences around the world. But most important for me is that we share times of rest and short vacations together, where I know Ché and Sue Ahn outside of public ministry. Their interests, values and motivations for life quickly come to the surface and, as is the case with each of my closest friends, they are the same in and out of the pulpit.

It's refreshing to see how God is raising up leaders who don't just know how to stir up the people of God with a good sermon—as important as that is—but who also know how to live life well and impart that grace to all who will receive it. Such is the case with the author of this wonderful book, *The Grace of Giving*. Ché Ahn lives life well and has something profoundly important to impart in this challenging hour. He truly has a prosperous soul.

Ché has an unusual anointing with the subject of money. It doesn't matter if it's personal finances, the finances of a ministry, or what is needed for business; he has a grace to impact each of these worlds with true Kingdom insights. Many have a grace for generosity, while others are brilliant with investments, and still others have the God-given gift to generate biblical wealth through entrepreneurial abilities. Ché has the most complete Kingdom approach of anyone I know. That's why I'm so happy to see this book finally get written, as he carries a breakthrough in this realm that must become the possession of every believer.

Money is one of the most difficult subjects to deal with well. While Jesus had no problem bringing up this topic, many leaders today live in reaction to the latest fad or error. We've all had our fill of those who teach that our spirituality is measured by how much money we have or make. As nauseating as that is, reaction to it has created another error that is no less demeaning. But Ché doesn't live in reaction. He lives in response to a biblical mandate and has an unusual ability to hear what God is saying in the moment. As a result, he has tapped into the purpose of prosperity and has released that grace to his whole church family. They model this beautifully. It's time for the rest of us to step into this Kingdom reality.

Whenever God raises up one of His generals with a message, it is because He wants the entire church to benefit from their insight and experience. When it comes to wealth, jealousy and accusation permeate much of the Church, while others seem to have a "lottery" mentality, hoping that lots of money will suddenly appear and everything will be okay. Ché brings us into a healthier lifestyle by challenging the mindsets that do not represent the kingdom of God. He will challenge you and ultimately take you on a journey that could change the rest of your life. Money really is a big deal, and knowing how to have that part of our life completely under God's dominion is refreshing and exhilarating!

I expect to hear extraordinary reports and testimonies from people who will read this book and have their lives changed. This is one of the timeliest books I've seen in years.

Bill Johnson
Pastor, Bethel Church
Author, *When Heaven Invades Earth* and *Hosting the Presence*

KNOW THE MOs

You've probably heard the term "MO," *modus operandi*, applied to a person's behavior patterns, as in, "That's his (or her) usual MO." Well, God also has some characteristic patterns of behavior—some MOs—that let us understand what we can consistently count on in Him. For example, God is unchanging. He is true to His word and He is a covenant maker. He is a lover and consummate giver who takes pleasure in blessing His children.

Why do we sometimes misunderstand the covenant quality of God's promises to us? Because we have all inherited an orphan spirit and are in the process of discovering and learning to live in our privileges as children of our heavenly Father. At times we can sabotage His efforts to bless us by our feelings of unworthiness or our fear of trusting completely in Him.

This first section is the foundation for everything else we will consider about giving and displaying a generous heart like the Father's. It is important that we not only understand, but also truly believe in and trust the characteristics of God—His MO. Otherwise, His promises to us will appear unobtainable, and His instructions impossible to do. At the heart of our difficulty is our distorted sense of identity. We have lost a clear vision of our original design in the image of God. Too frequently, we allow ourselves to be limited by our fallen orphan identities, and we try to perform our way into God's favor.

In our striving and uncertainty, we miss the revelation of God's grace. We forget that His first words to us were a blessing and a commission (see Gen. 1:28-30). He never changes, and His words always produce what He sends them forth to accomplish. That means our Father God has never given up on our original created purpose and destiny. Through the death and resurrection of Christ, and the redemption we now have from sin, God has planted His Holy Spirit within us, the seed of His kingdom. Like any good seed, this Seed contains its own inherent power to increase and grow within us, transforming and conforming us into the image of God.

This is totally a work of God's grace within us. Through faith we believe and trust in our Father God's love, His goodness, His

blessing and intention to completely restore us to our original position of authority, dominion and prosperity. Our Father God is a
giver, and His greatest desire is that we should be just like Him. In
His love He extends an invitation to us to discover the power of a
generous heart that will transform us, and through us, restore His
kingdom on the earth.

I encourage you to take your time in Section 1. We are laying
foundational truths here, and you must be rooted and grounded
in them in order to receive everything your Father God desires to
give you. If these truths are not established in you, you will be like
the man building his house on the sand. No matter how magnif-
icent and well built the house is, there is no foundation to support it, and it will not last. Take time and build a sure foundation
on these truths and watch how God transforms your life!

1

YOUR FATHER GOD LOVES YOU

The LORD appeared to us . . . saying: "I have loved you with an everlasting love, I have drawn you with loving-kindness."

JEREMIAH 31:3

ANGRY REBEL ON A PRECIPICE

The steel cell door rolled open with a metallic clank. Chains rattled as the inmate shuffled along on his way to final judgment. It was the closing scene of *Dead Man Walking*. However, the inmate was not Sean Penn shuffling to the execution room, but me slowly climbing the stairs as I approached my father's study. Each of my feet felt as if it had a 20-pound weight attached, and I was filled with an intensifying sense of dread.

How had it come to this? For years now there had been no love lost between my father and me. In fact, I loathed him and everything I felt he stood for. True, when I was four years old and newly arrived in the United States with my mother and older sister, I had been eager to rejoin my father, whom I had hadn't seen in two-and-a-half years. I remember feeling shy and overwhelmed, as the man who met us bore little resemblance to the framed, two-dimensional image on my mother's dresser in Korea.

Initially, my father tried to be a dad and spend time with us, but he had limited patience and a quick, intense temper. Besides that, his church work occupied most of his time. Although I craved his attention and approval, I learned to stay out of his way.

Unfortunately, things got much worse after I began school. My sister excelled academically, but I couldn't follow in her footsteps, even though I tried.

The real abuse started when I was in third grade and received my first bad report card with letter grades. I could still see my father's white-fisted knuckles as he grabbed my arm and shouted at me, "You stupid, careless boy!" Then, before I could take a breath, he began beating me harshly. What had I done to deserve this reaction? I had brought home a report card with two Cs.

For the next two years, I tried my best at academics, but I disappointed my father with every report card. I learned to take the verbal and physical abuse that went with every report card day, and slowly the eager little boy inside of me shut down and died. By the time I reached fifth grade, I had quit trying and was already experimenting with alcohol and smoking. In junior high I became involved in the drug culture, and by high school I was a drug dealer.

I was popular and had money, nice clothes and a car. Increasingly, I flaunted my rebellion openly with my father. I even turned my older sister on to drugs, and her grades slipped. I actually enjoyed seeing the disappointment this caused my dad. His shining academic star had become a shooting star.

Even now as I thought about this, a bitter smile of triumph spread over my lips. I hesitated at the door of my father's study. It had been nearly three weeks ago that we had another one of our confrontations about my grades. Like so many times before, I had left the house in an angry rage and gone for a drive. However, this time I hadn't come back for three weeks. I knew my father would never report me as missing, because that would not be the Korean way to handle an incident like this.

My father sat at his desk, his face looking drawn and tired. Actually, he looked a good 10 years older than when I had seen him three weeks earlier. I couldn't be sure, but it seemed that the light was glistening off what might be tears in his eyes. Yet his face remained expressionless. If I had hoped to hear something about missing me or being concerned, I would have been disappointed. His first words were, "Why did you come back?"

I stared at the floor, put on my most contrite look and mumbled, "Gee, Dad, I was really hoping that things could get better somehow." The real truth was I had run out of options and no longer had a place to stay.

After what seemed like an eternity, my father slowly straightened in his chair. Looking directly at me, he said, "I'm going to say okay on one condition. You must never bring drugs into this house again, and you have to stop using drugs." I agreed, knowing I was lying through my teeth. That was the end of our discussion. The incident was never brought up again.

I thought I had reestablished the status quo, but little did I know that I was on the edge of a precipice and would soon have the most dramatic encounter of my life: a confrontation with the love of Father God.

IMAGE DISTORTIONS: ORPHAN WOUNDS

When you hear the word "father," what comes to mind? For too many people, their image of "father" is a negative one. Perhaps you had a father who was absent because of divorce or death or a demanding career like the military. You may have had a father who was present but emotionally distant. Perhaps your father was controlling, or he was a demanding authoritarian. Maybe he was even emotionally, physically or sexually abusive. All of these types of early encounters will lead to distortions in a person's image of "father."

Unfortunately, negative experiences like these etch deep scars on the heart. God originally created us to be transparent and totally trusting. He made us this way so that we could love deeply and without reservation. But once we are hurt and wounded, our trust is broken, and we become fearful, insecure, cautious, performance oriented and often angry and rebellious. We feel as if our survival depends on us, and we are willing to do whatever it takes to look out for ourselves. In effect, we lose our identity as God's children, and we become orphans—alienated and alone.

Instead of building on a positive foundation, we build our identities on this faulty orphan foundation, and it becomes the base from which we learn what is possible and from which we develop our relationships with others. Even if love is offered to us, we often find it difficult to receive or trust it. If we are ever to recover from this distortion of our true identity, we must have an accurate image of God as "Father" restored to us.

How can this take place? I think Stephen K. De Silva states the answer very succinctly in his book *Money and the Prosperous Soul*: "It was a breach of trust that brought sin, and all that is come of it, into the world. Thus, the heart of God's plan for healing the world of sin is not only to forgive us, but also to restore our trust—and, through restoring our trust, to restore all that we are."[1]

ROOTED AND GROUNDED IN LOVE

Not getting the love we needed wounded our hearts, and only by getting the love we need can we mend them again. How can God restore our trust? We must have a personal encounter with a revelation of Father God's love. Heart wounds sink deep roots in our soul and ground us in a distorted image of ourselves. We can be set free only by being rooted and grounded in Father God's love and rediscovering who we truly are.

The apostle Paul reflects this in his letter to the church at Ephesus: "For this reason I bow my knees to the Father of our Lord Jesus Christ, from whom the whole family in heaven and earth is named, that He would grant you, according to the riches of His glory, to be strengthened with might through His Spirit in the inner man, that Christ may dwell in your hearts through faith; that you [may be] rooted and grounded in love" (Eph. 3:14-17, *NKJV*).

Among the world's religions, Christianity reveals a unique understanding of the relationship of God to us as a father. While the Koran mentions 99 different attributes of God, not one of them is "father." However, God is addressed as "Father" 264 times in the Bible's New Testament, and Jesus constantly referred to God as "My Father." Paul confirms this relationship: "For you did not receive a spirit that makes you a slave again to fear, but you received the Spirit of sonship. And by him we cry, 'Abba, Father.' The Spirit himself testifies with our spirit that we are God's children. Now if we are children, then we are heirs—heirs of God and co-heirs with Christ" (Rom. 8:15-17).

God makes it very clear that He is not only a Father but also a *loving* Father. Consider these verses:

> Yet my unfailing love for you will not be shaken nor my covenant of peace be removed," says the LORD, who has compassion on you (Isa. 54:10).

> But God demonstrates his own love for us in this: While we were still sinners, Christ died for us (Rom. 5:8).

> But because of his great love for us, God, who is rich in mercy, made us alive with Christ even when we were dead in transgressions. . . . In order that in the coming ages he might show the incomparable riches of his grace, expressed in his kindness to us in Christ Jesus (Eph. 2:4-5,7).

> How great is the love the Father has lavished on us, that we should be called children of God! And that is what we are! (1 John 3:1).

> We know and rely on the love God has for us. God is love (1 John 4:16).

The apostle Paul tells us that the love of God for us is so incomprehensibly vast that we need to have a revelation of how great it is: "[I pray that you] may have power, together with all the saints, to grasp how wide and long and high and deep is the love of Christ, and to know this love that surpasses knowledge—that you may be filled to the measure of all the fullness of God" (Eph. 3:18-19).

We cannot comprehend God's love with our intellect; and simply reading Scripture verses will not open our hearts to receive God's healing love. We need to have a personal revelation of how much God loves us, and this revelation can only come through the

Holy Spirit. Paul prayed, "I keep asking that the God of our Lord Jesus Christ, the glorious Father, may give you the Spirit of wisdom and revelation, so that you may know him better. I pray also that the eyes of your heart may be enlightened in order that you may know the hope to which he has called you, the riches of his glorious inheritance in the saints" (Eph. 1:17-18).

MY REVELATION OF THE FATHER'S LOVE

By the time I reached my junior year in high school, I had seen and done it all. While I was still partying and trying to have a good time with my friends, inside I was growing increasingly empty and bored. One Saturday night, I was at a party at a friend's house. We had gotten high and were drinking, but in the middle of all the activity, I just felt hollow inside. I wandered into a vacant bedroom in the back of the house and sat on the bed.

I wanted to have a good time, but I wasn't. I was craving something but couldn't identify what it was. Inside, I was longing so much that it hurt. I found myself beginning to talk to God. To this day, I remember what I said. In an audible voice I cried out, "God, I don't know if You exist. But if You do exist, and if what my parents told me as a little boy is true, that You love me so much that You died for my sins, I want You to reveal Yourself to me and show me the truth."

The words just slipped out, and the moment I uttered them, I felt a surge of warm energy envelop my body. It was a sensation of warmth and love like I had never experienced before. At the same time, my mind cleared of all the drugs and alcohol. In that moment I knew that Jesus was real, that His death on the cross was a real event, and that His act of love was directed to me.

As I sat there surrounded by this warm love, I was overwhelmed with how much God loved me, and I wept uncontrollably. For the next three days, waves of God's love continued to grip me so strongly that I cried repeatedly. I began telling all my friends what was going on, even though it was difficult to put into words. But it was so good, so positive and joyful, that I wanted to share it with everyone, and I have never stopped doing that. When God reveals His love to you, it is life changing. You have encountered your true identity, and your life can never be the same again.

My cry to God was desperate and sincere, but I wasn't expecting anything in particular to happen. I now realize that God promises to reveal Himself if we will seek Him. Jesus told us, "So I say to you: Ask and it will be given to you; seek and you will find; knock and the door will be opened to you. For everyone who asks receives; he who seeks finds; and to him who knocks, the door will be opened" (Luke 11:9-10). His first and best gift was the Holy Spirit through whom the Father reveals His love to us (see Rom. 8:5).

Not only will God reveal Himself to you, but He will also reveal Himself in a unique way that meets your particular needs. He understands the distortions in your image of "father." He is able to respond to you and encounter you in a way that will enable you to have a genuine experience of the love He has for you.

PUTTING IT ALL TOGETHER

Many of us have deep heart wounds that distort our image of ourselves and of God as our loving Father. Our hearts need the healing we can only receive from a personal revelation of God's love for us through the work of His Holy Spirit.

ASK YOURSELF

1. What is your image of "father"? How does it affect the way you view God?

2. Read over the five Scripture passages a couple of pages back that describe God as a loving Father. Right now, which verse speaks the loudest to you? What personal message from Father God is it revealing to you?

3. Think of a financial concern that you currently have. If you believe Jeremiah 31:3, how does this change the way you feel about this concern?

LIVE IT!

Have you received Christ as your personal Savior? God wants to reveal His love to you. He will never force a decision on you. You must open the door of your inner self and invite Him in. If you have never done this, are you willing to do it now?

If you are ready, please know that there is no set formula on how to invite God in. You can use your own words, or if it's helpful, you can say the following prayer:

> *God, I want to know You. I accept Your gift of love to me, the death of Jesus on the cross and His resurrection from death that reversed the curse of sin and death in my life. I repent of my rebellion against You and going my own way. I surrender control and give up doing it my way. I want to follow You, God, the rest of my life. I want to reconnect with You and discover my true identity and destiny through Your Spirit of life. I want to have a direct revelation of Your love. Please reveal Yourself to me now. Thank You for hearing me and answering my request. Amen.*

If you have already received Christ as your personal Savior, ask God for a fresh personal revelation of His love for you.

Note

1. Stephen K. De Silva, *Money and the Prosperous Soul* (Grand Rapids, MI: Chosen Books, 2010), p. 80.

Ché Ahn

2

GOD'S FAVORITE LOVE STORY

There was a man who had two sons.

LUKE 15:11

Rembrandt, the seventeenth-century Dutch painter, is well known for both his depictions of Bible characters and his portraits of contemporary life in Holland in the 1600s. He frequently used himself as a subject in his paintings, and they tell a story of his life. He enjoyed great success early in his career, earning large amounts of money. But he would spend most of it immediately.

During that period, he painted one self-portrait in which he showed himself drunk and surrounded by several prostitutes, which was an accurate reflection of his life at the time. He continued his lavish style of living and eventually died penniless. However, it does appear that Rembrandt may have had a change of heart. Before his death, he painted "The Return of the Prodigal Son," in which he depicted himself as the prodigal.

Most of us know the story of the prodigal son from Luke 15, but you may be surprised to learn that God is the real prodigal. The definition of "prodigal" is "extravagant," "lavish," "unrestrained" and "copious." The son was a prodigal with his sins, but the father was a prodigal with his love. I think Jesus told this story to paint a picture of God the Father and His love for us. Let's look at the story in depth.

THE STORY OF THE PRODIGAL FATHER

There was a man who had two sons. The younger one said to his father, "Father, give me my share of the estate." So the father divided his property between them.

Not long after that the younger son got together all that he had, set off for a distant country and there squandered his wealth in wild living. After he had spent everything, there was a severe famine in that whole country and he began to be in need. So he went and hired himself out to a citizen of that country who sent him to his fields to feed his pigs. The son longed to fill his stomach with the pods that the pigs were eating, but no one gave him anything.

When he came to his senses, he said, "How many of my father's hired men have food to spare, and here I am starving to death! I will set out and go back to my father and say to him: Father, I have sinned against heaven and against you. I am no longer worthy to be called your son; make me like one of your hired men." So he got up and went to his father.

But while he was still a long way off his father saw him and was filled with compassion for him; he ran to his son, threw his arms around him and kissed him.

The son said to him, "Father, I have sinned against heaven and against you. I am no longer worthy to be called your son."

But the father said to his servants, "Quick! Bring the best robe and put it on him. Put a ring on his finger and sandals on his feet. Bring the fatted calf and kill it. Let's have a feast and celebrate. For this son of mine was dead and is alive again; he was lost and is found." So they began to celebrate (see Luke 15:11-24).

In this story, God paints a picture of Himself. So often we concentrate on the son, but I want to go back over this story with you and concentrate on the father. Let us observe his actions and reactions. As you consider the father, listen to him; feel his heart break; sense the depth of his relentless love.

THE FATHER IS APPROACHABLE

Notice that the younger son did not hesitate to go and ask his father for his inheritance. He would never have asked for it if he had been uncertain about his father's response, especially in an

Asian culture. The father had absolute rule and authority in his household, and no one dared question him. I know, for I grew up in an Asian home and I was afraid of my dad. If I wanted something, I would tell my mom, but never my dad.

You may not be aware of it, but in that culture the son was expected to work for his father until his father died, and only then would he inherit his portion. So when this younger son approached his father and demanded his inheritance, he was literally telling his father, "I can't wait for you to die, Father. I wish you were dead now, so give me my inheritance." What an insult! How this must have hurt the father's heart, knowing that his son no longer wanted to live under his guidance or even be associated with him.

THE FATHER IS RESPECTFUL

After receiving so much disrespect from his son, the father could easily have put the son in his place by refusing his request and lecturing him on his position as a son. He could even have used his authority to punish the son for his insolence; but he doesn't do this. Instead he treats his son with respect as an equal. I'm sure the father knew his younger son's personality very well and was quite aware of what the son would do with his inheritance. Yet the father's magnanimous response was immediate: "so he divided his property between them" (Luke 15:12).

If you are a parent, especially of a teenage child, you are well aware of the father's dilemma. You need to allow your child to become more of an adult and experience the consequences of his or her choices, but deep inside you long to spare your son or daughter any pain. However, you've lived long enough to know that sometimes we have to have what we want in order to discover what we really need. The father was willing to let the son go and pursue his own agenda. He loved his son too much to restrain him, even though he could have. He knew that controlling another person is not love. He knew that type of possessiveness is not love. True love can only possess what it releases.

THE FATHER DISPLAYS
UNCONDITIONAL ACCEPTANCE

After the son wasted his inheritance and decided to return home, what was the father's response? We are told of five of the father's actions that speak louder than any words. "While he was still a long way off, his father saw him" (v. 20). Here we see the heart of this father. He is patiently waiting and anticipating his son's return. He has never given up on his son, never stopped hoping that he would come back. Every day he patiently watches and asks himself, "Is this the day my son returns? I hope so!"

As soon as he sees him, the father's heart is filled with compassion for his son. There is no anger and no resentment, no hint of feeling any alienation from his son. Instead the father is immediately filled with tender love, for at last his son is coming home to him! This is the day he has been anticipating for so long!

His lavish love is immediately expressed in action: "he ran to his son" (v. 20). The word actually means he raced. He couldn't get there quickly enough! In order to run like this, he had to hike up his robes and reveal his undergarments, an action that was completely undignified for an adult male in that culture. But this father didn't care. He gave no regard to propriety but was willing to make a fool of himself. He was so eager to greet his son.

We can only imagine how disgusting this son looked and smelled. His clothes were tattered and covered with dried pigsty dung. His hair was rumpled and greasy, and he hadn't bathed in weeks, but his father didn't care. He was so overjoyed that he threw his arms around his son, drew him close and hugged him. But even this wasn't enough for this loving father. He repeatedly kissed his son, welcoming him back with such joy.

THE FATHER LAVISHES HIS LOVE ABUNDANTLY

Notice what the father does next. The son tries to give his rehearsed speech about returning as a servant, but the father doesn't even hear him. He immediately turns to his servants and says, "Fetch the robe and put it on him." In that culture the robe was a festive ceremonial garment used only for visiting dignitaries. By putting the robe on his son, the father was telling him, "I completely forgive you. You are still valuable and precious to me."

The father didn't stop there. He said, "Put a ring on his finger." The ring the father was speaking of was the family signet ring. Putting this back on the son's finger signified that the father was accepting him back into the family as a full-fledged member. He was restoring him to his place as his son.

But even this was not enough for the father. He saw the dirty bare feet of his son, a sign of the poverty into which he had fallen. He commanded, "Put sandals on my son's feet." He was saying, in effect, "He is no longer poor but has everything he needs!" The father's joy was boundless and must be expressed, so he commanded his servants, "Kill the fatted calf and let's celebrate!"

This was extravagant love. Abundant and excessive? Yes! Especially when you consider the son's complete disrespect and wasted inheritance. Clearly the son did not deserve this kind of love, but the father lavished it on him anyway.

What Is God Saying to You?

This story is a love letter from the heart of God to each one of us. No matter what you have done or what you have been through, God is yearning for you and longs for a relationship with you. He is always approachable and respectful. No matter how long it's been since you've communicated with Him, He will never lecture you or put you down. He wants to cover you with the robe of righteousness that you have in Jesus Christ and let you know how valuable and precious you are to Him.

He also wants to put the family signet ring on your finger. He wants you to know that He has reopened relationship and restored your position as His adopted child. The apostle Paul knew this, and his words encourage each one of us to believe it: "Praise be to the God and Father of our Lord Jesus Christ, who has blessed us in the heavenly realms with every spiritual blessing in Christ. For he chose us in him before the creation of the world to be holy and blameless in his sight. In love he predestinated us to be adopted as his sons through Christ Jesus, in accordance with his pleasure and will" (Eph. 1:3-5).

Father God also wants to lavish His love on you by abundantly providing for you. He wants you to understand that He will take care of your every need and give you your heart's desires. There's no way that any of us deserve this kind of extravagant love. That is the mystery and wonder of it all—that He has thrown the door of His heart open wide and longs to embrace us with His unconditional love.

PUTTING IT ALL TOGETHER

This prayer of St. Augustine's summarizes what you have read in this chapter. I have taken the liberty to slightly reword it in order to make it personal.

God my Father, I find it difficult to come to You, because my knowledge of You is imperfect. In my ignorance I imagined You to be my enemy; I have wrongly thought that You take pleasure in punishing me for my sins; and I have foolishly conceived You to be a tyrant over my life. But now that Jesus has revealed You to me, I know that You are a loving Father and that my fear of You was groundless.

ASK YOURSELF

1. How does the father in this story compare with your earthly father?

2. Which attribute of the prodigal father is the most difficult for you to believe and receive from your Father God?

   • Being able to approach Him
   • Being respected by Him
   • His unconditional acceptance of me
   • His complete forgiveness of me
   • Adopting me as His child

3. Think about a financial concern you currently have. Imagine
    your Father God running to greet you. What might the robe, the
    ring and the sandals signify to you in your current situation?

LIVE IT!

Most of us have put on the robe, been to the courtroom and received our pardon. In other words, we have received the forgiveness of our sins through the death and resurrection of Jesus Christ.
We know that we are justified through Christ's righteousness, and
we are born again. But for many of us that's where it ends. We have
never received the ring and entered the living room. We have never
received our adoption as God's child and opened ourselves to receive His love as our Father.

Spend a few minutes every morning and evening during the
coming week and carefully read over the prayer of St. Augustine.
Better yet, say it out loud to yourself. Our minds tend to believe
more quickly what we hear our own voice saying, so read the
prayer and open a pathway for your heart to respond fully to the
Father's love.

3

Your Father Is a Giver

For God so loved the world that he gave his one and
only Son, that whoever believes in him shall not perish but
have eternal life. For God did not send his Son into the world
to condemn the world, but to save the world through him.

John 3:16-17

The Original Giver

A few years ago, Dr. Gary Chapman wrote a highly popular book called *The Five Love Languages.* In it he identifies five major ways that we give and receive love. They are: (1) words of affirmation, (2) giving quality time, (3) acts of service, (4) touch, and (5) giving gifts. When I look at the actions of God in Scripture, I can see Him using all of these ways of expressing His love, but He especially enjoys giving gifts.[1]

Our Father God is the original giver. The first thing He did after our creation was to bless us. Blessing someone is a relational act. It indicates that one party is bestowing favor and benefit upon another, the recipient of the blessing. In blessing us, God gave us power to increase and be successful in every area of our lives. He bestowed prosperity upon us, gave us dominion over all the earth, empowered us to subdue anything that would harm us, provided a perfect environment for us, and offered us His companionship and the opportunity to partner with Him. He provided everything we could possibly imagine and desire to enjoy (see 1 Tim. 6:17).

Just looking at the created world reveals the giving heart of God. Even though the earth has fallen under a curse due to mankind's disobedience, and no longer displays the full majesty in which it was created, we still see abundant beauty everywhere. Think of the incredible splendor of the Grand Canyon of Arizona, or the beautiful vistas at Yosemite Park in California, or the power of the massive Niagara Falls in New York.

God loves abundance and variety. No one knows how many species of plants and animals exist on the earth, but researchers estimate anywhere from 7 million to 50 million or more. More than 1.5 million animal species have been identified, a million of which are insects. Currently, 10,000 new animal species are identified each year. When it comes to decorating, our Father God is lavish. There are more than 270,000 different types of flowers on earth. Creation certainly reveals that God loves to give!

God is so eager to give that we're told His eyes are constantly running to and fro throughout the whole earth seeking those He can bestow blessings upon (see 2 Chron. 16:9). The Godhead itself is a community of extravagant giving generated by a dynamic of unending love. This limitless love propels God to extend His gifts to us with everything He is and everything He has. This is His supreme joy. Our ultimate destiny, as beings created in His image, is to become one with Him in this community of boundless love and joyful giving.

THE BLESSING OF ABRAHAM

After we chose to go our own way in the Garden of Eden, we were separated from intimate fellowship with God and cut off from His blessing. But God had no intention of accepting that as status quo. Even before Adam and Eve left the garden, God promised them that a day of restoration would come (see Gen. 3:15). Until that time of restoration, God wanted to reestablish a relationship with humanity and bless us, so He chose one man, Abraham, and made a covenant with him.

One of God's essential characteristics is that He is a covenant maker. He always keeps His side of the covenant whether we do or not. God came to Abraham and promised to be his God, to establish him upon the earth and make him a great nation. In return He asked Abraham to walk before Him and be blameless. In his later years Abraham is described as blessed by God in every way. He became very wealthy, having many sheep and cattle, much silver and gold, menservants and maidservants, camels and donkeys (see Gen. 24:1,35).

Later, under Moses, God described the many blessings of Abraham that He desired to give to all His people. They are listed in Deuteronomy 28:1-14 and include:

- Blessed wherever we live
- Our children will be blessed
- Our business or employment will be blessed
- We will have abundant prosperity in all areas
- We will be lenders, not borrowers
- We will be the head, not the tail
- We will be at the top, never at the bottom

Even as He did in the Garden, with Adam and Eve, when God presented these blessings to Israel, He offered them a choice: "This day I call heaven and earth as witnesses against you that I have set before you life and death, blessings and curses. Now choose life, so that you and your children may live" (Deut. 30:19).

We can see that Father God reopened the way for physical, material and financial blessing, but they were still spiritually dead and struggling with sin. The covenant that God made with Abraham had no power to restore life to our dead spirits and change us from within. It would take a new and better covenant to accomplish this.

THE NEW COVENANT IN CHRIST JESUS

God made a new covenant that would accomplish everything that could not be attained under the old covenant with Abraham. Jesus—God in flesh—was the answer. Early in His ministry, Jesus entered the synagogue and read from the prophet Isaiah: "The Spirit of the Lord is on me, because he has anointed me to preach good news to the poor. He has sent me to proclaim freedom for the prisoners and recovery of sight for the blind, to release the oppressed, to proclaim the year of the Lord's favor" (Luke 4:18-21).

Jesus' actions in His three years of ministry on earth demonstrated the fulfillment of this prophecy. He healed the sick, delivered those who were oppressed by demons, opened people's spiritual eyes to the truth of the Scriptures, and revealed the loving and giving heart of Father God to His followers.

In order to help us understand God's giving nature, Jesus said, "Ask and it will be given to you; seek and you will find; knock and the door will be opened to you. For everyone who asks receives; he who seeks finds; and to him who knocks, the door will be opened. Which of you if his son asks for bread, will give him a stone? Or if he asks for a fish, will give him a snake? If you, then, though you are evil, know how to give good gifts to your children, how much more will your Father in heaven give good gifts to those who ask him!" (Matt. 7:7-11).

If you have children, this description of a loving, giving father needs no explanation. Parents will go to great lengths to give their children not only what they need, but also what they want. Every parent knows the joy of seeing his or her children's faces light up when they open a present that contains something they have been wanting for a long time. Jesus is telling us that this is how our Father God feels. God wants us to trust Him and be receptive to His gifts. "I am the LORD your God, who brought you up out of Egypt. Open wide your mouth and I will fill it" (Ps. 81:10). "Those who seek the LORD lack no good thing" (Ps. 34:10).

Of course, God demonstrated His greatest gift in giving us His Son, Jesus Christ, whom He offered up as the sacrifice for our sins on the cross to redeem us from sin and restore our relationship with Him. The magnitude of this gift is incomprehensible. I have friends and relatives I dearly love, but I can't imagine giving up my only son, Gabriel, for any one of them. It would be the supreme gift. Any other gift I could give would pale by comparison! The apostle Paul challenges us to trust God's intentions toward us with these words: "He [Father God] who did not spare his own Son, but gave him up for us all—how will He not also, along with him, graciously give us all things?" (Rom. 8:32). God has given us His ultimate, so He will not deny us lesser gifts.

Jesus made it clear that He will not do so: "Therefore I tell you, do not worry about your life, what you will eat or drink; or about your body, what you will wear. Is not life more important than food, and the body more important than clothes? Look at the birds of the air; they do not sow or reap or store away in barns, and yet your heavenly Father feeds them. Are you not much more valuable than they? . . . So do not worry, saying, 'What shall we eat?' or 'What shall we drink?' or 'What shall we wear?' For the pagans run after all these things, and your heavenly Father knows you need them. But seek first his kingdom and his righteousness, and all these things will be given to you as well" (Matt. 6:25-26,31-33).

A Better Covenant with Better Promises

In Christ Jesus we have all the blessings of Abraham: "Christ hath redeemed us from the curse of the law, being made a curse for us: for it is written, Cursed is everyone that hangeth on a tree: That the blessing of Abraham might come on the Gentiles through Jesus Christ; that we might receive the promise of the Spirit through faith . . . And if ye be Christ's, then are ye Abraham's seed, and heirs according to the promise" (Gal. 3:13-14,29, *KJV*).

However, the new covenant far exceeds the blessings of Abraham. Jesus repeatedly declared that Father God was offering to restore us to our original position of dominion and authority in partnership with Him. He told His disciples, "Do not be afraid, little flock, for your Father has been pleased to give you the kingdom" (Luke 12:32). The Father wants to give us His kingdom, which is His rule and reign, and restore our fellowship with Him. Our new covenant in Jesus Christ is a better covenant founded on better promises, for we are permanently set free from all our sins, and our spirit is reborn and restored to a right relationship with Father God.

Scripture tells us, "This is the covenant I will make with the house of Israel after that time, declares the Lord. I will put my laws in their minds and write them on their hearts. I will be their God, and they will be my people. . . . They will all know me, from the least of them to the greatest. For I will forgive their wickedness and remember their sins no more" (Heb. 8:10-12). This is full restoration of everything we lost through our disobedience in the Garden. We have a new spirit and the ability to function as we were created, in the image of God. The way back into God's presence has been opened. In every conceivable way, Father God has demonstrated to us that He is a giver and that we are the objects of His giving heart.

PUTTING IT ALL TOGETHER

In all of His interactions with us, Father God consistently demonstrates that He is a giver. From the abundant variety and beauty contained in creation, to His initial blessing of us in the Garden of Eden and subsequent covenant making with Abraham, He displays His giving nature. But of course, His greatest gift was the sacrifice of His Son, Jesus Christ, to fully redeem us from sin and restore us to our original purpose and destiny.

ASK YOURSELF

1. Can you remember a time when you were surprised by receiving a gift that you really wanted? What was it and how did you feel about the person who gave it to you?

2. Read over Deuteronomy 28:1-14 carefully. Which blessing do you need most in your life right now? Do you believe that God is willing to give this gift to you? Why or why not?

3. We are all familiar with the words of John 3:16, but often we have never really considered the verse that follows. In verse 17, God gives us the gift of removing all condemnation from us.

Is there anything you feel guilty about or for which you condemn yourself? Can you release it to God now and receive His total forgiveness? Will you forgive yourself?

LIVE IT!

Increase your receptivity to God's blessing. Take a few moments at the end of each day to identify at least one gift you have received from God. It may have been that parking spot in front of your favorite restaurant, the kudos you received from a coworker, the smile that came your way in a down moment or the phone call from an old friend. Learning to recognize these as God's gifts will help you discover that they are not just coincidence, and it will increase your awareness of the steady stream of gifts God is sending to you on a daily basis.

Note
1. Gary Chapman, *The Five Love Languages* (Chicago, IL: Northfield Publishing, 1995).

4

DIVINE CHARADES:
THE MO OF FATHER GOD

Moses said to God, "Suppose . . . they ask me, 'What is His name?' Then what shall I tell them?" God said to Moses, "I AM WHO I AM. . . . This is my name forever, the name by which I am to be remembered from generation to generation."

EXODUS 3:13-15

Did you ever play the game Charades? You had to get people to correctly guess what you were trying to say by acting it out. You couldn't speak, but you could use gestures to give clues. So you would use gestures to capture some characteristics that represented the person or thing you were trying to portray.

We all have characteristic mannerisms, actions and words that identify us to others. We call these various behaviors an MO, or modus operandi. For example, suppose you wanted to get people to say the name "Santa Claus." You might put your hands in front of you as if on an imaginary extended belly and throw back your head, pretending to laugh. People would probably quickly guess the name "Santa Claus" because we have all seen him portrayed as acting this way. We might describe this behavior as part of the MO of Santa Claus.

Each of us has our own MO that makes it possible for others to know what to anticipate in interactions with us. Whether or not we realize it, we expect a person's MO to remain relatively consistent and stable over time. This allows us to create a sense of order and, to some extent, security in our personal environment.

Have you ever thought about the fact that God has an MO too? The Bible makes it very clear that there are some characteristic ways in which God behaves and interacts with people. We've already discussed two ways: God's Father heart of love and His generosity as a giver. It's important that we understand God's MO, for it is part of a firm foundation in which we can put confident trust.

I Am the Lord, and I Change Not

Repeatedly in Scripture, God reassures us that He does not change (see Mal. 3:6; Jas. 1:27; Ps. 102:26-27). He does not change in His essential being, in His attributes, the principles by which He operates or His plans. He is immutable, and He is the only being in the entire universe that is changeless. Since we live in a world surrounded by constant change, it is difficult for us to understand clearly what God's unchanging character really means.

It means that the sun will come up tomorrow; the days will continue to be 24 hours in length; the tides will continue to rise and fall; and all the operations of the universe will continue to function predictably as they have ever since creation. It means that God is not moody. We won't ever catch Him having a "bad hair day." He is 100 percent dependable, and His track record for reliability is perfect.

He never wavers or has a second thought, and He never doubts Himself. Throughout all eternity He will remain changeless. He is completely trustworthy and transparent in His intentions. He will never behave in random, unpredictable ways. Can you imagine what it would be like if you had even one human relationship that was this way? You could have complete confidence in that person and trust him or her implicitly. You could count on that person to remain constant and stable, and you would feel secure relating to him or her.

The Words of the Lord Are Pure as Silver Refined in a Furnace Seven Times Over

Pure words are true words. They do not have a double meaning and they are never deceptive. God reassures us that His words are pure (see Pss. 12:6; 33:4; Prov. 30:5). He says exactly what He means and He means exactly what He says. We never have to wonder if He has a hidden agenda. We can trust that He is telling us the truth, and that just as He is changeless, His words are also changeless.

This means that as we compare His words, we will not find contradiction. He doesn't say something at one point in time and then reverse it later. His words constitute reality as they tell us the essence of "what is." We can count on that revealed reality remaining stable and secure.

We can trust Him to tell us everything we need to know. He is not keeping secrets from us. On the last night with His disciples, Jesus told them, "No longer do I call you servants, because a servant does not know what his master is doing; but I have called you friends, because all that I have heard from the Father I have made known to you" (John 15:15, *Weymouth*). God wants to make Himself known to us, and we can believe what He tells us. We can stake everything we have on what God tells us in His Word.

GOD SENDS HIS WORD FORTH AND IT NEVER RETURNS TO HIM VOID

God never engages in small talk. His words are full of power and they always produce the desired effect (see Isa. 55:11). When He says something, it is as good as done. The Bible is very clear that God's words have incredible creative power. The entire universe was brought into existence through God speaking. God always backs up His words, and they are never futile or unproductive.

His words are alive, and they penetrate deep into the heart of every matter. The writer of the book of Hebrews describes God's word this way: "For the word of God is living and active. Sharper than any double-edged sword, it penetrates even to dividing soul and spirit, joints and morrow; it judges the thoughts and attitudes of the heart" (Heb. 4:12). God's words reveal His heart to us and our own hearts to ourselves.

GOD KEEPS HIS COVENANTS

The word "covenant" is a term familiar to anyone who has been in a church setting any time at all. But do we really know what a covenant is? A covenant is much more than a contract. In our day-to-day world, we don't have anything that even begins to approach covenant status.

In ancient times, covenants were considered sacred and unbreakable. Two parties would enter into a covenant in which they mutually agreed to exchange things that were needed and desired by each one. For example, two tribes might enter a covenant agreement with the stronger tribe agreeing to protect the weaker tribe, while the weaker tribe might allow the stronger tribe's flocks to graze on their land.

The mutual benefits of the covenant would be clearly discussed, and the tribal leaders would both swear an oath that they would keep the covenant. Then they also both invoked a curse upon themselves if they broke the covenant. They sealed the covenant, usually by shedding blood, either by making a cut in their own flesh or by sacrificing an animal. Once this was done, there was no turning back. The covenant stood, with the parties mutually bound to each other.

God established an everlasting covenant with Abraham and his descendants from generation to generation (see Gen. 17:7). He promised Israel, recorded in Deuteronomy 7:9, "Know therefore that the LORD your God is God; he is the faithful God, keeping his covenant of love to a thousand generations of those who love him and keep his commands." God proved true to His covenant. Time and time again when Israel deserted the Lord, He remained faithful to His covenant with them, coming to their protection and delivering them, even when they went into bondage for periods of time.

Then God did an amazing thing. He established a unilateral covenant with humankind through the blood of His Son, Jesus Christ. The making and fulfillment of this covenant rests solely on God's initiative; and instead of an oath agreed between two parties, God swore by Himself that He would keep this covenant forever. In this covenant, God provides complete redemption for us and an invitation to fellowship and joint loving service with Him throughout eternity. Jesus referred to this covenant when

He took the cup at the Last Supper and said, "This is my blood of the covenant, which is poured out for many for the forgiveness of sins" (Matt. 26:28).

What an incredible assurance we have! God has bound Himself to an everlasting covenant with us that He will never violate or change. And He has sealed this covenant with the blood of His own Son, Jesus.

THROUGH HIS COVENANT, GOD PROVIDES US ALL THE BLESSINGS OF ABRAHAM

As we have seen, a blessing bestows favor upon us and allows us to receive all of God's promises. Some of these promises include righteousness (right relationship) with God, abundant life, prosperity and eternal salvation (see 2 Sam. 7:29; Pss. 3:8; 24:5; 133:3). God assures us that even though at one time we were estranged and cut off from any covenant with Him, we have now been brought into an eternal covenant with Him through the blood of Jesus (see Eph. 2:12-13). "Through Christ Jesus, God has blessed the Gentiles with the same blessing he promised to Abraham, so that we who are believers might receive the promised Holy Spirit through faith" (Gal. 3:14, *NLT*).

We have difficulty comprehending what this means, because we really don't know what the blessing of Abraham is all about. As we move together through the rest of this book, we will be looking at many aspects of that blessing. It's important to establish here that the blessing belongs to us, too, for it is part of God's eternal covenant with us.

OUR RESPONSE TO HIS CHARACTERISTICS

Our response to God's characteristics is critical, for it determines what we can receive from Him. When we know and believe that these characteristics are the truth, we will diligently seek to understand His Word and put it into practice.

I'm going to ask that you agree with me to observe the rule of context and practice the operation of faith. Because we believe that God's Word is true and that He wants to make Himself known to us, it is important that we always consider the complete context in which He is speaking. It is tempting, and easy, to take a piece of text out of its context, but we risk losing the full meaning when we do this.

When we take "text" out of "context," we are left with a "con." We certainly don't want that! We want to accurately understand what God is telling us, because we know it's true and it contains power that can change our lives.

Our faith in God is put into operation through the following three-step process:

1. **Revelation:** Faith comes by having the word of God revealed to us through the Holy Spirit (see Rom. 10:17).

2. **Personal Conviction:** Faith is produced as we are firmly convicted of the truth and power of the word of God that has been revealed to us (see Heb. 11:1).

3. **Action:** Faith gives results as we act upon our firm conviction regarding the revealed word we have heard (see Jas. 2:17).

If we want to grow in the grace of giving, and become more firmly established in the Lord, we must always remember to observe the rule of context and practice the operation of faith. Throughout this book, I will be encouraging you to do this. If you do, you will come to know your Father God in a much deeper, more intimate and productive way.

PUTTING IT ALL TOGETHER

Staying focused on God's MO builds in us a confident faith as we become progressively more intimate with the one who empowers us with His grace to become all He created us to be.

Ché Ahn

Ask Yourself

1. Review the five characteristics of God. Which ones are the easiest for you to believe? Which ones are the most difficult?

2. Do any of the characteristics of God seem to contradict what you routinely expect of Him or what you've heard about God in the past? If so, how?

3. Pick out one characteristic of God. If you were 100 percent convinced that God is truly this way, would it change your daily life or behavior in any way? If so, how?

Live It!

Pick a characteristic of God that you currently have difficulty with. Focus on it for one week by doing the following:

-   Write out the Scriptures cited in the section under that characteristic.
-   Read these Scripture verses three times a day.
-   Ask the Lord to reveal their truth to you.
-   Record any insights God gives you.

5

THE ORIGINAL DESIGN:
OUR FIRST MO

Then God said, "Let us make man in our image, in our likeness."

GENESIS 1:26

I've been to Hawaii numerous times, and I always enjoy being there. The white sandy beaches, the crystal-blue ocean and the near-perfect weather are wonderful. I'm always relaxed when I'm there, and I feel like I'm at home. It truly is a paradise, and deep inside I long to stay. I've met many people who feel the same way after visiting the islands.

CREATED FOR PARADISE

Sometimes I wonder if it's easy to feel this way about Hawaii because we were originally created to live in a paradise. It's important to know our original design or MO to understand who God created us to be.

The first two chapters of Genesis contain a description of God's creation activity. While not detailed, the account certainly indicates that God created the earth with us in mind, and that a special place, the Garden of Eden, was specifically designed to be a perfect environment for us.

The word "garden" implies planning and organization. A garden is not just a bunch of foliage and shrubs; it is a deliberate and intentional array of various plants and flowers to capture their natural beauty. God Himself was the landscaper, so we know this had to be the most exquisite garden ever designed! This is suggested in the name "Eden," for the word means "delight." So the Garden of Eden was actually the garden of delight.

The Genesis account indicates that God filled the garden with all kinds of fruit to eat, ample water to drink, and gold and precious stones for our pleasure. "Then God said, 'I give you every seed-bearing plant on the face of the whole earth and every tree that has fruit with seed in it. They will be yours for food'" (Gen. 1:29). "And the LORD God made all kinds of trees grow out of the ground—trees that were pleasing to the eye and good for food. . . . A river watering the garden flowed from Eden; from there it separated into four headwaters. . . . (The gold of that land is good; aromatic resin and onyx are also there)" (Gen. 2:9-10,12).

It is clear that God designed this garden to meet our every need and to provide everything we could ever desire. But we were created for more than to simply live in paradise; God had a divine MO and purpose in mind for us.

CREATED TO BE LIKE GOD

One of the most incredible revelations in all of Scripture is the description of our true identity. Genesis makes it very clear that we are a unique, unparalleled order of God's creation. We were originally created in God's image, after His likeness (see Gen. 1:26). An image is a copy, a replica of the original. It captures the essential nature, both the external and internal characteristics, of the original. To have been created in the image and likeness of God means that we reflected God's perfection, His holiness, righteousness, knowledge and dominion. We were created to reflect the glory of God. "What is man that You are mindful of him, the son of man that You care for him? You made him a little lower than God and crowned him with glory and honor" (Ps. 8:4-5).

Our creation is told in detail in the first two chapters of the book of Genesis. Obviously, in giving us this detail, God wants us to understand some specifics about our created identity. It is very clear that God made both male and female in His image and likeness (see Gen. 1:27). Even though woman was created after man, and then brought to him, she was not an afterthought. She was as fully an expression of the glory of God as was the man.

"The LORD God formed the man from the dust of the ground and breathed into his nostrils the breath of life, and the man became a living being" (Gen. 2:7). We need to understand what we are being told in this verse. Up to this point God used His word to speak into existence all the other creatures. But when it came to us, the record states that God created us in a "hands-on" manner. He skillfully and artfully formed man's body from the dust of the ground, and then He breathed His own spirit life into him. This distinguished man (and woman) and made them unique in all the created order of being.

The Hebrew words for this passage read, "He breathed the breath of lives (plural)" into us. He animated our entire being, spirit, soul and body, with His very life. It is easy to describe our body. It is the part of us that is material and is in contact with and conscious of the physical world around us. Describing the spirit and the soul is more challenging. Both spirit and soul are the immaterial and invisible part of us that can exist separated from the body. Actually, there is no equivalent translation of the Hebrew idea of the soul in the English language. Both the soul and the spirit can be thought of as the seat of our human personality, or our being, by which we perceive, reflect, feel and desire.

In Hebrews 4:12, the author describes how difficult it is to distinguish between our spirit and soul: "For the word of God is living and active. Sharper than any double-edged sword, it penetrates even to dividing soul and spirit, joints and marrow; it judges the thoughts and attitudes of the heart." One distinction we can make between soul and spirit is that with our soul we are self-conscious, and with our spirit we are God conscious. It is clear from cumulative evidence in various Scriptures that we are a tripartite being, having a spirit, a soul and a body (see 1 Cor. 2:11; 2 Cor. 5:4; 1 Thess. 5:23; 2 Pet. 1:13-14).

As we were originally created, we had a unity of being. Our spirit, soul and our body operated as a unified whole. We were at complete peace within ourselves, unified in our purpose not only internally but also with each other. It is clear that initially the man and the woman operated as a unit. When the man first saw the woman, he said, "This is now bone of my bones and flesh of my flesh; she shall be called 'woman,' for she was taken out of man" (Gen. 2:23). They were in such unity and oneness that *their name* was Adam. They did not have individual names, for there was no need for them to be individually distinguished. It is difficult, if not impossible, for us to understand this degree of agreement and harmony.

CREATED FOR COMPANIONSHIP

Companionship is essential for us. God Himself was the first to state this fact when He said, "It is not good for man to be alone. I will make a helper suitable for him" (Gen. 2:18). We are social beings who are designed to live in family and community. We must never forget that God is a triune community of being, and we are created in His image.

The man and the woman had such deep companionship that we are told they were both naked and felt no shame (see Gen. 2:25). I don't think this primarily refers to physical nakedness as much as it refers to inner transparency. There was such oneness between them that there was nothing in either one of them that was hidden. They were totally transparent to each other and completely comfortable with that degree of vulnerability. There was no shame, because there was nothing to hide. None of us can imagine what it is like to be totally known and accepted by another human being in this way.

They also had companionship with God. In Genesis 3, we are told that God was walking in the garden in the cool of the day (see Gen. 3:8). The verb tense in Hebrew indicates that this was a habitual practice, so we can assume this was a customary time that God spent fellowshipping with the man and woman. We have no idea if this went on for weeks, months or years, but it obviously was an ongoing pattern of behavior for all three of them.

Have you ever wondered what their fellowship was like, what they discussed? We are not told, and of course there's no way to know for sure, but I think that at least part of their discussions focused on our God-given purpose and destiny. When God created them, His first words to them were a blessing and a commission: "God blessed them and said to them, 'Be fruitful and increase in number; fill the earth and subdue it. Rule over the fish of the sea and the birds of the air and over every living creature that moves on the ground'" (Gen. 1:28). "The LORD God took the man and put him in the Garden of Eden to work it and take care of it" (Gen. 2:15). Many of us have heard this creation story so many times that it becomes easy to gloss over these words without considering their true meaning.

CREATED TO REIGN

Immediately after blessing His creation of us, God declared for all time our purpose and destiny. We were to prosper, to multiply in number and penetrate the entire earth with our presence. So even though we began in the Garden of Eden, it was always God's plan that we would rule and reign over the entire earth. Note that we were given dominion, not domination. We were to rule and reign over everything that moved on the earth, but we were also told to take care of our dominion. This implies that we were to tend it and nurture it.

We were also to protect it. An interesting part of our commission that is frequently overlooked is the command to "subdue the earth." To subdue means to humble or to bring low. It implies subduing enemies. We were given the authority and the responsibility to exercise loving dominion over everything on the earth, but this command indicates that there would be opposition we would have to put down. Ultimately, we were called to bring Satan down. We know that he was already in the Garden (see Gen. 3:1). I believe our initial commission was really one of training for reigning. Through our fellowship with God and the decisions we made, we were to grow into the commission He gave us. The Garden of Eden was our prototype. We were to take the blessing that God had given us and bless the entire earth through our dominion.

We were given an incredible resource, the tree of life, to provide us with a continual flow of the life and Spirit of God into our being. Accessing this resource would provide us with the ongoing wisdom and knowledge of God and His blessing of perpetual abundance. Blessing, dominion, abundance, unity and companionship were all part of our original design. Every aspect of fulfilling the purpose and destiny of our original design was to work through our relationship with God.

While it is clear that something has dramatically changed for us here on earth since the creation of Adam and Eve, understanding our original design is not just a lesson in history. Don't forget God's divine MO. He never changes, and He establishes everything through His word that never returns to Him without accomplishing the purpose it was sent forth to achieve. God's original design remains His eternal purpose for us. We need to study it carefully to understand what He intends to accomplish in us and for us.

PUTTING IT ALL TOGETHER

Our original design and purpose is to prosper and live in abundance; multiply and occupy the earth; have authority and dominion over every other creature and every aspect of life on earth; defeat anything that would challenge our dominion (i.e., Satan); live in unity and harmony with one another; and walk in ongoing fellowship as companions with God.

ASK YOURSELF

1. Do you feel out of control in your relationships with family and friends, finances, job or career, health, or any other area? If so, focus on that area. What would exercising dominion in this area look like, feel like?

2. Think of a current significant relationship in your life. How much transparency do you enjoy with this person? What prevents you from experiencing even more transparency?

3. Pick one of the aspects of our original design described above. If this aspect was operating fully for you today, how would your life be different?

LIVE IT!

What are your personal goals? According to God's original design for you, what is His purpose and destiny for you? Do you need to make revisions in your lifestyle? What are they?

6

A Generation of Orphans:
Our Broken MO

*Remember that at that time you were separate from Christ, excluded
from citizenship in Israel and foreigners to the covenants of the promise,
[you were orphans] without hope and without God in the world.*

Ephesians 2:12

Training for Reigning

When God created man and woman, we were designed to prosper,
multiply, subdue any foe, and exert a loving dominion over all the
earth and everything in it. We lived in complete transparency and
unity with each other, with God and within ourselves. We lived
from the inside out; that is, our spirit in partnership with God's
Spirit was the source of our wisdom, knowledge and experience of
the truth. Our soul and our body were automatically aligned under the direction of our spirit.

We knew and experienced everything through our predomi-
nant sense that was faith, the sense of our spirit. This was how we
walked and talked with God daily. We could see into and experience the spirit realm without any difficulty through faith. Faith
was the sense that instructed all of our other senses in our experience of the physical realm. We were not directed by our five physical senses, but by our faith.

Scripture does not tell us how long we remained in this state
of transparency, unity and partnership with God, but we do know
that we accomplished at least one major task: "Now the LORD God

had formed out of the ground all the beasts of the field and all the birds of the air. He brought them to the man to see what he would name them; and whatever the man called each living creature, that was its name" (Gen. 2:19-20).

Don't make the mistake of thinking that Adam simply applied labels to the creatures. To give something a name was to determine its nature and character; so Adam was actually participating in the creative process with God. How could Adam operate in such knowledge and insight? He did it in partnership with God through faith. It was the beginning of humankind's training for reigning. I think God's intention was to take us through a process of increasing responsibility and dominion, to mature us to a place where we would reign over the earth, even as God reigns over the heavens and the universe. Unfortunately, we got off track.

THE SUPER SCAM

We are all familiar with the word "scam." You only have to turn on your computer and you will be greeted by pop-ups and spam email that often contain fraudulent offers. A scam is a deception, something that appears to be what it is not. It often sounds too good to be true, and if we fall for it, we are the worse for it. This is exactly what happened to the man and woman in the Garden of Eden.

We were not created preprogrammed for a particular set of behaviors. We were given the power of true freedom of choice. This was part of being created in the image of God. Scripture describes our free will: "In the middle of the garden were the tree of life and the tree of the knowledge of good and evil. . . . And the LORD God commanded the man, 'You are free to eat from any tree in the garden; but you must not eat from the tree of the knowledge of good and evil, for when you eat of it you will surely die'" (Gen. 2:9,16-17).

God did not place these two trees in the Garden as a temptation. They represented the real choice that we always have because we were created with a free will. The man and woman's choice was to be directed from within by their spirits in partnership with

God's Holy Spirit (the tree of life), or to be directed from the outside by their five physical senses and human reasoning (the tree of the knowledge of good and evil). God was not keeping any knowledge from them. His intention was that, in partnership with Him, their faith would instruct their physical senses to discern good and evil without ever having to directly experience evil itself (see Heb. 5:14).

Their choice to eat the fruit of the tree of the knowledge of good and evil represented a shift within from being God-centered to being self-centered. In a moment of time, they (and we) severed their trusting relationship with God and became separated from Him, from His life, from His wisdom, from His authority and from His power. Seeking to become more like God through their own knowledge and willpower, they actually became less than the image of God they were created to be (see Rom. 1:21-23,28-31; Eph. 4:17-19).

THE TRAGIC DIVIDE

The consequences of that choice went far beyond anything we could possibly imagine. Mankind went from living with blessing to bringing a curse upon themselves (see Deut. 28:15-68; Jer. 17:5-6). Our willful disobedience dramatically changed how we would live our lives from that day on. Let's consider a few of these changes. What did we lose?

SEPARATION

We lost our unity with God. Our separation from God meant that we were cut off from His presence and shut out from realizing His purpose and destiny for us. This is spiritual death, and it happened to us immediately when we made our choice. We continued to be alive physically, but spiritually we were dead. We experienced this incredible loss with a sense of shameful vulnerability (see Gen. 3:7-10; Isa. 59:2).

We lost our unity with each other. Until this choice, the man and woman had lived in total harmony with each other in unity of spirit and purpose. Now they became divided, two distinct individuals with differing intentions and purposes. This was reflected in the fact that Adam subsequently called the woman "Eve," giving her an identity completely separated from his own. Instead of harmony, there was now discord as two self-centered individuals pulled in different directions. There was no longer trust or transparency; there were attempts to hide oneself and accusations directed toward one another (see Gen. 3:12-13).

We also lost unity within our own selves. Instead of our understanding and actions being directed by our spirit in partnership with God, through our soul to our body, we became fragmented within. Our spirit was dead and the focus of our understanding and action shifted to our body through its five physical senses and to our soul through our passions. This fragmentation meant that at times we would be torn in different directions, having divided purposes even within ourselves. Another term for this is being double minded (see Rom. 7:18-24; Jas. 1:6-8).

Reason Instead of Wisdom

We no longer had access to the spiritual realm. We were limited to the physical world and what we could learn and observe through our reason. This meant that we were cut off from God's wisdom and the knowledge of His truth, which is the essence of reality. We were stuck trying to put together a myriad of facts, never knowing how much truth and error they contained. Instead of the unity of God's wisdom, we were left with the dichotomy of constantly differing opinions created through our individual understandings (see Rom. 1:19-22).

Fear Instead of Faith

We lost our spiritual sense of faith and became bound to our five physical senses. Our experience was dominated by our circumstances. We soon learned that there were many circumstances we could not influence or control through our senses. We felt vulnerable and fearful of many things. We no longer had the assurance of God's authority and power working within us. We were on our own, and our abilities were limited.

Toil Instead of Work

Our original purpose and destiny were to tend the garden, enjoy abundant prosperity, subdue our foes, and employ loving dominion over all the earth. This was creative work and was intended to give us enjoyment and blessing. Our choice had consequences beyond ourselves. We shifted our allegiance from God to the alien spirit, Satan, whose lies we believed. Our dominion of the earth was now corrupted and polluted, and even as we had rebelled against God, the earth began to rebel against us. The garden was gone. We had to toil incessantly to get the ground to yield a harvest to us. Our lives became characterized by hopeless bondage to toil (see Gen. 3:17-19).

We Are Broken Orphans

In the recent movie *Hugo*, a young boy finds an old automaton machine, shaped like a human, with a windup mechanism that is broken. The boy is not sure what the machine is designed to do and wants to fix it to find out. He says to his friend, "Everything has a purpose. Clocks tell time, and trains take you places. They do what they're meant to do. Maybe that's what makes me so sad about broken machines. They can't do what they're meant to do. Maybe it's the same with people. If you lose your purpose, it's like you're broken. I wonder what my purpose is."[1]

This little boy's words sum up our essential dilemma. Separated from God, we have lost our purpose, and we are broken. We try to understand who we are with our limited reasoning abilities. But we are cut off from the truth of our created identity, and we are like someone looking in a flawed mirror we see only distortions of who we might be. We no longer know our identity. We are alone in the world as orphans, without hope and without God. We have lost our identity as God's children. We can contrast these two identities this way:

Child of God (Original MO)	Orphan (Fallen MO)
secure	insecure
trusting	mistrustful
relationship-oriented	performance-oriented
unified	double-minded
transparent	ashamed
operates through wisdom	operates through reason
self-accepting	self-rejecting
God-centered	self-centered
practices dominion	practices manipulation
faith-based	fear-based
works creatively	toils in bondage
lives with purpose and destiny	lives with conflicting passions
has a sense of belonging	has a sense of alienation
is blessed	is cursed

We must understand both our original created identity and our broken identity as orphans. Our orphan identity reveals the challenges and difficulties we face when we come to Father God and hear His promises to us. Our original created identity helps us grasp God's purpose and destiny for us, which have never changed.

PUTTING IT ALL TOGETHER

By a choice of our own free will, we severed our connection with God and lost our original purpose and destiny. We lost our blessing; and without God, we fell into fear. By choosing to experientially know evil (eating from the tree of the knowledge of good and evil), we brought a curse on ourselves, on the earth and every-thing in it.

ASK YOURSELF

1. What effects of the curse are operating in your life right now? (Take some time to think about this—there may be more effects than you realize!) How would your life be different if these were areas of blessing instead?

2. As you compare the two identities (Child and Orphan), which descriptors do you see most clearly in yourself?

3. We frequently hear the phrase "seeing is believing." Is this true wisdom? Why or why not?

LIVE IT!

Assess yourself and your activities. For three days, at the end of each day, take 5 to 10 minutes to reflect and write down several decisions you've made each day. How frequently did you consult with God's Spirit in making your decisions? Use this process to help you become more aware of opportunities to walk and talk with God.

Note
1. Martin Scorsese, director, *Hugo* (Los Angeles, CA: Paramount Pictures, 2011).

7

LIKE FATHER LIKE SON

Anyone who has seen me has seen the Father.

JOHN 14:9

As he is, so are we in this world.

1 JOHN 4:17, *KJV*

A few weeks ago, I was in a local sporting goods store when I noticed a father and his young son. They were both dressed in matching LA Lakers T-shirts, and the father was trying to find a basketball that was the appropriate size for his son, who was probably about three or four years old. The father leaned back and put his hands on his hips, and his son immediately did the same thing. As I continued to watch them, I saw several more times when the son directly imitated his dad. He was watching his father with such admiration and enjoying every moment of his dad's attention. And his father looked down at him with such obvious pride.

That little boy was trying to reflect his father in every way, and the father displayed such enjoyment in attending to his son. In a simple way, it was like a visual representation of the relationship between God the Father and His Son, Jesus Christ. Scripture doesn't tell us much about their relationship before Christ came to earth, but we are given one hint at the baptism of Jesus in the Jordan. Before Christ entered His public ministry or ever performed a single act, His Father pronounced, "You are my Son, whom I love; with you I am well pleased" (Mark 1:11). This indicates a relationship based on love, not performance.

PERFECT UNITY: THE FATHER AND SON

The Gospels provide a record of the activity of Jesus' ministry on earth. "Jesus went throughout Galilee, teaching in their synagogues, preaching the good news of the kingdom, and healing every disease and sickness among the people. News about Him spread all over Syria and people brought to him all who were ill with various diseases, those suffering severe pain, and the demon-possessed, those having seizures, and the paralyzed, and he healed them" (Matt. 4:23-24). His ministry of instruction, encouragement and healing attracted enthusiastic crowds that followed Him.

As we previously discussed in the story of the prodigal father, Jesus frequently told parables to illustrate the character of Father God. A primary mission of His ministry was to reveal the heart of the Father to us. He did this not only in the stories He told, but also through His own life and actions. Jesus let us "see" the Father: "He is the image of the invisible God" (Col. 1:15).

Repeatedly, Jesus told His listeners that He came to do the will of the Father, as we see from the following verses:

> For I have come down from heaven not to do my will but to do the will of him who sent me (John 6:38).

> I tell you the truth, the Son can do nothing by himself; he can do only what he sees his Father doing, because what ever the Father does the Son also does. For the Father loves the Son and shows him all he does. . . . By myself I can do nothing; I judge only as I hear, and my judgment is just, for I seek not to please myself but him who sent me (John 5:19-20,30).

> For I did not speak of my own accord, but the Father who sent me commanded me what to say and how to say it. I know that his command leads to eternal life. So whatever I say is just what the Father has told me to say (John 12:49-50).

We see that Jesus only did what He saw His Father do, spoke only what He heard His father command, judged only as He heard from the Father, and lived to do His Father's will. His obedience was motivated by complete agreement in purpose, will and action with His Father. There is never any indication of coercion or any need to perform for His Father. Jesus described His life and actions as being one with the Father (see John 10:30). Therefore, we know that Jesus was willing to come and lay down His life for us.

Because the heart of God's nature and character is love manifested through giving, Jesus' entire ministry was one of giving, fueled by His great compassion for people. For example, when Jesus heard the news that John the Baptist was beheaded, He wanted to pull away from the crowds and get some rest. Instead, He had compassion on the multitude and blessed them by feeding them. He continually gave in abundance (see Matt. 14:15-21). His ministry on earth was best expressed in His own words: "I have made you [Father God] known to them, and will continue to make you known in order that the love you have for me may be in them and that I myself may be in them" (John 17:26).

At the last supper, Jesus revealed to the disciples His total unity with the Father: "Don't you believe that I am in the Father, and that the Father is in me? The words I say to you are not just my own. Rather, it is the Father, living in me, who is doing his work" (John 14:10). If you want to understand the Father's love, look at Jesus. If you want to understand the Father's giving heart, look at Jesus. If you want to know what the Father's will is here on earth, look at what Jesus did in His ministry. Jesus' life is an open book about the Father, for He and the Father were and are completely one in will, purpose and action.

GOD'S GREATEST DESIRE

Have you ever wondered what God wants more than anything else? It isn't a secret. It is plainly revealed in the prayer of Jesus found in John 17. His prayer includes you and me, for we are at the center of God's greatest desire: "[I pray] all of them may be one, Father, just as you are in me and I am in you. May they also be in us so that the world may believe that you have sent me. I have given them the glory that you gave me, that they may be one as we are one: I in them and you in me. May they be brought to complete unity to let the world know that you sent me and have loved them even as you have loved me" (John 17:21-23).

Father God longs for us to be His children, and to be one with Him, just as Jesus is. We were created to be included in the love communion of the Trinity itself. God has never backed off from His original intention for us. In giving Jesus as a sacrifice for sin, Father God was sowing to reap an abundant harvest—a multitude of children who would become like His Son. This is God's work of grace within us, not something we can achieve through our own efforts. Through His grace of giving Christ to the world, God has placed within those who choose to receive it, His own eternal, incorruptible seed—the Holy Spirit. We now contain His divine DNA within our re-created human spirit, which is His Kingdom in seed form. His Kingdom begins within us (see Luke 17:21).

God understands the principles of giving, for He established them. In planting the seed of the Holy Spirit within us, He knew He was initiating a process of growth and steady increase that would eventually result in the complete restoration of His kingdom on earth (see Isa. 9:7). Multiplication and increase is one of the principles of giving. Like the tiny mustard seed that becomes a huge bush, His DNA quickening our re-created human spirit constantly increases in its transformational power within us, making us more Christlike from the inside out.

The apostle Paul expressed this divine grace of giving when he said, "So all of us who have had the veil [of unbelief] removed can see and reflect the glory of the Lord. And the Lord—who is the Spirit—makes us more and more like him as we are changed into his glorious image" (2 Cor. 3:18, *NLT*). Our ultimate purpose is to reflect Father God's image in the world, even as Jesus did, "because as He is, so are we in this world" (1 John 4:17, *NKJV*).

As we are internally transformed, we become increasingly Christlike. We regain our internal unity and harmony and begin to operate as a unified whole again—spirit, soul and body. This unity allows us to partner harmoniously with the Holy Spirit, to use and direct His power to reassert our authority and dominion over the earth, and to subdue any powers that oppose us.

We now choose to walk in partnership with Father God, not out of fear, performance or desire for reward, but because we are increasingly united with Him in our will, purpose and plan, even as Jesus is. Like plants desiring the sun and water, we hunger and thirst for His presence, and our love for Him grows. As we yield more to His love within us, our hearts overflow with His love, and we give that love unconditionally to all.

Through our surrender to His love, we learn to become Christlike givers. As we give ourselves to Him, He increasingly fills us with Himself, His abundance and blessing. We become conduits of His nature, motivated by His love growing within us. We mature in Christlike giving, becoming increasingly like our Father; and through our giving, we reveal His kingdom to the world (see 1 John 4:15-17).

GIVING: LIKE FATHER LIKE SON

Father God's divine attributes are emphasized repeatedly throughout Scripture. He is wise, holy, righteous, omnipotent and omniscient. He is also generous and giving. Every one of His attributes reveals Father God's heart. As His grace works its transforming power within us, His attributes infiltrate our character and we become more and more Christlike.

Throughout the rest of this book, we will be looking at God's attribute of generosity and giving, and how it reflects the character and nature of God to us and in us. He calls us to share in His grace of giving, and to unleash the power of a generous heart. As we do, we show that we are His children, and we actively participate in restoring the earth to His kingdom, regaining our original destiny and purpose.

PUTTING IT ALL TOGETHER

Jesus came to earth to reveal the heart of Father God, redeem us from sin, and restore us to our original purpose and destiny. Father

God has given us His Spirit to transform us and conform us to His image. He calls us to a life of generosity and giving. As we become Christlike givers, we reveal His heart to others and restore the earth to His kingdom.

ASK YOURSELF

1. How is imitating Father God actually a form of worship?

2. Compare your feelings in the following two situations: giving a gift or receiving a gift. Which do you enjoy more, and why?

3. In what ways can our giving reveal the kingdom of God to others?

LIVE IT!

Father God has established principles of giving in Scripture. Write down all the principles you know and save them to use later. How do the principles you identified apply to your daily life?

GOD WANTS YOU TO PROSPER

In the first section of this book, we considered the characteristics of God, who God originally designed us to be, and what happened to us after our sin separated us from God. We reviewed the truth that our Father God is a lover and a giver, and He has done everything to redeem us and restore us to our original blessing and commission.

Part of His restoration to us is to provide abundantly and prosper us. This section provides a framework for prosperity and giving from God's perspective. The solid biblical bases for prosperity and wealth establish the truth that God wants to prosper His children in order to bless them personally and help them advance His kingdom.

Our security in God's provision rests on His promises that He is willing and desires to provide all our needs with His limitless riches in Christ. As we open our hearts to believe and actively receive God's promises, His grace works within our hearts, transforming us into Christlike givers. He may provide for us in unconventional ways and ask us to do things that don't make sense to our reasoning. These are actually His opportunities for training us to reign in His kingdom. As we trust Him and act on His directives, we grow in our confident expectation of Him, and we learn the power of being content in Him.

8

GOD WANTS YOU TO PROSPER

*"For I know the plans I have for you," declares the
LORD, "plans to prosper you and not to harm you,
plans to give you a hope and a future."*

JEREMIAH 29:11

WHAT IS PROSPERITY?

Every year, the "Forbes 400" lists the richest people in the United
States. Currently topping the list is Bill Gates, net worth $66 bil-
lion. In fact, the top 100 richest people are all multi-billionaires.[1]
When we think of prosperity, we typically think of money and material abundance. But is this God's idea of prosperity?

The Greek word for prosperity actually means "to be led along
a good road." I like this definition because it doesn't emphasize
the accumulation of things, but a way of living: "This is what the
LORD says—your Redeemer, the Holy One of Israel: 'I am the LORD
your God, who teaches you what is best for you, who directs you
in the way you should go'" (Isa. 48:17). God desires to lead us
along a good road that will prosper us in every area of our lives—
spiritually, emotionally, physically and materially (see 2 Pet. 1:3).

Consider the prosperity mentioned in these verses: "Both high
and low among men find refuge in the shadow of your wings. They
feast on the abundance of your house; you give them drink from
your river of delights. For with you is the fountain of life; in your
light we see light" (Ps. 36:7-9). Do you think the abundance of

Ché Ahn

God's house is limited to just spiritual prosperity? Think again, and remember that the streets in heaven are paved with gold!

That's not the only type of prosperity we are promised. Psalm 92:12-15 contains this wonderful promise: "The righteous will flourish like a palm tree, they will grow like a cedar of Lebanon; planted in the house of the LORD, they will flourish in the courts of our God. They will still bear fruit in old age, they will stay fresh and green, proclaiming, 'The LORD is upright; he is my Rock, and there is no wickedness in him.'" Here we have an abundance of health promised to us that will last us even into our old age!

Let's look at one last promise: "Nevertheless, I will bring health and healing to it; I will heal my people and will let them enjoy abundant peace and security" (Jer. 33:6). Here we see that physical health is combined with emotional wellbeing, a joint promise of abundance in both of these areas.

Probably the best way to answer the question "What is prosperity?" is to look at God's purpose in creating us and at His original commission to us. We were created in the image of God, so prosperity is anything and everything contained within that image. I think God's commission to us describes it beautifully. He told us to prosper and have abundance, be in health and increase in number, have authority and dominion on the earth and power over all our adversaries (see Gen. 1:28). That's complete prosperity! If you want a more detailed list, God provides specifics in Deuteronomy 28:2-14.

FRAGMENTS OF PROSPERITY

While God looks at prosperity in an all-encompassing way, we don't. All too often we look at prosperity promises and interpret them as relating to only the spiritual area. We have lived so long with a distorted image of ourselves, in this subnormal world under the curse of sin, that we accept its limitations and constraints as the norm. We accept fragments of prosperity when we could have total abundance in every area. We need to remember that Father God's original intention and purpose for us have not changed. In His gift of redemption to us through Jesus Christ, He is offering us the restoration of all the prosperity we lost in our disobedience. This means prosperity in every area of life.

For the rest of this book, I will be focusing on financial and material prosperity, not because it is the most important, but because it is the least accepted and most misunderstood area of prosperity. We need to stop grieving the Father's heart and start receiving everything He desires to bestow upon us.

It Takes a Change of Heart

God really wants us—He wants you—to prosper materially. Do you believe it? He really does! In order for you to start prospering, you must let go of your distorted self-image by gaining clearer insight into who you truly are in Christ. We read in the book of Ephesians, "I pray also that the eyes of your heart may be enlightened in order that you may know the hope to which he has called you, the riches of his glorious inheritance in the saints, and his incomparably great power for us who believe" (Eph. 1:18-19).

Jesus was opening the eyes of our heart when He said, "Repent, for the kingdom of heaven is near" (Matt. 4:17). He was saying we could have heaven here on earth. Since there are no financial shortages in heaven, there don't need to be any for us here; but in order to experience this, we first must repent. Does that surprise you? When most people think about repentance, they think about turning from their sins; but the Greek word for "repentance" is *metanoeo*, which means "to change your thinking." Today we would say, "You need a paradigm change."

Many in the church have a hard time believing that God is a good God who loves and even likes them and that He wants them to prosper financially. There are various reasons for this, but a major one is that many people have deep heart wounds and an orphan mentality that make it difficult for them to receive good things from Father God. They need a deep inner transformation that can only occur as their heart changes in profound ways. We will look at the central importance of our heart in this process shortly.

God Said It and That Settles It

The first step in true repentance, or a paradigm change, is to hear God's truth. Remember, God's words are true, expressing His unchanging intention, and they contain no hidden agenda. The power of His words always accomplish His purpose. So let's look at a few verses on financial prosperity and see what Father God is saying to us. Keep in mind that these are only a few of the many verses on the subject contained in Scripture.

" 'For I know the plans I have for you,' declares the LORD, 'plans to prosper you and not to harm you, plans to give you hope and a future' " (Jer. 29:11). This is one of my favorite Bible verses. God loves us so much that His heart's desire is to prosper us and give us hope for our future. Hope is the confident anticipation of good in every area of life. God told this to the nation of Israel, when they were in captivity by the Babylonians, due to their disobedience. Even in the middle of discipline, God offered them hope and communicated His heart to prosper and not harm them. Since God never changes, the same is true for us. What a good God we serve!

"The LORD will grant you abundant prosperity—in the fruit of your womb, the young of your livestock and the crops of your ground—in the land he swore to your forefathers to give you" (Deut. 28:11). This verse is taken from one of the most powerful chapters on prosperity in the Old Testament. When God speaks of prospering "your livestock and the crops of your ground," He is talking about financial prosperity, because for the farmer these were valuable financial commodities.

"When the righteous prosper, the city rejoices; when the wicked perish, there are shouts of joy" (Prov. 11:10). Why do people rejoice when the righteous prosper? Because the righteous, those who are right with God and others, are generous and will share their prosperity with the poor and needy. They are Christlike givers who know that God has blessed them to be a blessing to others.

"Let them shout for joy and be glad, who favor my righteous cause; and let them say continually, 'Let the LORD be magnified, who has pleasure in the prosperity of His servant' " (Ps. 35:27, NKJV). I love this passage because it reveals the Father heart of

God, who takes pleasure when we prosper. Just like I want my four adult children and their spouses to prosper, how much more our heavenly Father wants us to prosper!

In case you are still struggling with the idea that Father God wants to bless you with financial prosperity, consider these final two verses.

"But remember the LORD your God, for it is he who gives you the ability [power] to produce wealth, and so confirms his covenant, which he swore to your forefathers" (Deut. 8:18). The word "power" in Hebrew is the same as the root word for the chameleon lizard. A chameleon changes the color of its skin with the environment to protect itself from predators. Here God is saying we will have supernatural power to change, adapt and prosper, no matter if we're in a recession or hyperinflation. We are to prosper in every circumstance so that we can bring forth His covenant promises that He made to Abraham.

"The blessing of the LORD brings wealth, and he adds no trouble to it" (Prov. 10:22). We have only to look at the daily news to realize that wealth frequently brings great difficulty to people. Every year we see more tragic deaths of celebrities who, despite their wealth, are desperately unhappy. God promises us that money will be a blessing instead of a curse, because we know that money is simply a tool, a means to achieve our God-given purpose. We will truly prosper as we become aligned with Him and use our resources for His purposes.

PUTTING IT ALL TOGETHER

I hope it is clear from these few verses from Scripture that God wants you to prosper abundantly. Too often we accept prosperity fragments and deny ourselves the total abundance God would give us. We need to discard our distorted identity and let God do a work of inner transformation by opening the eyes of our heart. The first step is to receive a revelation of the truth through God's Word.

ASK YOURSELF

1. What is the definition of prosperity that dominates our culture today? How does it compare to God's definition of prosperity?

2. Read Deuteronomy 28:2-14. What specific example of prosperity, described there, do you need most in your life right now?

3. Do you really believe that God takes pleasure when you prosper? Why or why not?

LIVE IT!

Most of us need *metanoeo*, or a "change in our thinking," regarding prosperity. For many reasons, we have developed habitual ways of thinking that can hinder us from believing that God wants to prosper us. What ideas about prosperity have you believed that make it difficult for you to accept that God wants to materially prosper you? Write them down and we will consider them later.

Note

1. "The Richest People in America," *Forbes*, 2012. http://www.forbes.com/forbes-400/gallery.

9

PROSPERITY . . . FOR WHAT?

*I press on toward the goal to win the prize for which God has
called me heavenward in Christ Jesus.*

PHILIPPIANS 3:14

SOMETHING FROM NOTHING?

When I was a very young boy in Korea, I used to like to watch one
of our groundskeepers who was a wood-carver. He was highly
skilled and could carve very ornate figurines. He would take a block
of wood and begin shaving it with his carving knife as I watched,
transfixed. I would always ask him, "What are you making?"

He would only smile at me with his twinkling eyes and say, "I
don't know. We'll see what wants to come out of the wood." It
might take days, but gradually an animal would emerge, and I
would begin trying to guess what it was. I would feel triumphant
when I finally identified it and informed the wood-carver, who always acted surprised.

Back then it seemed like a magical process the way something
would come from nothing, and I actually thought I discovered its
identity before the wood-carver did. Of course, now I realize the
wood-carver always knew from the very beginning what he intended to make. Every shaving of his knife had a purpose behind
it. I was the only one living in the mystery of what that purpose
was until I could identify it.

It is often said that God made the world out of nothing. In one
sense this is true, for God created the material from the immaterial.

But God is not a tinkerer, and creation is not an experiment. Everything God does is purposeful. Read the creation story in the book of Genesis and you will see that every word God spoke was specific and directed to a purpose. His MO was no different when it came to our creation. God's purpose was to create human beings in His image, who would reflect His glory and partner in unity with Him. This was and still is His ultimate intention, and everything else He has ever done for us supports this central purpose.

Purpose Confers Meaning

Purpose gives meaning to a person, event or thing. Imagine if basketball was only an activity with two hoops at either end of a court, players on each team, and a ball, but no goal of competing to win. What kind of a game would that be? Certainly not a game that would have multimillion-dollar franchises like we know today!

When it comes to prosperity, we need God's revelation of His purpose for it in our lives. Prosperity is not a formula where we observe certain rules and obtain wealth; nor is it a reward system whereby we get rewarded for being obedient children. Prosperity is one aspect of the nature and character of God; as His royal children, it is ours as we walk in agreement and unity with our Father.

When, in faith, we receive God's grace of giving, we become Christlike givers who prosper. Our prosperity has three major purposes: to glorify our Father God (that is, to manifest His nature, character and power); to train us for temporal and eternal reigning as His children; and to advance His kingdom. Let's look at each of these.

Our Prosperity Glorifies Father God

God wants to prosper us because He loves us. He repeatedly assures us that He wants to meet our needs and fulfill our desires (see Matt. 6:31-33; 7:11; Phil. 4:19). Our prosperity gives Him pleasure (see Ps. 35:27) and it showcases His love for us. What would you think of billionaire Donald Trump if you saw that his children were thin and emaciated, and wearing old, worn-out clothes? Knowing that he could do much better for his children than that, you would think, "What a horrible father he is!"

What do you reflect about Father God and His love if you are living paycheck to paycheck and just struggling to have your needs met? Jesus told us, "I have come that they may have life, and that they may have it more abundantly" (John 10:10, *NKJV*). What does an abundant life mean? I believe it means an abundance of love, joy and peace; but I also think it means abundance of finances so that we can enjoy our life. Paul states, "Command those who are rich in this present world not to be arrogant nor to put their hope in wealth, which is so uncertain, but to put their hope in God, who richly provides us with everything for our enjoyment" (1 Tim. 6:17). Paul makes it clear here that God is the source of our prosperity and provides us with everything for our enjoyment!

Let's not get super-spiritual and think that God doesn't want us to have an enjoyable vacation, good food or a good life. The writer of the book of Ecclesiastes tells us, "Moreover, when God gives any man wealth and possessions, and enables him to enjoy them, and to accept his lot and be happy in his work—this is a gift of God" (Eccles. 5:19).

PROSPERITY BUILDS CHARACTER FOR REIGNING

Probably nothing reveals character as quickly as how we handle money. Jesus made it very clear that if we cannot be trusted with material possessions, God will not entrust us with His greater spiritual possessions (see Luke 16:10-13). God uses prosperity to cultivate our self-control, as well as to help clarify our spiritual maturity. As we yield to His grace, our character becomes progressively more Christlike in the way we handle money and determine financial priorities.

God expects us to manage our prosperity responsibly and meet our obligations. We are to provide adequately for our family and children: "If anyone does not provide for his relatives, and especially for his immediate family, he has denied the faith and is worse than an unbeliever" (1 Tim. 5:8). These are strong words. What does providing for one's own entail? I think it is more than the basics of food, shelter and clothing. I think it is also providing for a child's education and personal advancement. Wouldn't it be wonderful to send your kids to college and, when they graduated, not be under the burden of massive student debt? I believe that God wants to so prosper you that, with wise financial management, you can send your children to college without having to go into debt. By God's grace, we have sent all four of our children to college without having to borrow a penny.

God also wants to prosper us so that we can leave an inheritance for our children. Proverbs 13:22 instructs, "A good man leaves an inheritance for his children's children, but a sinner's wealth is stored up for the righteous." The psalmist says that God wants you to spend your days in prosperity and then leave your property to your children when you die (see Ps. 25:13). God approves of this prosperity and calls it the action of a "good man."

Prosperity Enables Us to Advance God's Kingdom

A major part of our original commission was to have authority and dominion in all the earth. Dominion implies rulership over a domain, and Jesus made it clear that we have been given the responsibility of advancing His kingdom here on earth. The kingdom of God is not a geopolitical kingdom centered here in this world. Neither is it only in heaven. It is a kingdom in the spirit dimension (see John 18:36). Jesus said that the kingdom of God exists within each one of us in seed form. As we learn to be Christlike givers, and we make Jesus King and Lord of our life, God's rule and reign come into our lives (see Luke 17:21).

The Kingdom is also the realm of His blessing, the restoration of everything we lost in our disobedience. It is heaven on earth. That's why we have been praying for more than 2,000 years, "Thy kingdom come, Thy will be done on earth, as it is in heaven" (Matt. 6:10, *KJV*). Father God wants people to experi-

ence on earth what is in heaven. To advance God's kingdom is to
bring more of heaven to earth.

One aspect of advancing God's kingdom is to fulfill the Great
Commission. Jesus has been given all authority in heaven and on
earth, and He desires that all persons should come to know Him.
We are to make disciples of all the nations (see Matt. 28:18-20).
It takes enormous amounts of wealth to fulfill this commission:
money to support missionaries, plant churches, build church
buildings, care for orphans, build Christian schools and univer-
sities, establish homes for the homeless, and more.

When Christians define prosperity as "just having your needs
met," I don't think they understand the implications of that
mindset. Money can be a powerful weapon in the hands of the
Christian to reach the lost. Robert Morris, in his wonderful book
The Blessed Life, shares how he and his wife reached out to a wait-
ress by giving her an outrageous tip (the bill was $10, and they left
a tip of $50) that impacted her so greatly, she and her husband
ended up giving their lives to Jesus.[1] We advance God's kingdom
by becoming a blessing to others (see Gen. 12:1-3; 2 Cor. 9:11).

Another important way that we are to advance God's kingdom is to help build the local Church. Throughout all Scripture,
God always commands that others meet His ministers' needs (see
Matt. 10:10; Luke 10:7). We are told that "the laborer is worthy of
his wages" (1 Tim. 5:18, *NKJV*); and Paul writes at considerable
length on giving to the church in his second letter to the Corinthians, encouraging them to give liberally with joy (see 2 Cor. 8-9).

A final aspect of advancing God's kingdom is to eradicate
systemic poverty. God places the welfare of the orphan, the
widow and the stranger (the person without a family) squarely
on the shoulders of His people. This aspect of kingdom building is so important to the Lord that He makes Himself indebted
to us when we give to the poor (see Prov. 19:17; 28:27). He describes this in James 1:27 as "pure and undefiled religion" (*NKJV*).
Jesus made it clear that taking care of the less fortunate divides
the believers from the unbelievers at the final judgment (see
Matt. 25:31-46).

Thus, we can see that not only does God want to prosper us, but also that prosperity is absolutely essential if we are to fulfill our God-ordained purpose and commission here on earth. God does not prosper us to satisfy our personal whims or greediness. While He wants to satisfy our needs and supply us with abundance to give to others, He does not endorse a lavish or wasteful lifestyle. We are never to look to our provision for security, but always to trust in our heavenly Provider. For many of us, this is difficult if not impossible to do. We will need to look at our hearts to understand why this is so.

PUTTING IT ALL TOGETHER

God wants us to prosper for a purpose. He uses our prosperity to reflect His glory and to build a Christlike character within us for reigning and advancing His kingdom here on earth. We are to use financial prosperity to provide for our families and the poor, to bless others, to fulfill the Great Commission, and to build the local Church.

ASK YOURSELF

1. In what ways has God materially blessed me? Try to think of as many examples as possible.

2. What do you see as your responsibility in planning to provide for your present or future children's education? For their inheritance? Do you need to rethink your position?

3. In what ways are you involved in meeting the needs of the poor? If you haven't been involved, how can you begin now?

LIVE IT!

In 2 Corinthians 8 and 9, Paul takes up an offering for the needs of the Church. Read these two chapters as if they are being written to you personally. What feelings come up as you read his exhortation? Do you usually give cheerfully and willingly? Or do you give begrudgingly, feeling under pressure? Why do you feel this way?

Note
1. Robert Morris, *The Blessed Life* (Ventura, CA: Regal Books, 2002), pp. 85-86.

Ché Ahn

10

CAN GOD AFFORD IT?

And my God will meet all your needs according to his glorious riches in Christ Jesus.

PHILIPPIANS 4:19

WHAT'S THE FOCUS: PROBLEM OR PROVISION?

"Can we afford it?" In these past few years of the "Great Recession," this has become an increasingly common question. For some people the focus is on issues like, "Can we afford the family vacation this year?" or "Will we be able to keep the kids in private school?" For others the belt tightening is more austere, with concerns like, "Will the car get repossessed?" or "How will we pay the light bill?"

We have all become more aware that we live in a world of limited resources, and lack is never far away. Many people who felt reasonably secure a few years ago now find that their lives have been upended. Some have lost employment and are still unable to find work. Others have had to default on their mortgages, and many now live in homes that are worth less than the mortgage they still owe.

Our church, HRock, is located in one of the most affluent areas in the nation. Compared to many other areas, we have come through the recession relatively unscathed. While most home values fell 20 percent, and even 30 percent to 40 percent in some parts of the country, property values here decreased by only 10 percent. Yet, when we took a survey recently within a five-mile radius of our sanctuary, Ambassador Auditorium, and asked residents,

"What are your greatest needs?" the second most common answer was finances.

With so much anxiety in the culture, it is easy to focus on limitation and lack from the fearful perspective of an orphan heart. Christlike givers, however, see their situation, whatever it is, through Father God's abundance to them as His children. In Philippians 4:19, we have been given the following wonderful promise: "And my God will meet all your needs according to his glorious riches in Christ Jesus." God reminds us that we are not to allow fear to distort our focus so that we see only our limitations; we are to trust in the unending abundance of God's provision. Our Father God has a limitless supply, and He definitely can afford it.

The promise is short, simple and direct, but it is one of the most amazing, all-encompassing promises in the Bible. It is God's guarantee regarding our finances. Because we are so familiar with it, it is easy to overlook the depth of meaning it contains. This promise is packed with rich assurance, so let's take a few minutes and unpack it.

- "God will." It doesn't say, "He *might* meet your needs." The Word says, "He *will*." This is a fact, an absolute guarantee. God is staking His character and reputation on it. We know that all of God's words are true words, and we can stake everything we have and are on what He tells us. There is no fine print here, no "escape clause." Father God is simply telling us what He is willing to do.

- "God will meet *all* . . ." It doesn't say, "I'll meet *some* of your needs." The promise says all your needs. Would that include your car payment? Education expenses? Braces for your kids? Your house mortgage? Yes! He is interested in and wants to meet all of these needs.

- Needs, not greeds. What about the new jet skis you've been drooling over, or that plastic surgery you've been secretly coveting? God never promises that He will supply our every whim. There's a difference between needs, which are necessities, and wants, which can be greeds. Think for a moment. As a parent, do you give your children everything they ask for and want? I doubt that you do, and I certainly hope that you don't, because you will spoil them. Our heavenly Father is a good parent. He's not going to give us everything we want, but He will supply all our legitimate needs.

• "According to His riches." This promise is not based on my assets, thank God! It's based on what God has, and His resources are unlimited. There is never a recession or shortage in heaven! However, God knows that we frequently get shortsighted, so He often reminds us in Scripture about who He is and what He has. " 'The silver is mine and the gold is mine,' declares the LORD" (Hag. 2:8). Actually, He wants us to understand that not just the silver and the gold, but everything belongs to Him. "For every animal of the forest is mine, and the cattle on a thousand hills. . . . The world is mine, and all that is in it" (Ps. 50:10,12). We will never have a need that can exhaust God's supply. He can afford it!

• "In Christ Jesus." It's very important that we pay attention to these three little words, for God is directing His statement to a certain group of people. This is a promise only for believers, not a promise for everyone. It's for those who are "in Christ Jesus." In other words, God is saying, "If you're one of My children, in My family, I promise to meet all your needs." God has never promised to meet all the needs of humankind. But He has always made it abundantly clear that He will take care of His own children, those who receive and trust in Him. "I have been young, and now am old; yet I have not seen the righteous forsaken, nor his descendants begging bread" (Ps. 37:25, NKJV).

Paul's words in Philippians 4:19 make it clear that God our Father is both willing and abundantly able to provide everything we need. He can definitely afford it, and He wants to do it. *That's great, you may be thinking, so why do I still have so many financial needs? Is God ignoring me, or has He changed His mind? Maybe this only refers to "spiritual" needs, not my material or financial needs.* When we get discouraged, thoughts like these often plague us. We must remember what God is like, even when we are tempted to think otherwise. Our heavenly Father is changeless, totally trustworthy, and He keeps His covenants with us.

We know from earlier discussions that God is a lover and a generous giver. He even sacrificed His only Son, Jesus, to reconcile us back into a right relationship with Himself. He tells us in Romans 8:32, "He who did not spare His own Son, but delivered Him up for us all, how shall He not with Him also freely give us all other things?" (*NKJV*). If God the Father was willing, out of His love, to give the supreme sacrifice of His Son to redeem us, would He withhold anything else to meet our other needs when He can so easily supply them?

Then why aren't all of our needs met? We know that the financial principles that God has laid out in His Word are eternally true. Like Him, they are changeless, powerful and totally effective. God has done everything on His end to provide for all our needs. If we are to receive anything from Him, we must open our hearts to believe and receive all the good things our Father has for us. Next, we will look at how we believe and receive.

Putting It All Together

God is willing to supply His abundant provision for every type of need we may encounter in our lives.

Ask Yourself

1. Do you currently have a financial need? What is it? Spend a few minutes looking at your need through the lens of God's abundant supply. How does this change the way you view your need?

Ché Ahn

2. What hinders you from confidently expecting God to meet your financial needs? Are you disqualifying yourself for some reason? What is it? Try to be as specific with yourself as you can.

LIVE IT!

Your understanding of God's heart will deepen as you meditate on His Word. Actively meditate on Philippians 4:19 for the next few days. Ask God to reveal His heart to you as you meditate.

One way to actively meditate is to repeat the verse several times, emphasizing a different section each time. For example, you might begin this way:

My God *will* meet
All my needs
According to *His glorious riches*
In Christ Jesus.

As you repeat each section of the verse, give special focus to the emphasized words. Repeat each section several times before going on to the next section. This will only take a minute or two, so try to do it several times a day. After several days, ask yourself how the verse has changed in its meaning for you. You may want to write a few notes that will remind you of this change.

11

THE POWER TWINS: BELIEVE AND RECEIVE

Do not be anxious about anything, but in everything, by prayer and petition, with thanksgiving, present your requests to God.

PHILIPPIANS 4:6

A SUBTLE ATHEISM

Do you believe that God will provide for your needs? Faith is a trusting relationship with a good heavenly Father; but due to our early experiences with our earthly parents, many of us act like spiritual orphans. Even when we want to, it is difficult for us to trust in God's goodness. In His Sermon on the Mount, Jesus reassures us repeatedly about God's goodness and trustworthiness (see Matt. 6:25-34). He tells us to look at the birds. They don't spend time worrying about where their next meal will come from, for God supplies what they will need. Jesus asks us to consider that if God takes care of the birds, don't we think He'll take care of us if we trust Him? Of course the logical answer to this is yes.

Belief, however, is more than mental assent regarding facts. When God tells us to believe Him, He is insisting that we place our confidence and total trust upon Him. This means that we rely on Him, not merely that we give credence to His words. We need to realize that our degree of trust in our heavenly Father reflects our relationship with Him. The more intimately we know Him, the more deeply we will trust Him.

One measure of our trust in God is how frequently we worry. Actually, worry is a form of atheism. Every time we worry, we're acting like atheists. In effect, we're saying, "If it's to be, it's up to me." We may say we believe in God and His ability to provide, but in the final analysis our actions demonstrate that we are still depending on our own efforts and resources to carry us through difficult situations. We must always remind ourselves that our security is not our bank or savings account, our investments or any other resource, no matter how much we have. Our only true security is in our heavenly Father. We need to avoid the subtle atheism that tells us we must take care of ourselves.

WE WILL ACTIVELY RECEIVE WHAT WE BELIEVE

Belief always involves action. This is where receiving comes in. Many people have the mistaken idea that receiving is the passive action of waiting for something to appear. Actually, receiving is the active response to believing. When we receive, we ask and give thanks, then take and obtain what we have requested. One definition of "receive" is to look for, take in full, give space to and make room for. This means we are actively involved.

The first step in receiving is actively asking. The Bible is clear that in everything we are to ask God and make our requests known (see Phil 4:6). We ask, expecting God to answer. One of my favorite verses is "You do not have, because you do not ask God" (Jas. 4:2). God is waiting for us to ask. In fact, we are instructed more than 20 times in the New Testament to ask for what we need and want. God never shuts His storehouse until we shut our mouths. He wants to help, but the problem is that many of us don't ever ask.

Think for a moment. The last time you needed a car, did you ask God for it or did you just go out, get a loan and buy it? My guess is that you probably didn't ask for it; you just went out and bought it. God wants to supply your needs, but active asking is an important part of receiving. One of the reasons why we so seldom see miracles in our lives is that we do not ask for them. Would you like to see God work supernaturally in your life more often? Start asking!

A second important key to receiving is to make your requests specific. Imagine that your millionaire uncle, Tex, decides to buy a car for you. He tells you that you can have anything you want. Do you just take him to the nearest dealership and let him pick out anything on the showroom floor? Not hardly! You would take him to the exact dealership that has the make and model you want. You would pick out the color, the accessories and every detail about the car. You wouldn't leave any of it to chance, because you know this is a sure thing.

We wouldn't hesitate to be specific with Uncle Tex, but often we make vague requests to God. Dr. Paul (David) Yonggi Cho, now retired, who was the Korean pastor of the world's largest church, told this story: During the 1950s, he was in Bible college and needed a bicycle. He brought his request to God, but nothing happened. He persisted in asking for his need and still nothing happened. Finally, in frustration he confronted God, insisting that he really needed a bike. The Lord asked, "What type of bicycle do you really want?" He was believing for any bike, but God wanted him to be specific.

Although he didn't possibly see how he could ever afford it, Dr. Cho then described his desire for an American 10-speed Schwinn bike (the best available at the time), in the color blue. Shortly after his specific request, a retiring missionary gave him a nearly new bicycle before leaving Korea. And guess what it was? An American 10-speed blue Schwinn!

Sometimes, God wants to give you good things you haven't even asked for. A number of years ago, my family and I were settled in a very nice home in Pasadena. We liked that home and had no plans to move. But we received a prophetic word that we should seek another residence. The word came from Cindy Jacobs, who is a dear friend we know to be a true prophet of God. Although we didn't understand it, Sue and I wrote down what we wanted in a new home. We asked for a five-bedroom house with four bathrooms that would accommodate our large family and allow us to host out-of-town visitors. God gave us a beautiful, new, six-bedroom house with five bathrooms for less money than we anticipated!

We moved into our new home on Thanksgiving Day 1998. Since that time, even with the recession, our home has tripled in value. The Lord gave us a generous gift that we hadn't even requested. By the way, the model home was called "Revival." So we moved into "Revival" on Thanksgiving Day 1998! Perhaps you will experience more of His reviving presence by giving thanks for what He has given you. Let's look at this in more depth.

THE LANGUAGE OF FAITH

Giving thanks is the third step in active receiving. When we truly trust God, we will bring everything to Him in prayer, thanking Him for providing for us. Thanksgiving has been dubbed the "language of faith." When I make a request to God with thanksgiving, I am actually demonstrating that I believe God will meet my need even though I don't see it yet. My belief in God and His goodness prompt my expectant request for my needs to be met. When I make my request to God, I know that it is as good as done. I actually see myself receiving, and this makes it easy for me to thank Him.

Believing and receiving are the power twins. They are faith in action. We cannot receive what we do not believe, but our receiving must be active. We must refuse to worry, trust in God's goodness, make specific requests when we ask, and thank Him in advance, knowing that He will provide.

This is a hallmark of joyful living. Jesus told us, "You have not asked for anything in my name. Ask and you will receive, and your joy will be complete" (John 16:24). Why does God want us to ask? So that He can give to us. Why does He want to give to us? So we can receive. Why does He want us to receive? So that we will be full of joy! God wants to give to us and increase our joy because He is a loving Father. Loving fathers love to bestow gifts on their children.

PUTTING IT ALL TOGETHER

Believe and receive by doing the following:

- Refuse to worry.
- Take everything to God.

- Make your requests specific.
- Thank God in advance for His provision.

Ask Yourself

1. Think about the last time you asked God for something. Was your request specific or general? If you were to be specific about what you really wanted, what would you request?

2. Do you thank God when you make your requests? If you do thank Him, is it because you genuinely believe that He is going to provide for you?

3. Do you pay for it before you pray for it? Do you take everything to God in prayer or do you only ask Him for the really "big" needs that you don't know how to handle yourself?

Live It!

The next time you have a need, believe and actively receive. See what God will do for you when you stop worrying and decide to start living the joyful life.

1 2

A Divine Airline Reservation

*Jesus said to him . . . "Go to the lake and throw out your line. Take the
first fish you catch; open its mouth and you will find a four-drachma coin.
Take it and give it to them for my tax and yours."*

MATTHEW 17:26-27

A New Testament Example
of Training to Reign

When we think of God supplying our financial needs, usually we
think of more money coming into our hands, perhaps through a
new position at work, a pay raise or an unexpected bonus check.
But God is not limited to conventional means to prosper us financially. He can do very unusual things to increase our material blessings. He uses many situations as opportunities to train us to reign.

Remember when Peter came to Jesus with a financial need—the
question of the temple tax? Jesus indicated that they should pay,
and His ministry had a purse for expenses. He clearly could have
gotten the money from there. But He gave Peter most unusual instructions. He literally told him to go fishing for the money!

Apparently, Peter had been around Jesus long enough to not
question His strange directives. Peter simply obeyed what had to
seem like an unreasonable action, caught the fish and found the
tax money! We need to follow Peter's example. When we bring our
need to the Lord, we must be prepared to follow His leading, no
matter how unconventional it might be. We may be tempted to
rely on our own reasoning, but we simply need to believe that

however He does it, God will meet our every need, even as He promised He would.

A PERSONAL EXPERIENCE
IN TRAINING TO REIGN

I'd like to share an incident from my life that illustrates this. Because I travel a lot, many times I have seen God meet my travel needs supernaturally. One of the most memorable times was when I was to fly from Inchon, South Korea, to Singapore on Singapore Airlines. I was cutting it close when I had to catch a morning flight and then speak later that same evening to 12,000 people at a major event called the Festival of Praise.

When I got to the airport, there was no record of my itinerary anywhere. I had to show them my copy of the itinerary, and because I'm a frequent flier, I have a Global Service status for United Airlines. I called the United Global Service office in the US to confirm my business class seat on the flight. I even had the Global Service agent talk to the manager of Singapore Air. The manager acknowledged that the mistake was on their end, but the problem was that there was not one single seat on that particular flight, even in economy class. They were totally sold out, and everyone had checked in.

The manager apologized and offered me a first class seat on the next flight, but that flight was at 4 PM, and I would miss the speaking engagement. I asked the manager if they could put me on another carrier that was going into Singapore, but all the airlines were totally booked or they had already taken off for Singapore.

It was the month of July, when summer travel was at its peak. The closest city I could get into was Kuala Lumpur on a Malaysian Airline flight, but there wasn't one seat available on the connecting flight to get into Singapore. Once there, I could rent a car, but it was a three- to four-hour drive into Singapore, depending on the rush hour traffic on a Friday evening. I knew I couldn't make it in time by driving.

My human reasoning started telling me that perhaps this wasn't meant to be. So I called my host, thinking that perhaps it wasn't God's will for me to speak. Maybe someone else could take my place. But when I talked to my host, he explained that there was no other speaker. *I was the only speaker* they had advertised in advance, and I *had* to do whatever it took to come that night. I don't need to tell you that my stress level went sky high! I told the Singapore Airlines manager that I would take the Malaysian Air into Kuala Lumpur, with the hope that one seat would open up on the 5:00 PM connecting flight into Singapore. It would be a tight fit since I would be arriving at 4:20 PM.

CHOICE POINTS IN TRAINING FOR REIGNING

While on that first flight, I prayed a lot for that empty seat on the connecting flight. As soon as I arrived into Kuala Lumpur airport, I ran to the Malaysian Air connecting desk. There was a Muslim woman wearing a burka (a head covering), standing behind the desk. I asked if a seat had opened up for my flight into Singapore at 5:00 PM. She smiled and said, "This is your lucky day. One seat has opened. It is economy class, but it is available."

I let out a big "Hallelujah!" right in front of her as joy flooded my heart. Father God had done it again! Driving would not have been an option. Time wise, after getting my bag and clearing customs, I would have had to drive at least three hours; and even if the traffic was good, I would still have missed my speaking time, which was exactly at 8:00 PM.

Have you ever noticed that just when everything seems resolved, a dark cloud appears on the horizon? The agent started to make the changes on the computer to rebook me, and then she paused and gave a somber look at the computer and told me, "It says here that you have a checked-on bag, and there is no way I can put you on that next flight without your bag."

I said, "Madam, I don't care about my bags. You can put them on the later flight. I need to get on this flight!"

She replied, "I am so sorry, sir, but after 9/11, our policy is that a person cannot be separated from his or her luggage. You must have your luggage on the next flight. And to get your luggage and put it on will take at least one hour, and you only have a half hour to catch your flight!"

I felt a sinking sensation in my gut. I couldn't believe that I was so close to making the connection, only to be grounded by my baggage! For just a moment, I resigned myself to the situation. After all, I'd given it my best shot; what more could I do? Deep within, I felt the Lord nudge, "Ask Me."

Suddenly my mind cleared, and I remembered who my Provider is. The Lord had opened the seat; He could get me on the next flight. I replied to the agent, "I know you are a Muslim, but I am going to pray to Jesus right now and ask Him to find my bag and put it on the 5:00 PM flight."

She gave me a strange look as I prayed aloud, but I didn't care. I was desperate! I asked her to call down to the baggage area and see if they could find my luggage and place it on the 5:00 PM flight. She told me it was futile, but I pleaded with her to just ask. So she called and gave my name with the instructions to find my bag off the previous flight, and to call her if they found it.

During this whole time, I was praying in the Spirit under my breath. It was hard not to be anxious, but a gentle peace began welling up inside me. Within five minutes, the phone call came to the desk. They had found my luggage! She immediately told them to rush and deliver it to the Singapore flight that was departing at 5:00 PM. I only had 15 minutes to catch that connecting flight. She printed out my boarding pass, and I ran to the Singapore departure gate with another prayer under my breath, that this would be a sign to that Muslim lady that *Jesus* answers prayer!

I got on the plane as they were shutting the door. I arrived in Singapore by 6:00 PM, with my luggage in tow! The host driver immediately drove me to the arena, and without changing or taking a shower, I walked up on the platform ready to speak. I didn't smell or look good with my disheveled clothes, but by God's grace, He supernaturally got me there!

God truly met all my needs that day, according to His glorious riches in Christ Jesus! He met both my needs and the conference's financial needs through a series of events that I know were not coincidence, but divine intervention. In retrospect, I recognize the event as another opportunity for my training to reign. We serve a loving and gracious heavenly Father whose desire is to give us His kingdom (see Luke 12:32). He wants to bless and profit us in every circumstance!

PUTTING IT ALL TOGETHER

God is concerned about your financial needs in every situation. Ask Him to intervene, and believe that He will come through for you. Expect the unexpected! Remember that every event in your life is an opportunity for God to train you to reign in His kingdom.

ASK YOURSELF

1. Can you remember a time when you had a financial need, and a "coincidence" occurred just at the right time? Take a few moments and reflect on it. Can you see God's hand at work?

2. Do you routinely bring your financial needs to God in every situation? Why or why not?

3. If God instructed you to do something unusual in answer to a requested need, would you do it? What might hold you back?

LIVE IT!

Start a financial prayer journal. Record the date and your requested need. Watch the Lord provide, and record when and how He met your need. Be prepared for "blessed coincidences"! Review your journal often. Remembering how God has met your needs in the past will help your faith grow in the present.

13

THE POWER OF CONTENTMENT

I know what it is to be in need, and I know what it is to have plenty.
I have learned the secret of being content in any and every situation,
whether well fed or hungry, whether living in plenty or in want.

PHILIPPIANS 4:12

At first glance, Philippians 4:12 appears to be a contradiction. How could the apostle Paul be content in any situation if he was in want or need? Surely we can only be content when we have sufficient provision and are comfortable in our circumstances. While it sounds reasonable, this concept of contentment is outwardly focused, and ignores the fact that true contentment is an inward process. Contentment is the state of being delighted, full of joy, gratified and having peace and ease of mind. When we see our contentment as being dependent upon our circumstances, we actually set ourselves up to be discontented.

THE DECEPTION OF "WHEN, THEN AND MORE"

We are all familiar with the feelings that accompany being discontent. We experience frustration and the sense that we lack control in our lives and are powerless to change our circumstances. We become fearful and anxious and often spend time worrying about what we don't have. We fall into the "when/then" mode of thinking. "When I get such and such, then I'll be happy." "When I get that promotion at work" or "When I get the bills paid off, then everything will be great."

We become future oriented. We imagine that when we can re-
tire or when we get the house paid off, things will be better. Our
contentment always lies someplace else and out in the future
when things are different. We don't realize it, but this future ori-
entation robs us of the pleasure of enjoying our lives now; and
the idea that something more will bring us contentment is in itself an illusion. Somebody once asked the millionaire Howard
Hughes, "How much does it take to make a man happy?" Hughes
replied, "Just a little more."

Often, we begin comparing ourselves to others and end up
feeling "less than." We fall into the trap of "keeping up with the
Joneses" and imagine that if we only had comparable possessions,
we would be happy. The apostle Paul cautions us against making
comparisons of ourselves with others. He warns, "When [people]
measure themselves by themselves and compare themselves with
themselves, they are not wise" (2 Cor. 10:12).

Comparing ourselves to others never produces contentment,
because it is focused on the wrong thing: what we possess. We live
in a culture that puts tremendous emphasis on the acquisition of
material goods. We've all seen the bumper sticker "He Who Has
the Most Toys Wins." It is easy for us to fall into the mentality that
more will produce contentment.

Thinking that "more is better" is not new. In his letter to the
young minister Timothy, Paul directly addressed this delusion:
"Godliness with contentment is great gain. For we brought nothing into the world, and we can take nothing out of it. . . . People
who want to get rich fall into temptation and a trap and into many
foolish and harmful desires that plunge men into ruin and destruction" (1 Tim. 6:6-7,9).

The reality is that no amount of "more" will ever produce contentment. The story of Adam and Eve powerfully illustrates this.
They were created in perfection, had intimate access to God, and
were given complete dominion over everything on earth. They lived
in a perfect place, "Eden," where they had everything they could
possibly imagine, and there was absolutely no lack. Yet, while in
perfect abundance, they became discontent. How did this happen?

Despite the abundance that surrounded them, Adam and Eve became convinced that there was something that could be added to their lives that would make them even more content. They wanted to become self-sufficient and be like God.

Self-sufficiency is the ultimate delusion that leads to discontent, for we imagine that if we can only control our circumstances, we can ensure our contentment and security. But we can never attain true self-sufficiency, and our futile quest for it leaves us frightened and insecure, dominated with a survivalist mentality. We ignore the fact that God created us to be dependent upon Him and in constant fellowship with Him. We can never attain true contentment until we experience the security of knowing our identity as Father God's beloved child.

RELATIONSHIP, NOT SELF-SUFFICIENCY

True contentment can only be found in relationship, for joy and grace come from participation in the giving and receiving that occur in ongoing relating. Contentment is an inward sufficiency that is produced by our surrender to God in every circumstance. We surrender, not because of some fatalistic attitude, but because we know that our God is all-powerful and on our side. He has promised to supply our every need, and we believe Him completely (see Heb. 13:5-6).

We can be content in any and every circumstance because we know our Father God will never leave or forsake us, and He is working every situation for our good. It is this abiding in a trusting relationship with Father God that produces contentment in us, not in our circumstances. We know that "nothing is impossible" with our God (see Luke 1:37) and that "in all things we are more than conquerors through [Christ] who loved us" (Rom. 8:37). We take our God at His word and rest securely in His promises, which we know are true and enduring and will never fail.

Even when we do not like our present circumstances, or their purpose seems hidden from us, we can still trust in our Father God's abundant provision, knowing that He will not withhold any good thing from us. This understanding allows us to remain content in any and every situation.

CONTENTMENT IN HENAN

As president of HIM, an international apostolic network, I travel all over the world, and I've had many opportunities to be discontent. One particular incident comes to mind, when I traveled to the Henan province of China to conduct some meetings. Getting to Henan involved traveling more than eight hours on poorly paved roads, without air conditioning, in weather that was in the 90s, with 100 percent humidity. By the time we arrived, I was a hot, sticky mess and felt totally wilted. All I wanted was some air conditioning and a nice shower!

I got out of the car into what looked like a schoolyard. It was a closed-off compound, and the building that I was led to had no air circulation. There was only one available toilet located outside the compound, and the stench from it was unbearable. It was early evening, and the mosquitoes were out in full force. As I began settling in, I realized there would be no shower, and no relief from the heat and humidity.

I suggested that I could stay in a nearby motel. Clearly, the accommodations could not be worse, and there was a chance there might be some air-conditioning and the opportunity to shower in a motel. I was immediately informed that option was not possible due to security reasons. That night, on top of the heat and humidity and my showerless state, I had unrelenting diarrhea. I don't mind telling you that I was really tempted to complain long and loud to the Lord.

But the Lord brought to my mind the situation of the apostle Paul and Silas and how they were imprisoned in Philippi (see Acts 16:22-40). They certainly could have complained about their situation, but instead they gave thanks to God. In the middle of their singing and praising, God released them from their captivity. They didn't take the opportunity to escape, but stayed to witness to their Philippian jailor, who accepted Christ as Savior and Lord.

Clearly, my situation was not as bad as theirs, so I quietly determined to be thankful and tried to get some sleep.

The next day, during the meeting, I saw some of the greatest miracles I had ever seen up to that time. A deaf woman's hearing was completely restored. A man with stomach cancer was instantly healed, which led to both he and his family being saved. As I watched God do these and other wondrous things, I realized that my discomfort in my circumstances was nothing compared to what God had in mind to accomplish through my visit. I learned that when you trust God and are content in any circumstance, like Paul and Silas were in prison, you get incredible breakthroughs.

PUTTING IT ALL TOGETHER

The true heart of contentment is setting your affections on things that are above, and not on things below, like circumstances. Jesus spoke the truth when He told us, "Seek the kingdom of God above all else, and live righteously, and he will give you everything you need" (Matt. 6:33, *NLT*).

ASK YOURSELF

1. Are you able to praise and give thanks to God in any situation? Why or why not?

2. What types of "when/then" or "more" thinking are you tempted to engage in when you are discontent?

3. Think of a current difficult circumstance you are facing. How could the power of contentment change the way you are experiencing that circumstance right now?

LIVE IT!

What means the most to you in your life? What do you feel would be irreplaceable? Is it circumstances or things, or is it people and

relationships? (Do I even need to ask?) Take time this week to focus on these relationships, and praise and thank God for them. As
you do, see if your contentment grows and your discontent with
current circumstances begins to shrink.

You Prosper
as Your Soul
Prospers

In the last section, we established that Father God wants us to prosper in order to bless us, bless others through us and advance His kingdom. As we believe and actively receive His promises and provision, we are trained to reign and to assume our rightful authority in His kingdom.

Scripture assures us that as children of God, we are new creatures in Christ; but this refers to the regeneration of our spirit, not our soul. There is a powerful connection between our mind and our heart, and we can only be transformed as our mind is renewed. Issues in your mind and heart can literally block the work of God's grace within you and prevent you from partaking in His promises and provision.

For many of us, believing and receiving Father God's promises and provision is difficult. Several factors contribute to our difficulty, including erroneous ideas about the piety of poverty; generational patterns of poverty; and distortions in our self-identity due to soul wounds and our orphan's heart. Most of us have some misconceptions about prosperity and confusion concerning God's relationship to it.

In this section, you will be asked to examine your attitudes and behaviors regarding prosperity, and your feelings of personal worthiness to prosper. There is a simple self-assessment tool that will help you in this process. Our attitudes and behaviors can actually become strongholds that must be addressed before we will allow God's goodness to reach us.

We will also look at a master key that reopens access to our lost authority in God's kingdom. Healing does not come through our performance, but through our choice to receive God's grace, hear God's Word and actively seek to understand it. God's grace will transform our hearts if we choose healing and pursue it. There are four essential phases of healing that God will lead and direct us through if we will actively seek and follow Him.

Our ability to believe and receive God's promises of abundance and prosperity are dependent upon His healing of our hearts and the renewing of our minds. Receiving His grace is the only thing that will produce the inner transformation of our souls and allow us to move forward and receive all the abundance God wants to give us. Please take time in this section to carefully consider each entry, giving much thought to the questions and application suggestions at the end of each entry. Your ability to benefit from the rest of the material in this book depends upon the condition of your heart and the prosperity (the healing) of your soul.

1 4

THE MIND-HEART CONNECTION

As [a man] thinks in his heart, so is he.

PROVERBS 23:7, NKJV

MONEY IS NOT YOUR PROBLEM

Probably everyone would agree that we currently have a money problem in America. Actually, it started before "the great recession of 2008." In 2003, Gallup poll reported that 64 percent of all couples argued over money. It is now the number-one cause of divorce--"till debt do us part." It is estimated that more than 54 percent of divorces are caused by conflicts over money issues.[1]

However, that is not our only money problem. Right now in America, consumer debt stands at $1.7 trillion.[2] That's not our national debt; it's our personal debt! That's more than three times the yearly gross national product of Russia. We live in the richest nation in the world, and yet so many of us are struggling with personal finances. So why do I start this section with the statement "Money is not your problem"? Let me explain.

Imagine that you have come to my home and find me in the backyard with a pair of garden shears. As you watch, I am pruning stalks and leaves from a huge weed that dominates my garden. You ask me, "Ché, what are you doing?"

I immediately reply, "I'm pruning back these stalks and leaves because they get overgrown from time to time."

What would you think of that strategy? Of course I can prune back the weed; but you know it will only grow back again, because

I'm not doing anything about getting to the roots. The only way to permanently get rid of the weed is to attack the roots and pull them out.

I submit to you that our money problems are not just fiscal management difficulties or lack of knowledge; they are issues of the heart. Focusing on strategies for budgeting and debt reduction will not produce permanent results. Our difficulty with money is a spiritual issue. We do not trust our Father God to provide for us, and without that solid foundation, we cannot truly prosper.

Several years ago, I met a woman who was once a top financial planner and made a six-figure salary by counseling exclusive clients; but her personal finances were in shambles. She had all the financial knowledge and expertise, but unfortunately, she also had character issues rooted deep within her heart that needed to be healed.

AT ODDS . . . WITH OURSELVES

Our choice in the Garden to separate from God and go our own way led to a cascade of results we never intended. One result that we have already mentioned is that we became fragmented within ourselves. As God originally designed man and woman, we operated as a unified whole—spirit, soul and body—with direction and purpose coming from our spirit. We had inner harmony, security, and the clarity of God's wisdom.

Eating the fruit of the tree of the knowledge of good and evil opened us to a new system of thinking, a new system of knowing and being in the world. Instead of God's wisdom revealing the truth to our spirit, we now had knowledge through our sense-based reasoning; but there was a problem with this new source of information. It was limited, and each of us experienced it a little differently. This led to disagreements with one another and uncertainty within ourselves. We often felt pulled in different directions at the same time, which led to feelings of insecurity, anxiety and indecisiveness (see Jas. 1:8). Our thoughts and feelings were at war with each other. We knew what our logic told us to do but found ourselves caught up in our emotions, behaving irrationally. We often had deep regrets over our actions but found ourselves doing them anyway.

When you and I became a Christian, the internal warfare only increased! Our spirit was now re-created in Christ, and we were once again in fellowship with Father God, but our soul and body still had the same tendencies to go their own way. In our spirit, we agreed with Father God's will and wanted to pursue His way, but we often found ourselves stumbling in the ruts of old behavior patterns we didn't want to do. The apostle Paul describes this internal battle in Romans 7:14-25.

We frequently resolved over and over again to make positive changes only to find ourselves slipping back into the old patterns. Does this sound familiar? Unfortunately for many Christians, this ongoing struggle is deeply discouraging. In order to overcome the old habits we find ourselves in bondage to, we need to understand that we are not battling in a vacuum. There are forces arrayed against us.

An Affair of the Heart

Your heart is the seat of your personality, also known as your reflective consciousness. It is the part of you that perceives, reflects, feels, imagines, desires and wills. It is what you know or identify as yourself when you say "I". In Scripture, the word "heart" is interchangeably translated in both the Old and New Testaments as "spirit" or "soul." Actually, the heart is influenced by both the spirit and the soul, and this is where the internal warfare rages. The battle is for your heart.

Once your spirit is re-created in Christ Jesus, you have access to the revealed wisdom of God through His Holy Spirit, but your soul also continues to exert influence with its knowledge and understanding. Many of us have hearts that have been deeply wounded by early experiences and traumas. While some of these negative circumstances may be due to abuse and neglect, other experiences can occur from being raised in poverty, being an ethnic minority or being bullied by peers, and the like. These experiences further distort how we understand our identity, our expectations of others and how we think our life works. Over time, we believe these distortions and perpetuate and re-create what we believe. "As [a man] thinks in his heart, so is he" (Prov. 23:7, *NKJV*).

These distortions become habitual ruts in our thinking. Because we have believed them for so long, they feel like reality to us and we don't see ourselves as able to choose different patterns of thought and behavior. Paul calls these habitual patterns "strongholds" (see 2 Cor. 10:3-5).

Simply stated, a stronghold is a belief system made up of a complex of thoughts, feelings and behaviors. Once established, strongholds serve as a filter for our reality and will only allow information that is in agreement to enter and remain in our hearts. For example, if as a child you were frequently disappointed and developed a stronghold of mistrust, you will find yourself suspicious of everyone's motives. It will be difficult for you to receive good things from others, including God, because the stronghold of mistrust is founded on a belief like, "Nothing good ever happens to me." Therefore, even though the present situation may look good, you know it can't be, and you are not open to receive it.

STRONGHOLD MASTERS

Strongholds are frequently established through heart wounds inflicted on us by circumstances and people in our lives. But there are other forces at work against us that can also produce powerful strongholds within our hearts. One is the culture or worldview of the family and society in which we grew up. We are taught by our parents, teachers, peers and media, and by movies and advertising, that certain values, behaviors, aspirations and ways of thinking are "right" or "desirable."

Examples of cultural influences in the United States that can become strongholds are the materialistic desire to accumulate things; the drive for power; the fascination with fame; valuing the superiority of science to all other types of knowledge . . . I think you get the picture. The apostle Paul called these cultural influences the wisdom of this world and made it very clear that it is foolishness to God: "Do not deceive yourselves. If anyone of you thinks he is wise by the standards of this age, he should become a 'fool' so that he may become wise. For the wisdom of this world is foolishness in God's sight. As it is written: 'He catches the wise in their craftiness'; and again, 'The Lord knows that the thoughts of the wise are futile' " (1 Cor. 3:18-20).

We also have a very real adversary, Satan, who seeks to steal from us, kill and destroy us (see John 10:10). One of his favorite tactics is to cripple our hearts with accusation, and self-condemnation, such as shame, guilt, inferiority or unworthiness. Other strongholds can masquerade as something admirable, such as self-reliance or the need to gain approval through our performance. All of these strongholds can hinder us from believing God's promises and fulfilling His purpose for our lives.

Paul warns us, "You were following the course and fashion of this world [were under the sway of the tendency of this present age], following the prince of the power of the air. [You were obedient to and under the control of] the [demon] spirit that still constantly works in the sons of disobedience [the careless, the rebellious, and the unbelieving, who go against the purposes of God]. Among these we as well as you once lived and conducted ourselves in the passions of our flesh [our behavior governed by our corrupt and sensual nature], obeying the impulses of the flesh and the thoughts of the mind [our cravings dictated by our senses and our dark imaginings]" (Eph. 2:2-3, *AMP*).

Our old ways die hard, but Father God has always offered us the choice of life or death, blessing or curse (see Deut. 30:19-20). No matter how fierce the battle rages within us, we are responsible to make that choice. We are told, "Keep and guard your heart with all vigilance and above all that you guard, for out of it flow the springs of life" (Prov. 4:23, *AMP*).

The good news is that we do not battle on our own. God has given us the gift of His Holy Spirit, who has freed us from every form of curse and condemnation (see Rom. 8:1-2). We are equipped to cast down every stronghold in our heart and walk in our privileges as God's children. Before we discuss how we gain victory over strongholds, we must honestly look at our hearts and identify the strongholds we find there.

Putting It All Together

Strongholds are habitual patterns of attitudes and behavior that take root in our heart and hinder us from trusting God and receiving the prosperity He desires to give us. They become established through negative circumstances and experiences with people, cultural messages from family and society, and self-condemnation prompted by our adversary, Satan. We must look honestly at our hearts to identify what strongholds we may be harboring there.

Ask Yourself

1. Read Romans 7:14-25. Can you identify with the struggle the apostle Paul describes? Is there any area related to finances where you've tried to break a bad habit but find yourself falling back into it? (Impulse spending, credit card debt, denying yourself little luxuries, and so on.) Write down the specific area you struggle with.

2. What was the financial philosophy of your parents, or the home you were raised in? How does that philosophy affect your attitude and behaviors with finances today?

3. Why do you think some people enjoy great financial prosperity?

Live It!

During the next three days, write down your thoughts (and what you hear yourself saying) about finances and money. Read them over. What do they tell you about what's in your heart regarding prosperity and finances?

Notes

1. Bruce Fleet, *Demystifying Wall Street* (Bloomington, IN: AuthorHouse, 2009), p. 151.
2. Tiffany Hsu, "Household Net Worth Jumps $1.7 Trillion in Third Quarter," *Los Angeles Times,* December 6, 2012. http://www.latimes.com/business/money/la-fi-mo-household-net-worth-20121206,0,4353086.story.

1 5

SOUL-SEARCHING: WHAT'S YOUR PQ?

Beloved, I pray that in all respects you may prosper and be in good health, just as your soul prospers.

3 JOHN 2, *NASB*

God intends to create within us the character of a Christlike giver in order to restore us to our original purpose and destiny. He invites us to take our place as His children, to become Christlike givers and joint heirs with Christ. In order to do this, we need to let go of whatever might hinder us. Jesus Christ called this process "deny[ing] yourself" (Matt. 16:24, *NKJV*), and the author of Hebrews described it as "lay[ing] aside every weight" (Heb. 12:1, *NKJV*). We need to examine our hearts and confront the strongholds (weights) we find there.

Let's begin the examination by doing a simple self-assessment that I call a PQ ("Prosperity Quotient"). Completing this assessment can help you identify some basic attitudes you may have about prosperity and reveal strongholds or beliefs and behaviors that can hold you back from becoming prosperous in the Lord.

A word of caution before we begin: This is not a scientific measure, but it is based on a number of different questionnaires regarding attitudes to prosperity and my own experience in counseling church members with financial concerns. It is divided into seven sections with seven statements in each section. Read each statement and decide if the attitude or action described reflects you. Give each statement a number from 1 to 3, based on the following scale:

1. Not like me at all
2. I'm this way sometimes
3. I'm this way most of the time

No one will see the results but you, but I will refer to the results throughout the rest of the book. Add the numbers in each section to give you a total for that section. The attitudes in the sections totaling the highest scores are the most like you. There is a brief summary at the end of the assessment to help you understand the results.

PROSPERITY QUOTIENT SELF-ASSESSMENT

SECTION 1

_____ I often lose sleep thinking about my finances.

_____ Whenever things are going too well, I know there will be a downturn.

_____ In making a major purchase, you can never get too much information.

_____ I could never start my own business. It's too risky.

_____ I must check the stock market daily to see how my investment portfolio is doing.

_____ You never know when disaster may strike.

_____ My unpaid bills are always on my mind.

Total score for Section 1: _____

SECTION 2

_____ I avoid balancing my checkbook like the plague.

_____ Several times, I have made budgets but then didn't use them.

_____ I always seem to be a day late and a dollar short.

_____ I usually pay my bills at the last minute, or even late.

_____ I should do more to plan for my retirement.

_____ I need to ask for a raise, but I find myself avoiding it.

_____ Sometimes I have overdrawn checks because I fail to deposit my paycheck on time.

Total score for Section 2: _____

SECTION 3

_____ If I really want something, I will raid my savings account to buy it.

_____ I make the minimum monthly payment on my credit cards.

_____ Shopping always cheers me up.

_____ I routinely buy a lottery ticket. You can't win unless you play.

_____ I do not have a monthly budget. It is too confining.

_____ Sometimes I buy things on the spur of the moment and later regret it.

_____ When I am moved to make a donation at a Christian conference, I put it on my credit card if I don't have the money.

Total score for Section 3: _____

SECTION 4

_____ A lot of people who don't deserve it are wealthy.

_____ Instead of buying fancy cars and clothes, wealthy people should give more to help others.

_____ You have to have money to make big money.

_____ Money is the root of all evil.

_____ I've returned an item I bought, because I knew I had spent too much on it.

_____ Rich people are conceited, thinking they're better than everyone else.

_____ The deceitfulness of riches will cause you to stray from your Christian commitment.

Total score for Section 4: ___

SECTION 5

_____ I'm a diehard clipper of coupons.

_____ If I were looking to buy a home, I'd check the foreclosure lists first.

_____ I keep track of each expenditure to the penny.

_____ A penny saved is a penny earned.

_____ I have a hard time discarding old things. You never know when they might come in handy.

_____ I don't care how special the occasion, I would never spend more than (you fill in the blank) for dinner.

_____ Buying three pairs of shoes on sale beats one expensive pair at regular price any day.

Total score for Section 5: _____

SECTION 6

_____ Poverty runs in my family.

_____ It's better not to aim too high; that way you won't be disappointed.

_____ Good things always happen to someone else, never to me.

_____ Because of my financial obligations, I feel chained to my job.

_____ My situation will never change because . . . (I'm too old, too young, not well educated, don't know the right people . . .)

_____ It's pointless to dream about the future, because mine won't change.

_____ I'm in a real financial bind, but I've made my bed. I'll just have to lie in it.

Total score for Section 6: _____

SECTION 7

_____ I believe that God wants to bless me and give me the best of everything.

_____ Never let a good financial opportunity pass you by.

_____ Most poor people are just lazy and want to milk the system.

_____ God helps those who help themselves.

_____ I'm a strong believer that in whatever measure you give, you will receive.

_____ If I had more money, I could give more to help other people.

_____ I make money the hard way: I earn it.

Total score for Section 7: _____

PROSPERITY QUOTIENT SELF-ASSESSMENT RESULTS

Please keep in mind that this is a nonscientific, informal assessment, but it can help you think about your attitudes and behaviors regarding prosperity. A brief summary of each section follows, but keep in mind that different people can display similar behaviors for very different reasons. Your attitudes and behaviors are signs and symptoms of underlying issues in your heart that go deep. Only by getting to the roots of your attitudes and behaviors can your heart be transformed and the hindrances removed to receiving what God wants to give you.

Section 1: Fearful and Anxious
Prosperity and finances are an area that makes you feel uncomfortable and anxious. You may not feel comfortable handling money or have much confidence in your ability to produce wealth. You spend too much time worrying about money and trying to anticipate potential setbacks. You may also have difficulty making major financial decisions.

Section 2: The Avoider
You have a tendency to handle your discomfort about prosperity and finances by avoiding the issue as much as possible. This avoidance expresses itself in procrastination. You simply put off doing things that you know need to get done, but you can't seem to break out of this habitual behavior rut.

Section 3: The Emotional Spender
You use prosperity and money to make you feel good. You have difficulty going to the mall without buying something, even if you don't need it. Instead of becoming responsible, you opt for "get rich quick" ideas. You are waiting for the big breakthrough, but you need to work at reducing your debt.

Section 4: Poverty Piety
You distrust wealth and people who have it. You are concerned that prosperity might draw you away from Christ. Prosperity and abundance may feel like a club you are excluded from, and you may doubt your worthiness to have wealth.

Section 5: The Miser
Prosperity and finances also make you feel uncomfortable and anxious. You tend to control your discomfort by being hyper-vigilant

about your expenditures and always trying to get a bargain whenever you can. In order to feel secure, you may unnecessarily go without or settle for cheap imitations when you could afford better quality.

SECTION 6: THE DESPONDENT

You tend to handle your financial difficulties by resigning yourself to the status quo. You may have struggled a long time and come to the conclusion that nothing can really change for you. You may look back on mistakes you've made and feel that you deserve your current situation. Your pessimism is causing you to miss out on the joyful life that hopeful expectation can give you.

SECTION 7: PROSPERITY RELIANT

You understand correctly that God wants to bless you with prosperity, but you don't understand the purpose for prosperity. Your focus is on your provision, rather than on your Provider. You may also have a tendency to be self-reliant in acquiring wealth.

PUTTING IT ALL TOGETHER

Most of us have issues related to prosperity and finances. These issues reveal a lot about our hearts, for Christ told us, "Where your treasure is, there will your heart be also" (Matt. 6:21). If we are to trust Father God and receive His blessings, we need to take an honest look at our attitudes and behaviors to identify wounds in our souls that need healing.

ASK YOURSELF

1. In what section was your highest PQ? Does this seem accurate to you? Why or why not?

2. Think of your spouse or someone you know well. What do you think his or her PQ might be? How do you see this PQ reflected in what he or she says and does?

3. In what way might your PQ hinder you from being blessed
    with prosperity?

Live It!

Name three ways you would like to see your attitudes and behaviors
related to prosperity become more positive. Be as specific as you can
and write them down. What would it take to make them happen?

1 6

A MASTER KEY TO THE KINGDOM

A sower went out to sow . . .

MATTHEW 13:3, *NKJV*

When I was a young child, I remember finding an old key while playing in the basement. I had no idea what the key might unlock, so I went and showed it to my older sister. We had just watched an old movie version of *Treasure Island* on TV. As my sister carefully fingered the key, looking very thoughtful, I asked, "Do you think it might go to a treasure chest?"

"Hmmm," she said with another thoughtful pause. She handed the key back to me with a little smile, and said, "You never know when you might find the key to a treasure, Ché. You just never know." I trusted my big sister. I knew she was very smart, so if she said it went to a treasure, I knew it had to be so. For the next week, I tried that key on every lock I found anywhere I went. Of course it never opened up anything, and eventually, I quit trying.

Imagine for a moment that you are given a key and told it will unlock a fabulous treasure. Would you just put it in a drawer and forget about it, or would you set it aside because you were too busy right now? Not hardly! You would take that key and go wherever needed to get that treasure and unlock it.

THE MASTER KEY

Jesus has given us a major key to unlock our authority in His kingdom. He knew that we would battle with strongholds caused by our distorted self-image, the culture of the world and the vicious attacks of Satan. He knew that these strongholds must be destroyed or they would block us from receiving the abundant life and prosperity Father God wants to give us. God has restored our dominion and authority in this earth, but we need a key in order to gain access to it.

Jesus frequently told parables about God's kingdom to explain truth or illustrate a divine principle by comparing it to something in everyday life. Probably the most well-known parable about the Kingdom is the parable of the Sower and the Seed. This parable is mentioned in the books of Matthew, Mark and Luke, so it obviously made an impression on the disciples (see Matt. 13:3-23; Mark 4:2-20; Luke 8:4-18). Jesus indicated that understanding this parable is the key to understanding everything He said about the Kingdom (see Mark 4:13).

That makes this parable an important master key. Even though this parable is a familiar one, I want to review it with you and see how it applies to unlocking our authority in God's kingdom.

The Sower and the Seed

"Then he told them many things in parables, saying: 'A farmer went out to sow his seed. As he was scattering the seed, some fell along the path, and the birds came and ate it up. Some fell on rocky places, where it did not have much soil. It sprang up quickly, because the soil was shallow. But when the sun came up, the plants were scorched, and they withered because they had no root. Other seed fell among thorns, which grew up and choked the plants. Still other seed fell on good soil, which produced a crop—a hundred, sixty or thirty times what was sown. He who has ears, let him hear'" (Matt. 13:3-9).

Notice that Jesus ends His story by talking about hearing. He says, "He who has ears, let him hear." He's not talking about physical ears and physical hearing; He is talking about hearing with our spirit, hearing in our heart. I like the way this is translated in the *Amplified Version*: "He who has ears [to hear], let him be listening and let him consider and perceive and comprehend by hearing" (v. 9). This makes it clear that the hearing and subsequent comprehending are a volitional act, something we choose to do.

Jesus frequently spoke to people in parables, but He almost never interpreted them except to His disciples. In Matthew we have an account of what went on behind the scenes after Jesus told this parable. His disciples asked Him why He spoke to the people in parables and Jesus replied, "The knowledge of the secrets of the kingdom of heaven has been given to you, but not to them" (v. 11). This sounds like Jesus is playing favorites with His disciples and refusing to reveal secrets to the crowds.

That is not the case, however, and Jesus goes on to explain: "Whoever has [spiritual knowledge], to him will more be given and he will be furnished richly so that he will have abundance; but from him who has not, even what he has will be taken away. This is the reason that I speak to them in parables: because having the power of seeing, they do not see; and having the power of hearing, they do not hear, nor do they grasp and understand. . . . But blessed (happy, fortunate, and to be envied) are your eyes because they do see, and your ears because they do hear" (vv. 12-13,16, *AMP*).

Jesus makes it very clear that we choose whether or not we will hear God's Word. We choose whether or not we will receive His grace to see, and seek to understand His Word. We are making active choices that open our access to authority in the Kingdom, or deny access. Jesus honored His disciples' desire to gain insight into the Kingdom, and that is why He interpreted parables and revealed the secrets to them.

THE KEY REVEALED

Let's look at Jesus' interpretation of this parable to understand the secret He is revealing. "Listen then to what the parable of the sower means: When anyone hears the message about the kingdom and does not understand it, the evil one comes and snatches away what was sown in his heart. This is the seed sown along the path" (vv. 18-19). Jesus clarifies here that the seed is God's Word, or the gospel. The soil is the choice we make about how we receive God's

Word, or we could say it is the condition of our heart. Remember, our heart is how we think, perceive, feel and act, and it determines what is reality for us (i.e., what can take hold and grow).

In the other Gospel accounts, the path is described as the well-traveled path or the roadside. It symbolizes people who choose to follow the dominant thinking of the culture around them. They don't grasp and understand the Word because they are not seeking it. God's Word doesn't make sense to the worldly wisdom they currently believe, so they easily toss it aside and forget it. Jesus makes it clear that they are under the influence of the evil one. They reject God's Word before it has an opportunity to take root.

This heart condition is described as the hard heart, and it is caused by different factors. Some people who have been traumatized and hurt become disappointed and shut down in an effort to protect themselves. They fear that God will be harsh or demanding, and they avoid Him. Some people with hard hearts are full of pride and can't admit to any problems. Their tough exterior frequently covers insecure feelings within. Some people let their hurts fester into bitterness, and they shut everyone out. They avoid pain; but nothing new can happen in their life. Their heart is barren and nothing can grow there.

"The one who received the seed that fell on rocky places is the man who hears the word and at once receives it with joy. But since he has no root, he lasts only a short time. When trouble or persecution comes because of the word, he quickly falls away" (vv. 20-21). This is the heart condition of the superficially interested person who lacks real commitment. These people may be experience seekers running from one religious event to another. They will believe as long as it is convenient, but if things get difficult, they become resentful and indignant. Instead of trusting and obeying God through a time of testing, they become offended and fall away. They would rather be comfortable than conformed to God's image.

"The one who received the seed that fell among thorns is the man who hears the word, but the worries of this life and the deceitfulness of wealth choke it, making it unfruitful" (v. 22). This is the person who makes a real heart decision to receive God's Word and begins to grow in relationship with Him. However, God's Word doesn't have first place in their life and their heart is divided. They become preoccupied with distractions such as anxieties, the desire for more material possessions, work and daily activities or recreational pursuits. These distractions begin to take over their life and crowd out the voice of God's Spirit.

"But the one who received the seed that fell on good soil is the man who hears the word and understands it. He produces a crop, yielding a hundred, sixty or thirty times what was sown" (v. 23). This is the person who not only hears and receives God's Word, but also trusts and believes in it. These people surrender to God's grace, perceive and recognize God's ways, and become progressively more experienced and deeply acquainted with Him. They actively seek God's companionship and see difficulties as opportunities to train for reigning. They choose to commit their undivided hearts to God, and patiently persevere as God creates a Christlike character within them. This choice puts them in the center of God's purpose and plan, and opens them to receive His abundant prosperity.

THE SEEKING HEART

The heart condition containing "good soil" is the seeking heart. It is the heart of the God chaser. God honors this type of person. "You will seek me and find me when you seek me with all your heart" (Jer. 29:13). The seeking heart has chosen to reestablish internal unity by once again putting the soul and body under the direction of God's Holy Spirit. This internal transformation is pleasing to God, for He makes it very clear that our heart condition is of utmost importance to Him. "For the LORD does not see as man sees; for man looks at the outward appearance, but the LORD looks at the heart" (1 Sam. 16:7, NKJV).

What, then, does this parable tell us about gaining access to our authority in God's kingdom? It tells us that the condition of our heart will determine how receptive we are to God's Word. If we want God's Word to take root in our heart and produce fruit that results in access to authority, we must receive more of the

Holy Spirit (see Eph. 5:18) that empowers us. We must seek His revelation, believe and receive what He reveals, and act on it. We cannot just mentally give assent to it; we must base our life and actions on His promises and direction. This involves actively trusting in His character and allowing Him to work the transforming power of His grace within us so that we once again reflect His image. We must realize that the choice is ours, has always been ours and will always be ours. We can choose the condition of our heart, and He encourages us to choose His life.

If we don't deal with the condition of our heart, no amount of other actions will produce lasting results. We can employ good financial management techniques, positive thinking and any number of investment strategies, but we will not prosper as God desires to prosper us. We must realize that God's first and foremost priority is to create a Christlike character in us, and that all the other blessings we seek from Him proceed from this place (see Matt. 6:33).

Putting It All Together

Our heart condition determines how we receive God's Word, and the results it can produce. We determine our heart condition by the choices we make. We can choose to receive God's gracious gift of life, and seek God and His transforming power, or we can shut Him out.

Ask Yourself

1. As you read the parable, which soil describes the current condition of your heart?

2. Read Colossians 3:16. List the ways to receive God's Word mentioned there. Which ways do you use? What ways can you try that might be new for you?

3. When was the last time you set aside time to listen to God? What did you hear?

LIVE IT!

Monitor yourself for three days and record what thoughts frequently dominate your thinking. How are these thoughts distractions in your relationship with God? Write down your answers.

17

A SPANNER FOR THE SOUL

Do not conform any longer to the pattern of this world,
but be transformed by the renewing of your mind.

ROMANS 12:2

When I was a teenager, my favorite rock band was the Beatles. I obtained a book written by John Lennon titled *A Spaniard in the Works*. It was a collection of quirky short stories and poems written by Lennon. He was dressed in a matador's cape and hat and was holding a wrench. I didn't understand the title and cover until someone informed me that in Britain, a wrench is called a spanner.

One story I will never forget was "No Flies on Frank." Frank is a grumpy man who lives with his even grumpier wife. One day, he gets tired of her constant complaining, so he bludgeons her to death with a skillet, in the kitchen. Relieved by the silence, he goes out to read his paper in the living room. After a while, however, he notices that there are some flies buzzing around. He goes into the kitchen to find his wife's body covered with flies, but there are no flies on Frank! As the days go by, more and more flies collect on his wife's body, but he proudly proclaims that there are no flies on Frank.[1]

The story is an allegory about how we often refuse to acknowledge our responsibility for things that are going on in our life. We distance ourselves from deep inner issues and overlook the fact that we have helped to create them. By ignoring the issues, we only allow them to fester and get worse, while we pretend they don't exist.

CHOICE, NOT PERFORMANCE

I think that story reflects a way of coping that is all too common today; if we simply ignore something, it will go away. That sounds good, but it doesn't really work, and Scripture reminds us, "There is a way that seems right to a man, but in the end it leads to death" (Prov. 14:12). Father God loves us and desires real healing for us. He wants to lead us in a better way, and He has a spanner to restore our soul.

As we have seen, our wounded hearts contain strongholds, habitual patterns of thought, feelings and behaviors that distort our image of self and others and hinder us from receiving the abundance Father God desires to give us. In the parable of the Sower and the Seed, Jesus tells us that we must choose to hear and seek to understand His Word. The responsibility of choice is ours. We cannot avoid it, and it will determine the condition of our hearts and what we receive from God.

Unfortunately, many Christians confuse choice with performance. God makes it very clear that we can do nothing on our own, for we were not created to operate that way (see John 15:5). When God tells us to seek Him and His Word, He is telling us to choose Him, His way, His plan and His purpose. He is not asking us to produce His works as an outcome of our efforts, but to surrender and trust the inflow of His grace to produce His works in us. His Word contains inherent power to till the soil of our hearts, progressively transforming us as it renews our minds. He is not asking us to make this happen, only to allow Him to work it in and through us.

I have met so many Christians who feel discouraged and burned out. They've been trying for years to measure up to what they see in Scripture, but they constantly fall short. They are struggling under a performance stronghold, trying to please what they think is an authoritarian Father God who is always demanding more from them. Satan keeps them feeling stuck and powerless, full of guilt or shame at their repetitive failures. Instead of a sense of freedom and joy, they feel heaviness and bondage.

Healing and permanent change in our heart condition is not a process of human effort that happens from the outside in, but a spiritual process that flows from the inside out. Our mind is renewed as the Holy Spirit reveals the truth of God's character and Word to us. We cannot simply stuff ourselves with information or try to adopt new behaviors. These are superficial changes, and like pruning back the stalks and leaves on a garden weed, they will not produce permanent change, because they do not get to the root issues in our wounded heart.

THE MONSTER IN THE CLOSET

Like many young children, I was afraid of the dark, especially after I saw the original Dracula movie at my best friend's birthday party. I remember one time being in bed and looking at the closet that was half opened. It looked like a huge, menacing dark figure was starting to come out of the closet, and I knew it was Dracula! I called out to my sister, who was asleep on the other side of the room. I told her that Dracula was in my closet. Needless to say, she was not too happy to be awakened and told me to go back to sleep. Not very comforting. But I was far too afraid to go to sleep. Fortunately, she got up and turned on the light, and I could see that "Dracula" was nothing more than my bathrobe hanging over the door.

The strongholds that keep our wounded hearts captive are like those childhood monsters in the closet. We acknowledge that they exist and that we are not able to demolish them on our own; but when we shine the light of God's truth upon them, we begin to understand that they are lies and deceptions. God's Word is His truth, and the most powerful weapon against lies is truth. We progressively recognize the counterfeit by allowing God to replace the core lies that form the root of our heart wounds with the core truth of His love for us. Knowing His truth sets us free (see John 8:32).

Too often, we try to change *what* we think before we allow God to change *how* we think. Instead of relying on our sense-based reason to figure things out, we must learn to trust Father God's love and direction. Instead of waiting to understand, we surrender in trust to His love and grace. We act on His truth revealed to us, because we believe Him, despite how we feel. In fact, it won't feel right to us at first, but He assures us that we are His workmanship re-created in Christ Jesus. He has a plan and He wants us to take the way He has prepared so that we will live the good life He has prearranged and made ready for us to live (see Eph. 2:10).

THE FOUR *R*s OF INNER HEALING

Inner healing is the process of cleaning out the mental and emotional garbage stored in our wounded hearts. There are four major phases in demolishing strongholds and healing our heart wounds. They occur as Father God guides and directs us to them. He knows exactly how to grow us through our healing process and what types of revelation and encounters will encourage us most. While all four phases are essential, there is no single template, no one-size-fits-all pathway to healing. We can trust Him to be both the author and the finisher of our faith (see Heb. 12:2). God's grace provides both the motive and the power to transform us and set us free.

REPENT

We need to acknowledge that our thinking and behavior are distorted and that we want to repent. No matter how the wounds have been inflicted, we take responsibility for our heart condition and make the active choice that we want to change direction. We confess our inability to make this change in our own strength and ask Father God to perform His work of grace within us. We fearlessly face the monster in our closet, knowing that our Father God will only reveal to us what He intends to heal.

We actively seek God and listen to His Word. We make this a practice, knowing that the more we focus on Him and His truth, the more He will keep us in His peace and conform us to the image of Christ (see Isa. 26:3; 2 Cor. 3:18). In this way, we actively cooperate with the Holy Spirit in tilling our heart, so that it progressively becomes the good soil that brings forth much fruit. We understand that this is a process, and we patiently persevere, knowing that the Lord's love will never fail us (see Jer. 31:3; 1 Cor. 13:8).

RELEASE

We release ourselves from the past and its bondage by forgiving others for the wounds they have inflicted upon us, intentional or not. We understand that this is an act of our will, not a feeling. As long as we hold on to unforgiveness, bitterness and judgments against others, we keep ourselves tied to the heart wounds associated with them. Like the ancient mariner with the rotting albatross hanging about his neck, we wear our woundedness, fettered by our bitterness and judgments. In forgiving others, we must make sure that we also forgive ourselves, and often we find this the most difficult forgiveness to extend.

RENOUNCE

We renounce the lies that have held our strongholds in place. We confess agreement with the truth of God's Word in prayer, through praise and thanksgiving, in worship and meditation (see Col. 3:16). We may need to work with someone experienced in inner healing or even deliverance to demolish the root of some of our strongholds. There are various resources and ministries that can assist us in this process.

RECEIVE

Like trusting children, we open ourselves to receive God's Spirit, His grace and His goodness, and stop performing to gain His approval. We receive help not only from the Holy Spirit but also from others as we walk out our healing. God never intended for healing to be a solitary journey. From the beginning, He declared that it is not good for us to be alone (see Gen. 2:18). He will bring people alongside us, at various times, who will be able to minister to our needs at that moment. We must keep ourselves receptive and open to the assistance He sends our way.

We proceed in confidence, knowing that He will provide everything we need to destroy the strongholds that have been established in our hearts (see 2 Cor. 10:4-5). As our healing progresses, we find it easier to trust and believe in His Word. We become more hopeful and optimistic. We find ourselves greeting each day with the expectation that it will contain good things. We learn to see our true identity more clearly, and we understand our purpose and how to accomplish it.

These principles are powerfully present in God's Word. We do not make them work; we activate them by choosing to hear and by seeking to understand His Word. As we do this, our mind is renewed, and we are transformed. Our heart becomes fertile ground for His power to flow in and through us, producing the prosperity and abundance that is ours. Only this type of transformation will set us free to walk in our dominion in God's kingdom.

In the next section, we will look at specific strongholds Satan has established to rob us of our God-ordained prosperity.

PUTTING IT ALL TOGETHER

We can't heal our heart wounds; we can only choose to hear and seek to understand God's Word that will heal us. God's grace will guide us through the four phases of healing: repent, release, renounce and receive. As we are healed, we trust God more and have confident expectation of His goodness and provision to us.

ASK YOURSELF

1. Are you getting burned out trying to be good enough for God? If so, what lies have you believed that make you feel that you must do this?

2. Have you ever experienced God's truth exposing a monster in your closet? How did it happen? Take a few minutes to remember and praise God for it.

3. Take a few minutes to look back over the four chapters in this section. Have you identified any attitudes and/or behaviors you do repeatedly but want to stop? Write them down.

LIVE IT!

Do you feel guilty and condemn yourself for the attitudes and behaviors you identified in question 3 of the "Ask Yourself" section? Will you make the choice to release the self-condemnation by forgiving yourself? If so, do it now.

Are you willing to admit to God that you need and want His power to change you from within? Meditate on Isaiah 26:3; 2 Corinthians 3:18; Jeremiah 31:3; and 1 Corinthians 13:8a. What do you hear God saying to you? Write it down. Repeat this for several days and look back over what you have written. When you seek God, He will talk to you. As you follow His directives, you are taking steps toward your inner healing.

Note

1. John Lennon, *A Spaniard in the Works* (Cutchogue, NY: Buccaneer Books, 1995).

PROSPERITY ROBBERS' MOST WANTED LIST

Historically, the message of prosperity has been challenged and polluted by two major forces that are powerful spiritual principalities: the spirit of poverty and the stronghold of Mammon. Monasticism and vows of poverty in the Middle Ages elevated poverty to a position of piety that still remains in much of the Church today. This section looks at common ideas about poverty that too often dominate our thinking and pass for wisdom and humility, including the belief that Jesus was poor. These widespread teachings are examined and discredited.

The various manifestations of the stronghold of Mammon are presented, including materialism, the spirit of greed, covetousness, pride, self-reliance and parsimony. A personal deliverance from the spirit of poverty is presented along with explanations of the process of both inner healing and spiritual deliverance.

You will be asked to examine your heart and identify possible strongholds regarding finances and prosperity. I encourage you to begin the process of both inner healing and spiritual deliverance. There is no condemnation in this process, as Father God's entire desire is that we should be set free from any stronghold that hinders us from receiving everything He desires to give us as His children.

Only by demolishing the strongholds that hinder us can we move forward to receive God's transformational grace and become the Christlike givers He longs for us to be.

1 8

THE SPIRIT OF POVERTY

The thief comes only to steal and kill and destroy . . .

JOHN 10:10

When you hear the word "saint," what comes to mind? Do you see some thin, emaciated person in a robe, living in a monastery? Or perhaps you think of a man or woman bravely facing a lion in the Roman Coliseum? Maybe you picture a person with a halo around his head, praying and looking toward heaven. One picture that I doubt comes to your mind is a happy, wealthy person. No matter how philanthropic a person might be, we typically do not view rich people as saints.

In fact, the church is the only place in modern society where success is measured by how little a person has. The thinking goes something like this: Christians are supposed to be spiritually minded because the spiritual world is holy. The material world is corrupt, and money is the most blatant symbol of material corruption, so it is definitely something Christians should not seek to acquire. After all, it's widely acknowledged that Christ was poor; therefore, His followers should adopt His example of asceticism by pulling away from involvement in the material world and focusing on the spiritual one.

POVERTY IN THE OLD TESTAMENT

Poverty and piety go hand in hand in this worldview. These religious ideas seem noble, and Christianity is full of them, but do they accurately reflect God's truth? If we look at the Old Testament and the lives of the patriarchs, the "make do with less" mentality is not a part of their culture. In fact, just the reverse is the case. Abraham, Isaac and Jacob were all notably wealthy individuals, and Scripture makes it clear that their wealth was a blessing from God (see Gen. 24:35; 26:12-13,16; 30:43). At no time in the Old Testament is any virtue associated with being poor. Actually, poverty is looked upon as a curse.

We first see it in the Garden of Eden, after Adam and Eve disobeyed and separated themselves from following God. With the loss of their authority and dominion, the earth was no longer able to produce in abundance for them. God told Adam, "Cursed is the ground because of you; through painful toil you will eat of it all the days of your life. It will produce thorns and thistles for you, and you will eat the plants of the field. By the sweat of your brow you will eat your food" (Gen. 3:17-19). God gives a comprehensive description of the curse of poverty in Deuteronomy 28:15-68. Here is a summary:

> You will be cursed in the city and cursed in the country. Your basket and your kneading trough will be cursed. The fruit of your womb will be cursed, and the crops of your land, and the calves of your herds and the lambs of your flocks. You will be cursed when you come in and cursed when you go out. . . . You will sow much seed in the field but you will harvest little, because locusts will devour it. You will plant vineyards and cultivate them but you will not drink the wine or gather the grapes, because worms will eat them. You will have olive trees throughout your country but you will not use the oil, because the olives will drop off. . . . Because you did not serve the LORD your God joyfully and gladly in the time of prosperity, therefore in hunger and thirst, in nakedness and dire poverty, you will serve the enemies the LORD sends against you (Deut. 28:16-19,38-40,47-48).

I think you will agree with me that this is a picture of utter destitution, and the text leaves no doubt that it is a curse. Ancient

Israel had a very clear understanding that abundance and prosperity were blessings from God, and want and poverty were a curse. To this day that understanding remains strong in the Jewish mentality. In his book *The Jewish Phenomenon*, Steven Silbiger describes the incredible success of Jews in the American culture. Despite the fact that Jews represent only 2 percent of the U.S. population, 45 percent of the richest people in America are Jewish. Jewish producers, directors and studio CEOs dominate the Hollywood entertainment industry. This level of outstanding achievement extends beyond the United States to the world scene as well. Forty-five percent of all the Nobel science awards, and 25 percent of all Nobel awards, regardless of category, have been given to Jews.[1]

POVERTY IN THE NEW TESTAMENT

Numerous passages in the New Testament make it clear that the same blessing that God bestowed upon Abraham was made available to Gentile believers through Jesus Christ. We are told that Christ became poor for our sake, so that we might become rich, and that all the blessings of Abraham, which includes prosperity, are ours in Christ Jesus (see 2 Cor. 8:9; 9:8; Gal. 3:13-14,29).

Contrary to popular belief, Jesus was not poor. He was an itinerant rabbi, but He had a large following and was supported by wealthy people, several of whom are named (see Luke 8:1-3). Influential members of society frequently entertained Him, and He had close friends such as Lazarus, who was rich. While Jesus cautioned against the idolatry of wealth, He never advocated poverty as a way of life. In fact, He gave hope to the poor by telling them they were blessed, for theirs was the kingdom of heaven. In essence, He was telling them, "Be happy, you who are poor, because the wealth of God's kingdom is yours."

If the emphasis on the piety of poverty did not come from God and Scripture, where did it come from and how did it gain such influence in the church? Jesus Himself gives us a major clue when He describes His purpose, and the purpose of our enemy, Satan. He states in John 10:10, "The thief comes only to steal and kill and destroy; I am come that they may have life, and have it to the full." No one would describe living in poverty as having life to the full! Jesus did not come to give us a life of poverty, but one of abundance.

However, Satan's primary objective is to destroy relationships. First and foremost, he wants to keep people from having an intimate relationship with God. But if he can't accomplish that goal, he wants to distort and pervert the relationship into a legalistic one, and he uses the spirit of poverty to accomplish this.

I believe this spirit of poverty is an evil spirit that works to keep people poor. It is different from a poverty mentality. The spirit of poverty does lead to a mentality of poverty, but I am talking about a literal demon principality whose objective is to keep people poor. It is an evil spirit released by Satan, not just a state of poverty. Systemic poverty is a fruit of this principality, and it is clearly a work of Satan.

Poverty is a curse that leads to all sorts of evil, and one type of evil is corruption. Whenever I travel in the developing countries where there is widespread poverty, there is overt corruption and greed. I remember when we brought $50,000 worth of children's vitamins to Mozambique for Heidi Baker, a missionary who runs a children's center there that serves thousands of children. The customs agent confiscated the vitamins and wanted a bribe, saying ludicrous things like the vitamins had traces of cocaine. We contacted Heidi and she said, "Do not give them a dime. I am trying to reform this nation and eradicate poverty and corruption." Unfortunately, you see this territorial spirit of poverty everywhere around the world.

THE SPIRIT OF POVERTY IN THE CHURCH

The spirit of poverty is firmly rooted in the philosophy of Plato, who elaborated a mind-body dualism that originated from many ancient sources. He maintained that the mind or soul and the body were two distinct substances. The body was connected to the material world, while the mind or soul was connected to the world of ideas and thus was immortal.

Before the end of the first century, this philosophy, in the form of Gnosticism, was already infiltrating the church. The Gnostics maintained that gnosis, or a higher, intuitive knowledge, was the way to salvation of the soul from the material world. The material world was seen as created by an intermediary being, not by God, and it was created evil and corrupt. This was clearly not a view that was biblical or Hebraic in origin. Their inevitable conclusion was that the more spiritual you become, the less material you will be.

The apostle Paul issued this warning regarding Gnosticism to the young minister Timothy: "Guard what has been entrusted to your care. Turn away from godless chatter and opposing ideas of what is falsely called knowledge, which some have professed and in so doing have wandered from the faith" (1 Tim. 6:20-21). The first epistle of John was written to counteract heresies related to Gnosticism.

When the church aligned with the Emperor Constantine in the fourth century, the door to a Greek rather than a Hebrew worldview opened wide. This only strengthened the influence of Gnosticism on the church. The virtues of the spiritual life, like fasting, praying and meditating on God's Word were to be pursued, while the world and everything associated with it was to be shunned. This led to what is known as the monastic movement. People who wanted to be part of this movement had to make a vow of poverty.

Nowhere in Scripture do you have to make a vow of poverty to follow Jesus. I have no problem if someone wants to give away everything and live a simple lifestyle. But this was not what was happening. All those who were serving in the church had to make a vow of poverty, which is legalistic. Eventually, piety became synonymous with poverty. The poorer and more sacrificial you were, the more spiritual you were. Down through the centuries this has led to the idea that ministers should be poor. The influence of this demonic spirit of poverty is widespread throughout the church today.

Next, we will consider the "wisdom" this spirit whispers to our hearts as it tries to influence all of us.

Putting It All Together

Historically, poverty became linked with piety through the Greek philosophy of mind–body dualism. Poverty is not considered pious in Scripture. It is actually viewed as a curse. Satan uses the demonic spirit of poverty to oppress people and nations and keep them poor.

Ask Yourself

1. Do you think there is something pious about being poor? If so, how do you believe you were influenced to think this way?

2. How might the spirit of poverty hinder a person's ability to have an intimate relationship with God?

3. In what ways has viewing poverty as pious made the church less effective in its ministry?

Live It!

Read the verses cited under the sections on poverty in the New Testament. What do these verses say to you personally? Is there anything contained in these verses that represents a new way of thinking about poverty or prosperity for you? If so, in what way?

Note
1. Steven Silbiger, *The Jewish Phenomenon: Seven Keys to the Enduring Wealth of a People* (New York: M. Evans & Co., 2009).

The "Wisdom" of Poverty

So for the sake of your tradition (the rules handed down by your forefathers), you have set aside the Word of God [depriving it of force and authority and making it of no effect].

MATTHEW 15:6, *AMP*

SINCERELY WRONG

When I first became a Christian, I was determined to "get it right." I read everything I could get my hands on about how to live a disciplined and consecrated life. I loved the Lord, and I sincerely wanted to serve Him with all of my heart. At the time, I was going to a conservative church that provided a lot of guidance and direction on how we were to live. As a young adult, I lived in a community setting, sharing housing with other Christian brothers. We shared our expenses, like utilities and food, and tried to live our lives simply.

At the time, Ron Sider's book *Rich Christians in an Age of Hunger* had just been published, and we all eagerly read it. It advocated that people in wealthy societies like the United States should strive to live more simply and give more generously to poor nations.[1] My friends and I redoubled our efforts to simplify our lives. We fasted frequently, rationed our incomes, piled on jackets rather than use our heat. We took every cost-cutting measure you can imagine. Without realizing it, we also developed a poverty mentality and began feeling pious about it.

We read lots of articles about social justice and Christian activism. The more I plunged into these ideas, the more I knew prosperity was not for Christians. How could we justify our standard of living when so many people in the world were living in abject poverty? I began to question all my purchases and tried to limit myself only to those things that were absolutely necessary. I wanted to be a good steward of the resources God placed in my hands.

Years later, when I was in the doctoral program at Fuller Theological Seminary, I smiled as I heard my professor and mentor, Dr. C. Peter Wagner, relate a story with a similar theme. For years after he came to Fuller, he shopped at the local Salvation Army Thrift Store for most of his clothing and household goods, even though he could afford much more. He was convinced that it was his responsibility, as a conscientious Christian, to live as frugally as possible so that he could give more.

I know now that we were both totally sincere, but we were sincerely wrong. We were listening to poverty's "wisdom." God does not call us to live on the edge of poverty in order to be able to give more to others. Instead He wants to bless us with abundance so that we may give abundantly.

Heart wounds and an orphan mentality can create strongholds that interfere with our receiving all the blessings God desires to give us. The demonic spirit of poverty can also create a stronghold in our heart if we listen to and believe the deception it whispers to us. How can you tell if you're being deceived? Let me share the most common deception the spirit of poverty will use against you.

THE PRIMARY DECEPTION: "IT'S ALL SPIRITUAL"

I think the spirit of poverty is one of the most deceptive because it is a religious spirit. Dr. Wagner defines a religious spirit as "an agent of Satan assigned to prevent change and to maintain the status quo by using religious devices."[2] It infiltrates the church and Christian thinking, and deposits noble-sounding religious ideas that are easily assimilated into doctrinal positions. But these religious ideas are not solidly rooted in the context of Scripture, even though Scripture may be quoted to support them. When Satan was tempting Jesus in the wilderness, he quoted Scripture to Him, but he took it out of context.

The religious spirit of poverty operates in much the same way. Let's look at an example that is frequently quoted, or should I say, misquoted. It's the passage found in 2 Corinthians 8:1-9. This second letter to the church at Corinth was probably written a few months after Paul's first letter. Paul was writing from Macedonia, and he reminded the Corinthian church that the believers in Jerusalem were in dire need of financial help. In the first 5 verses, he relates how the Macedonian church, even in the midst of severe tribulation, had taken up a very generous offering for the church in Jerusalem.

In 2 Corinthians 8:6-8, Paul encourages the Corinthians to match the generosity of the Macedonians, or even exceed it. He states, "I am not commanding you, but I want to test the sincerity of your love by comparing it with the earnestness of others" (v. 8). He continues on in verse 9: "For you know the grace of our Lord Jesus Christ, that though he was rich, yet for your sakes he became poor, so that you through his poverty might become rich."

Despite the fact that Paul has been talking about a monetary offering up to this point, nearly every major Bible commentary chooses to interpret verse 9 as referring to "spiritual prosperity," and not money or material prosperity. They follow the long-standing tradition in the Church of the piety of poverty. They take the verse to be saying "though He was spiritually rich, yet for your sakes He became spiritually poor, so that you through His spiritual poverty might become spiritually rich."

This interpretation is a total disruption of Paul's train of thought, for in verses 10-11 he continues with the theme of generous monetary giving: "And here is my advice about what is best for you in this matter: Last year you were the first not only to give but also to have the desire to do so. Now finish the work, so that your eager willingness to do it may be matched by your completion of it, according to your means."

Does it make sense that the apostle Paul would be discussing monetary giving and suddenly switch to an aside about spiritual prosperity? Since Paul is prompting them to give freely, I think in verse 9, he is lifting Jesus up to them as an example of generosity. He reminds them that Christ left the abundance of heaven, and on the cross, He took the curse of poverty upon Himself so that we could be set free to have God's prosperity. If Christ is such a generous giver, shouldn't we do the same? Then in verses 10 and 11, he prompts them to fulfill the commitment they made a year earlier, and give an abundant amount to the Jerusalem church.

In fact, if verse 9 is interpreted as relating to spiritual prosperity, then Paul is actually saying that Christ became spiritually poor, which is impossible. Christ was all God and all man. He could never have performed the miracles and signs that He did if He was spiritually poor!

WE ARE TO PROSPER MATERIALLY

Let's look at some additional verses that support the understanding that God intends for us to prosper materially:

Remember the LORD your God, for it is he who gives you the ability [power] to produce wealth, and so confirms his covenant, which he swore to your forefathers, as it is today (Deut. 8:18).

Wealth and honor come from you; you are the ruler of all things. In your hands are strength and power to exalt and give strength to all (1 Chron. 29:12).

His delight is in the law of the LORD, and on his law he meditates day and night. He is like a tree planted by streams of water, which yields its fruit in season and whose leaf does not wither. Whatever he does prospers (Ps. 1:2-3).

Blessed is the man who fears the LORD, who finds great delight in his commands. His children will be mighty in the land; the generation of the upright will be blessed. Wealth and riches are in his house, and his righteousness endures forever (Ps. 112:1-3).

The blessing of the LORD brings wealth, and he adds no trouble to it (Prov. 10:22).

God is able to make all grace abound to you, so that in all things at all times, having all that you need, you will abound in every good work (2 Cor. 9:8).

These are just a few of the many verses in Scripture that clearly demonstrate God intends to prosper us materially. However, we're not limited to Scripture to see God's intentions regarding wealth.

A REALITY CHECK FROM HISTORY

While I was a student at Fuller seminary, I was privileged to do some coursework under the late Dr. Donald McGavran, the founding professor of Church Growth. He taught a principle he called, "Redemption and Lift." Throughout Church history, wherever the gospel has gone forth, it brought salvation and redemption, and it lifted people out of poverty. I accepted the idea without too much reflection. Obviously, in today's world, economic growth is the most advanced in countries with a history of embracing Christianity.

Then in the year 2000, I read a secular book edited by two Harvard professors, Lawrence E. Harrison and Samuel P. Huntington, *Culture Matters: How Values Shape Human Progress.* They are sociologists and observed that when a nation embraced Judeo-Christian values like integrity and hard work, that nation prospered economically. They used South Korea as a case study, which got my attention, because I am a Korean. After the Korean War, the average South Korean made $30 per year. The doors were opened wide to the gospel and there were an incredible number of conversions to Christ. As Christianity spread, South Korea prospered. Today it is the thirteenth largest national economy in the world.[3]

You can make a similar case for China. Christianity is spreading rapidly in China, with currently 100 million to 150 million Christian believers. Within the next two decades, China will be the number-one economic nation in the world.[4] In India, 30,000 people come to Christ each day, and now India's economic growth is one of the fastest in the world. This is also true for Brazil and many other nations experiencing spiritual revival. Is this the result of embracing a Christian work ethic, or is this a macro illustration of the truth of 2 Corinthians 8:9: "For you know the grace of our Lord Jesus Christ, that though he was rich, yet for your sakes he became poor, that you through his poverty might become rich." I think it's the blessing of God coming upon nations as they receive Christ and come under His blessing of prosperity.

Next, we will look at additional deceptions the religious spirit of poverty employs against us.

PUTTING IT ALL TOGETHER

The primary deception of the spirit of poverty is to "spiritualize" the concept of prosperity in Scripture. There are many texts in Scripture that refer to material prosperity. Also, the economic history of nations reveals that God blesses nations with material prosperity as they come to Jesus Christ.

ASK YOURSELF

1. Consider these two sentences from the text: "God does not call us to live on the edge of poverty in order to be able to give more to others. Instead, He wants to bless us with abundance, so that we may give abundantly." How does God's way help to advance His kingdom more effectively?

2. Can you think of other examples where the traditions of the church have interfered with the correct understanding of Scripture? (Hint: "spiritualizing" promises of physical healing,

adding rules of conduct or dress to the free grace of the gospel, and so on.)

3. Consider Proverbs 10:22: "The blessing of the LORD brings wealth, and he adds no trouble to it." What trouble could wealth bring? How can receiving wealth in God's way avoid this trouble?

LIVE IT!

Do a little research. Go on the Internet and look up the average yearly incomes in the following countries: Sri Lanka, South Korea, Mozambique, China, Indonesia and Brazil. Look up the dominant religion for each country. What pattern do you see? Do you think the principle of "Redemption and Lift" is accurate?

Notes

1. Ronald J. Sider, *Rich Christians in an Age of Hunger* (Nashville, TN: Thomas Nelson, 1978).
2. Dr. C. Peter Wagner, *The Changing Church: How God Is Leading His Church into the Future* (Ventura, CA: Regal, 2004), p. 19.
3. Lawrence E. Harrison and Samuel P. Huntington, *Culture Matters: How Values Shaped Human Progress* (New York: Basic Books, 2000).
4. Spengler, "Christianity Finds a Fulcrum in Asia," Asia Times, August 7, 2007. http://www.atimes.com/atimes/China/IH07Ad03.html.

2 0

Additional "Wisdom" from Poverty

"For My thoughts are not your thoughts, neither are your ways my ways,"
declares the LORD. *"As the heavens are higher than the earth, so are my*
ways higher than your ways and my thoughts than your thoughts."

ISAIAH 55:8-9

False Humility

When I got married, I left the community living arrangement behind, but I took the deceptions of the spirit of poverty with me into
my marriage and ministry. It never occurred to me to question the
idea that, as a minister, I should live very modestly. Actually, it
wasn't too hard to do, because we weren't doing that well financially
anyway. But I strove to avoid even the appearance of prosperity.

I remember when my dad retired from his pastorate in Northern Virginia in 1993. I was asked to give the main address at his
retirement service. His congregation from the Antioch Korean
Baptist church really honored him. They bought him a brand-new,
top-of-the-line Lincoln Continental and gave him a gold watch.

Over dinner, as our family was celebrating my dad's retirement,
he said to me, "Son, they gave me a new watch, so I want to give
you my watch." And he proceeded to take off his chrome Rolex
watch and hand it to me.

I immediately pushed his hand back. "Dad, I can't receive this."

"What do you mean?" my dad asked.

"Dad, this is a Rolex watch," I replied, "and as a pastor, I can't wear a Rolex watch."

My father's response caught me a little off guard. "Look, son, I am a pastor and I have been wearing this watch. What's wrong with it? Besides, you're not buying it. It's a gift from me, and it's not even the top-of-the-line Rolex, it is the cheapest one you can get!"

I quickly realized that my dad was becoming offended by my lack of graciousness, so I took the watch and put it on. But that was the last time I wore it for years. In fact, I never wore it again until the Lord broke the spirit of poverty in my life.

I was living under the deception of false humility. I thought that as a minister it would be inappropriate to have anything— whether it was the clothes I wore, the house I lived in or the car I drove—that would suggest I was "too prosperous." As a Christian, I was supposed to be humble. In reality, instead of being humble, I was just being stupid. I was ignorant of God's Word and will concerning prosperity, and so I was living without it.

Over the years, I have met many Christians caught in the same deception. They are denying themselves because they think it's pious to do so. They feel guilty if they have something that's "too nice." They think the guilt they experience is God's Spirit nudging them to stay humble. They see other people who are able to enjoy high quality possessions, take nice vacations and drive new model cars, and they begin to resent that God places so many restrictions on them. They are mired in a quandary. They feel guilty if they have nice things and angry with God when they deny themselves. It's a terrible place to get stuck.

SMOKE AND MIRRORS

Some Christians are able to permit themselves to have nice things, but they have to rationalize what they're doing in order to justify to their minds how they're living. They can't just enjoy their prosperity; they must give it some spiritual overtones. I used to have this difficulty as well. I drive a Mercedes-Benz, and when people would say, "Nice car," I would reply, "It really is not mine; the church leases it out for me."

One day, the Lord began to deal with me and show me how I always had to justify owning anything nice. When people complimented me on something I was wearing, I made sure to let them know I got it on sale for 50 percent off. I would apologize and explain myself if I went on a nice vacation, say to Hawaii, by saying something like, "We're using my frequent flyer miles and staying at a timeshare." If anyone commented on how nice our home was, I would reply, "Our house has tripled since we bought it," emphasizing that the purchase was a good stewardship decision.

I could never just say, "Thank you," to a compliment, and I always had to spiritually justify any signs of overt prosperity. I really wasn't able to enjoy nice things. Underneath, I always felt somewhat guilty unless I figured out a way to convince myself that I was truly being spiritual after all. For example, if I wanted a nice leather briefcase, I would rationalize that it would last at least three times as long as a cheap one, so it was really financially prudent to buy it. I couldn't simply enjoy owning a quality briefcase. I played this little smoke and mirrors game with myself for years, but it never brought me any true peace.

A PROUD PIETY

Without realizing it, some Christians actually take pride in their piety. They deny prosperity for themselves and judge and criticize others who enjoy prosperity without guilt. They can always tell you the price of the clothes someone is wearing or the car he or she is driving and then translate that amount into the numbers of meals for hungry children those dollars could buy. They pride themselves on knowing where to get the best bargains for just about anything, how to get free goods and services, and which eateries are the cheapest. They're always eager to let you know just how little they paid for something or how much they saved on a deal.

They've taken the challenge of living simply and turned it into a type of self-discipline that is actually a form of bondage. Instead of trusting God's counsel and direction in their lifestyle choices, they are completely caught up in their own self-effort to be pious. Without realizing it, they are proving themselves to God by their performance of legalistic piety.

The apostle Paul warned us against falling into legalistic performance in any area of our lives, because legalism puts us in control and denies the grace of God. As Paul stated in his letter to the Colossians, "Since you died with Christ to the basic principles of this world, why, as though you still belong to it, do you submit to its rules: 'Do not handle! Do not taste! Do not touch!'? These are all destined to perish with use, because they are based on human commands and teachings. Such regulations indeed have an appearance of wisdom, with their self-imposed worship, their false humility and their harsh treatment of the body, but they lack any value in restraining sensual indulgence" (Col. 2:20-23).

Paul's words tell us that in an effort to put down the flesh, our legalism only makes the flesh that much stronger! Instead of living simply, we have bound ourselves with financial restrictions that limit our ability to receive God's blessing and become the Christlike givers He intends us to be.

The Idolatry of Poverty

We have already seen how Satan stole our identity in the Garden of Eden when he convinced Adam and Eve to choose their own way and reasoning over God's way and wisdom. We lost the reality of being created in God's image, and we became filled with an orphan mentality. Our self-image was further distorted by life circumstances and the influence of family, friends and culture on our thoughts and behavior. Taken all together, these factors create strongholds in our hearts that consist of habitual attitudes and behaviors that prevent us from trusting Father God's promises and receiving His blessings.

Remember the parable of the Sower and the Seed? Everything you are able to do and receive in God's kingdom depends upon the condition of your heart. If your heart contains poverty strongholds, it is like the rocky soil. You have no true depth of understanding concerning God's perspective on prosperity, and the truth of His promises to abundantly bless you cannot take root in your heart. You are separated from God's truth regarding wealth and, consequently, you are in bondage to poverty's deceptions.

The demonic spirit of poverty strengthens these strongholds by adding his deceptions. His purpose is to further distort our self-image by fueling feelings like shame, self-deprecation, a sense of powerlessness and hopelessness, and a deep suspicion, even fear, of wealth. Since Satan was not successful in preventing us from being redeemed by Christ, he can still destroy our effectiveness in God's kingdom by keeping us trapped in our distorted image regarding our right to be prosperous.

Robert Morris in his book *The Blessed Life* sums it up well: "The enemy of our souls works so hard to corrupt and distort our thoughts about money. The devil knows that God can take temporal money and turn it into eternal souls. He knows that the more money we give to the church, the more souls are going to be saved, the more the Kingdom of God is going to be advanced and the kingdom of darkness is going to fail."[1]

Satan knows that whatever we give our primary attention to is what we worship. If we organize our financial life around our self-determined efforts to live modestly and strictly control our finances, then we are worshiping poverty, and that is idolatry. In effect, we're saying that our own ideas and persuasions about wealth are superior to God's words and promises. Does this have a familiar ring? We're right back in the Garden of Eden, choosing our own reasoning and way over God's wisdom, purpose and plan for us. We need to remember that His ways and His thoughts are far above our ways and our thoughts (see Isa. 55:8-9). We need to worship Him and not our own ideas.

PUTTING IT ALL TOGETHER

The spirit of poverty seeks to deceive us in other ways by associating a false humility with living modestly. It creates a constant need to justify having nice things, and a pride in our piety as we judge others for their wasteful lifestyles. All these deceptions take hold in our hearts because we trust our own reasoning and way more than God's way and wisdom.

Ask Yourself

1. Have you ever been deceived by false humility? Do you feel the need to self-justify having nice things, or do you feel proud about your piety? How has this deception influenced your attitudes and behaviors? Be specific.

2. Have you ever felt that God was denying you the good things He was giving to others? Do you think this viewpoint is accurate? Why or why not?

3. Read Isaiah 55:8-9. Do you believe God's ways and thoughts about prosperity are higher than yours? If you do, then what prevents you from embracing His wisdom and living His way in the area of your financial life?

Live It!

Do you see any connections between the behavior and attitude of poverty's wisdom and those in your Prosperity Quotient identified from the self-assessment you completed in Section 3? What are they, and how do you think you acquired them?

Note
1. Robert Morris, *The Blessed Life* (Ventura, CA: Regal Books, 2002), p. 83.

2 1

WASN'T JESUS POOR?

But [Jesus] made himself of no reputation, and took upon him
the form of a servant, and was made in the likeness of men.

PHILIPPIANS 2:7, *KJV*

If you asked the average person on the street if Jesus was poor,
most would probably answer yes. He is commonly depicted in
movies, and from many pulpits, as living very simply, having no
home, sleeping under the stars and accompanied by a group of
uneducated fishermen. Many theologians teach that Jesus was
poor, and because they equate poverty with spirituality, in order to
really "imitate Christ," we need to be poor. But is this viewpoint accurate? Let's take a closer look at a few facts.

JESUS' BIRTH AND EARLY CHILDHOOD

Many people think that Jesus was poor because he was born in a
stable. Joseph and Mary traveled to Bethlehem to register for the
universal census ordered by Caesar. Scripture makes it clear they
intended to stay in an inn, so they obviously had some money, but
they were unable to find any accommodations. Jesus was born in
a stable, not because his parents were destitute, but simply because
it was the only place available to them.

One very common misconception is that the Magi came to the
birthplace of Jesus. This erroneous idea is reinforced by the many
Christmas nativities that have the Magi joining the shepherds at
the manger. Matthew's Gospel states, "On coming to the house,
they saw the child with his mother Mary, and they bowed down and

worshiped him. Then they opened their treasures and presented him with gifts of gold and of incense and of myrrh" (Matt. 2:11).

Several things are clear from this passage. Some time has passed since the birth of Jesus. He is referred to as a child, not a baby, and he is living in a house, not a cave or stable. His parents have decided to remain in Bethlehem for a while, and they are doing well enough to have some type of house. Again, this is hardly a destitute family.

The Magi were very wealthy and influential and came from a great distance, possibly as far away as Persia. They were obviously greeted as important, as they had an audience with Herod the king. They came to pay tribute to the newborn king (Jesus). Historically, when one gave a tribute of gold to another king, it would be a significant amount of gold, not just a few gold coins. We know that incense and myrrh were rare and costly ointments that might have rivaled the gold in value. I believe that the Magi's gifts were considerable enough to finance Joseph, Mary and Jesus' flight to Egypt, and to sustain them in Egypt for years to come.

Life in Nazareth

Just because Jesus had what we would consider a nonprofessional or non-aristocratic job does not mean He was poor. He was a craftsman with a highly developed skill and trade. Who is to say He only made furniture? Is it possible he also built houses?

If you are good at something, people will seek you out. We know that Joseph had quite a reputation as a carpenter. In referring to Jesus, Matthew 13:55-56 tells us, "Isn't this *the* carpenter's son? Isn't his mother's name Mary, and aren't his brothers James, Joseph, Simon and Judas? Aren't all his sisters with us?" (emphasis added). Note that Joseph is referred to as *the* carpenter. He may have been the only carpenter in town or just the best one, but he is completely identified by his reputation as a carpenter, so he most likely was successful.

Jesus would have learned His skills from Joseph, so it is safe to assume that He also was an excellent carpenter. Can you imagine

Jesus being a carpenter and making or building anything shabby? We don't know when Joseph died, but it apparently was before Jesus began His public ministry. In Middle Eastern tradition, the oldest son takes care of the family upon the father's death. Jesus had a large family—four brothers and at least two sisters. That makes a family of eight, including Mary, his mother. Scripture tells us that Jesus grew in wisdom and stature and in favor with God and man (see Luke 2:52). This is not the description of an economic failure.

JESUS' MINISTRY YEARS

Jesus was one of a number of traveling rabbis, which was a well-known and respected occupation at that time. Men of learning would walk from one town to the next, teaching in synagogues and gathering places. Those who found their teaching instructive would open their homes and host the rabbi, providing him with food and shelter and provisions for his journey as he traveled to the next town. Individuals eager for ongoing training would become disciples and accompany the rabbi on his journeys.

We think of Jesus as having 12 disciples who formed a small band and went everywhere with Him. It is true that Jesus personally designated 12 men to be His disciples, but there was a much larger entourage that followed Him. When He wanted to commission men and send them out to minister, Jesus had no difficulty finding 70 people in addition to the 12 disciples. He must have known and trusted these men, but where did He find them? They were part of a group that consistently followed Him. This traveling party was sizable!

Ever wonder who these people were and how they could afford to travel with Jesus? They were not homeless persons or religious fanatics who deserted their responsibilities and left their families without support to accompany Jesus. That kind of behavior would have violated basic tenets of the Law and would not have been condoned by Jesus. These were people of independent means, businessmen who could leave the family enterprise in the capable hands of others while they traveled.

Take the apostle Peter, for example. His home in Capernaum is one of the most well documented New Testament sites known today. Capernaum was a bustling, prosperous city with a large, elaborate synagogue. Peter's home was large and spacious, and very near the synagogue. This indicates that he was a well-to-do and influential person, as the most important people in a city lived the closest to the synagogue. Scripture refers to him, along with his brother, Andrew, as having boats and nets. He was not a simple fisherman, but the owner of a family fishing business. Scripture indicates that Jesus frequented Capernaum. No doubt prosperous Peter and his family often hosted Him.

MINISTRY FINANCES

Just how did Jesus and His disciples finance their travels? Some of the people who were followers were also financial supporters. The names of several supporters are listed in this passage from Luke 8:1-3: "Soon afterward Jesus began a tour of the nearby towns and villages, preaching and announcing the Good News about the Kingdom of God. He took his twelve disciples with him, along with some women who had been cured of evil spirits and diseases. Among them were Mary Magdalene, from whom he had cast out seven demons; Joanna, the wife of Chuza, Herod's business manager; Susanna; and many others who were contributing from their own resources to support Jesus and his disciples" (*NLT*).

These women were obviously well known and influential because they are referred to by name. We know that Jesus had wealthy friends—Lazarus, Mary and Martha from Bethany being one example. I think there is a strong possibility that Nicodemus and Joseph of Arimathea, along with other establishment members, were secret donors. But there were also many other nameless contributors who formed the financial backbone of His ministry.

The important point to note here is that the ministry had large enough finances to make mention of financial contributors. It was also prosperous enough to have a treasurer, Judas Iscariot. John's Gospel states plainly that Judas regularly helped himself to ministry money: "[Judas] was a thief, and since he was in charge of the disciples' money, he often stole some for himself" (John 12:6, *NLT*). Apparently, there was enough money so that his pilfering ways were not detected.

Jesus also wore some expensive clothes. "When the soldiers crucified Jesus, they took his clothes, dividing them into four shares, one for each of them, with the undergarment remaining. This garment was seamless, woven in one piece from top to bottom. 'Let's not tear it,' they said to one another. 'Let's decide by lot who will get it'" (John 19:23-24).

This type of garment would be the equivalent of wearing a made-to-order Armani suit today. Perhaps Jesus acquired it as a gift; but don't ministers today face criticism for accepting such expensive gifts? Whether He bought it or it was given to Him, Jesus obviously had no difficulty being seen in the clothing of a prosperous person. Considering all the facts presented here, what do you think? Was Jesus poor?

Putting It All Together

A religious idea like the piety of poverty can gain a life of its own and be applied inappropriately to situations without regard to the facts Scripture presents. Stay rooted and grounded in the Word!

Ask Yourself

1. If Jesus dressed like a prosperous person and also directed a prosperous ministry, what do you think His attitude toward prosperity might be?

2. Does the idea that Jesus was prosperous change your view of poverty in any way?

3. Why do you think so many Christians find it difficult to believe that God would want to prosper His children?

LIVE IT!

Reread the Sermon on the Mount found in Matthew, chapters 5-7, from the perspective that it is being taught by Jesus—a skilled, successful, former carpenter who directs a flourishing and prosperous ministry. Does this change the way you hear and interpret any part of it? If so, in what way? (This can also be done with friends or in a small group study.)

2 2

BREAKING THE POVERTY CURSE:
PERSONAL ENCOUNTERS

And you will know the truth, and the truth will set you free.

JOHN 8:32, *NLT*

The spirit of poverty often exerts its influence over us in subtle ways we would never suspect, keeping us in a "just getting by" frame of mind. To illustrate, I'd like to share two significant events that happened in my life and helped me to break free from the spirit of poverty. Both happened to me during my early pastorate at HRock Church.

THE FIRST ENCOUNTER

The first encounter was in 1996, as HIM, our apostolic network, was just getting started. I was invited to speak over a weekend at a church that was interested in becoming part of HIM. The pastor there was an old friend that I had known when he was part of a sister ministry back in the 1970s and '80s. At the end of the weekend, after I spoke, my friend pulled me aside and confronted me with this truth, in love.

He said to me, "Ché, since I have been with you over the weekend, I have picked up that you have a spirit of poverty." He went on, "I really believe God wants to prosper you." He then asked, "How much do you make annually?" I told him that I was making around $90,000 a year.

He replied, "Last year, I made over $300,000, and I have a smaller church than yours. Most of that came through honorariums. I

Ché Ahn

believe that God wants to break the spirit of poverty and start to prosper you. I want to do a prophetic act. I know that you only spoke one time, but I want to give you an honorarium for $5,000 [the largest I had ever received up to that time for one message]. This is prophetic to let you know that God does not want you to limit Him in any way in how much you make. Second, by giving you this, I break the spirit of poverty over your life!"

I was stunned and at a total loss for words. We had four children, mostly in their early teens, so extra expenses were always coming up. We had a nice home and were getting by, so it never occurred to me that God might want to give me more. We certainly were not poor, so how could I have a spirit of poverty? As I stood and received my friend's prophetic encouragement, I can honestly say that something shifted. I received by faith that God did want to prosper me, and I would never limit Him financially again.

THE SECOND ENCOUNTER

Sometime the following year, we were having our annual prophetic conference. Cindy Jacobs, who is a major prophet in the Body of Christ, and one of my dearest friends, was our keynote speaker. Right after the lunch break, before the afternoon session started, one of our church members came to me with an envelope in her hand and began to tell me how she had just gone through the worst week of her life. She had lost her job that week, and a few days later her husband lost his job. They had emptied out their savings account and she was bringing $2,000 as seed money to sow into the church.

I was touched by their generous and sacrificial gift, but concerned about their financial predicament. I thought my response to her at that time was wise and pastoral. I said, "Patricia, you and your family will need this money to hold you over until you find a job." I gave her back the envelope and walked away feeling "spiritual" for refusing the offering.

I didn't realize it, but Patricia walked away frustrated. She went into our resources center where Cindy Jacobs was doing some last-minute shopping before her afternoon session started. Patricia shared the whole story with Cindy, how she and her husband lost their jobs and how she brought seed money to me, which I had refused.

Cindy came running out of the bookstore with Patricia running right behind her. I have never seen her so mad in my life. She came storming up to me and got right in my face and asked, "Did you refuse this woman's offering?"

"Well, yes, but she lost her job and her husband lost his job, and they will need this money to hold them over," I replied, feeling confused and a little sheepish.

Cindy asked, "Ché, do you believe in the Bible?"

I didn't know where she was going with this line of questioning, but I said meekly, "Yes."

She said, "I don't believe you really do. The Bible says that it is more blessed to give than to receive. If you really believed, then you would have received this woman's offering and not deprived her of her blessing. You see, she was giving out of her need. Now, you receive this offering!"

I obediently received the offering. Then Cindy went on, "I think you have a spirit of poverty, and I command that spirit of poverty to leave you right now, in Jesus' name!"

Again, I felt something break off my life. I believe that I was delivered.

Cindy began the afternoon service by sharing the whole incident. I wanted to find a hole somewhere to crawl into! Then she had Patricia come up, and Cindy took up a spontaneous offering for her. I remember that more than $18,000 came in that afternoon, and the whole amount was given to Patricia. Later that week, Patricia got a better job, and her husband also found a better-paying job.

My life was forever changed that week. I was delivered from the spirit of poverty, and I also learned an important truth of how sowing and reaping can break a poverty spirit. Out of your need, you need to sow a seed. That is what Patricia did, and I almost hindered her blessing by initially refusing to receive her seed.

I had good intentions, but I was using worldly thinking, letting the wisdom of a spirit of poverty guide me. It seemed so reasonable and even compassionate, but it wasn't the truth, and it only strengthened poverty's grip in the situation. I was focusing on the $2,000 I could see as Patricia's available resource, instead of Father God's promise to supply all our needs according to His riches in glory in Christ Jesus (see Phil. 4:19). I had preached on that text and certainly thought I believed it, but when the situation stood before me in flesh, named Patricia, I didn't even recognize it!

PUTTING IT ALL TOGETHER

We need to be aware that poverty's wisdom will often sound very reasonable, but it is not the truth. Following it will only strengthen poverty's grip on us and lead us into deeper bondage.

ASK YOURSELF

1. Think about the last time you made a financial decision. What wisdom guided your thinking: God's or poverty's?

2. What are the ways you may be settling for "just getting by" financially? Do you really believe God wants to give you more?

3. What hope does Paul's words in Philippians 4:19 speak into your current life situation?

LIVE IT!

This week take time to really listen to your thoughts and words about money. What wisdom do you hear: God's or poverty's? Do you hear any consistent patterns of poverty's wisdom? If so, write them down to help you become more aware of the thoughts that are keeping you in bondage.

23

THE STRONGHOLD OF MAMMON

None is able to serve two lords, for either he will hate the one
and love the other, or he will be hold to the one, and despise
the other; ye are not able to serve God and Mammon.

MATTHEW 6:24, *YLT*

MAMMON IS A SPIRIT

Most people don't really understand the word "Mammon." Even
the various translators of the Bible use different words for Mammon. For example, consider two well-known translations. The *New*
International Version translates the word as "money," and the *New*
American Standard Version translates it as "wealth." The *New King*
James Version uses the right word, "Mammon," which comes from
the Greek word *mamona*, but fails to capitalize the word. The only
translation I have found that recognizes that the word is a proper
noun, and capitalizes it as "Mammon," is *Young's Literal Translation.*

Young got it right. Mammon is a proper name, like Satan or
Baal or Jezebel. It is, in my opinion, a major demonic principality
under Satan. It encourages us to become self-reliant as we put our
trust in wealth, rather than God. People deceived by Mammon are
obsessed with wealth. They may or may not be prosperous. Many
poor people struggle with this spirit. Satan uses Mammon as a pawn
to take the place of God. Mammon promises to give us things that
only God can give us, like significance, security, identity, power, authority and freedom. It promises everything and delivers nothing.

Money is not the same as Mammon. Money is an amoral tool,
a neutral object that can be used either for good or evil. The Spirit

of God or the spirit of Mammon can rest on money. If money is not submitted to God, it is by default dominated by Satan and the spirit of Mammon. Money submitted to God and His purposes is blessed and used to advance His kingdom. Money that has the spirit of Mammon is used to manipulate and control people.

One of the most common misinterpretations in Scripture is the saying that "money is the root of all evil." That is not what Scripture says, and it is not how God regards money. The Bible says, "For the *love* of money is the root of all kinds of evil" (1 Tim. 6:10, emphasis added). It is the love of money—not money itself—that is the root of all evil. This is further clarified in the rest of that verse: "Some people, eager for money, have wandered from the faith and pierced themselves with many griefs."

I remember when televangelist Jim Bakker went to prison in 1988 for financial impropriety in his ministry. He was in prison for seven years, and when he got out, HRock Church was one of the first churches to invite him to speak. We received a lot of criticism for that, but we believe that our God is a God of forgiveness and restoration. Jim had already repented and written his confession in the book *I Was Wrong*.[1]

I invited him to speak at our church because I had met him earlier and was genuinely impressed by his brokenness and repentance. He shared something profound with me that directly relates to 1 Timothy 6:10. Jim said, "Ché, in the seven years I was in prison, there was not one person there who was not there because of the love of money. No matter what crime they committed, the root evil was the love of money. The bank robber was there because of the love of money. The pimp was in prison for the love of money. The white-collar tax violator was there because of the love of money." He went on to mention other crimes that people committed and how they were all rooted in the love of money. I will never forget that conversation as long as I live. It showed me how strong the principality of Mammon is.

I believe the whole recession of 2008 was rooted in the love of money. The subprime loans given to people who did not qualify for those loans were a major trigger that brought on the recession.

I remember reading one news article about a man who was interviewed after having to foreclose on his home. He said, "I wouldn't have given me a loan. I was unemployed and in debt, but the bank still gave me a loan for that house." The lust for a good commission drove that broker to give a loan to someone who was totally unqualified. That obsession with the short-term gain available in commission checks—multiplied over thousands of subprime loans—led to the subsequent bank failures, stock market crash and highest unemployment rates since the Great Depression. When you are ruled by the spirit of Mammon, he will come and "steal and kill and destroy" (John 10:10).

THE MO OF MAMMON

Regardless of how Mammon presents itself, here are some basic characteristics that reveal when it is at work:

- An emphasis on sensual living and the pursuit of comfort
- A desire for more that is never satisfied, no matter how much is acquired
- Constant comparisons of self to others
- Using the power of money to acquire things and attract people
- Manipulating the need to be accepted and significant by buying connections to the "right people" and acquiring the "right image"
- Inflaming the desire to possess beautiful things and beautiful people
- Preoccupation with self; self is #1
- Compromises in integrity; self-justification
- Instead of possessing and controlling money, money possesses and controls the person

Materialism is the most common expression of the spirit of Mammon. Materialism is the devotion to material wealth and the accumulation of possessions at the expense of anything and everyone else. It is the sensually driven love of excessive comfort. I remember when I had lunch with a major leader of the Church in Hong Kong. He said to me, "Ché, you think you live in a republic in the United States, but you don't. You really have a monarchy in America. Your king is materialism, your queen is entertainment and your crown prince is sports." I reflected for a moment and knew he was right.

Our culture is driven by materialism. We are constantly bombarded by a stream of ads on TV, on the Internet, on our smart phones, on billboards . . . the list is endless. The ads tell us we're lacking if we aren't wearing the latest clothing and hairstyles; don't have the best star athlete-endorsed shoes; don't own the latest technological gadgets, and so on. There is no saturation point. George Otis Jr., founder and president of The Sentinel Group, a Christian research and information agency, says that materialism is one of the last spiritual giants. In his book *Last of the Giants*, Otis says that materialism is one of the major spiritual strongholds in the world. Its roots infiltrate every culture worldwide.[2]

MATERIALISM UNMASKED IN MY LIFE

I was convicted of materialism the first time I went to Toronto Airport Christian Fellowship, in October 1994, during their first Catch the Fire Conference. It was the morning session on the second day of the conference, and Mike Bickel, the founder of the International House of Prayer, was the speaker. He said that if we were drawing life and security from anything other than Jesus, we were engaging in idolatry. He ended by giving an invitation to the Holy Spirit to show us if we had given our hearts to anything other than Jesus. He led us in a prayer and then we were all dismissed for lunch.

As other conference participants drifted out of the room, I sat in my chair and asked the Holy Spirit if there was anything I was putting security in other than Jesus. I quickly heard a still, small voice. "Son, you have a stronghold of materialism." I immediately rebuked that voice and disagreed with what it said. I knew that it couldn't possibly be the real Holy Spirit. After all, we had just

started HRock Church, and I did not even receive a salary in the
first five months. My wife, Sue, and I had lived by faith for almost
a year and a half now. Those were not the actions of a materialistic person!

Then the Holy Spirit spoke to me again: "I want to show you
how strong this is in your life. I want you to take your retirement
money and sow it into My Kingdom." We had depleted our savings to provide our living expenses, but we had a little over $20,000
in our retirement account. When God spoke this to me, I immediately said, "No, Lord!" (Of course this is the ultimate oxymoron.
How can one call Jesus "Lord" and say "No"?!) But that is what I
said. And when it came out of my mouth, I realized how true God
is and how much materialism was a stronghold in my life. I wept
for the next two hours. In part, I was crying because I didn't want
to give my retirement money away; but most of my tears were honest weeping over my sins.

Finally, after two hours, I could see that God wasn't going to
change, so I said, "Okay, God. But this is not just my retirement
money; it also belongs to Sue. I have to call Sue and see if she will
agree." (To this day, Sue and I do not make any transactions, purchases or give more than $500 to any ministry without praying
and talking to each other about it first). I was actually relieved.
Sue wasn't at the conference, and this would be a cold call. She
would be shocked by this news and would never go for it, and I'd
be off the hook!

So I called her in Pasadena, California. When I told Sue what
I sensed the Lord had said, she paused for a few minutes to pray.
Then she said, "That is the word of the Lord. Let's do it!" I hated
her at that moment. Here I was in Toronto, experiencing revival,
and there she was 3,000 miles away. It took me two hours and a
flood of tears before I said yes. She said yes in less than two minutes of praying! But you see, this was not her problem. It was mine.

We didn't know it then, but God was testing our hearts; for in
the future, He was going to allow us to manage millions in the various ministries we serve. This was another opportunity for us to
train for reigning in God's kingdom.

Putting It All Together

Mammon is a demonic principality that encourages us to be self-reliant by trusting in wealth, rather than God. Money is just a tool that can be submitted to God or dominated by Mammon. Materialism, expressed in the desire for material wealth and the accumulation of possessions, is the primary expression of Mammon worldwide.

Ask Yourself

1. In what ways are you influenced by materialism?

2. Who do you think might be more deceived by materialism, someone who is wealthy or someone living in poverty? Why?

3. How would life in your city be different if the stronghold of Mammon was completely disabled?

Live It!

Look at the characteristics of Mammon's MO. Which characteristics do you see reflected in your attitudes and behavior? How did these influences gain an entrance into your life? Take time in prayer to see if God brings memories to mind that you may have forgotten. Write down the things that are revealed to you. They can help indicate the possible roots of strongholds in your heart.

Notes

1. Jim Bakker, *I Was Wrong: The Untold Story of the Shocking Journey from PTL Power to Prison and Beyond* (Nashville, TN: Thomas Nelson, 1997).
2. George Otis Jr., *The Last of the Giants* (Ada, MI: Chosen Books, 1991).

2 4

THE MANY FACES OF MAMMON

You may say to yourself, "My power and the strength of my hands have produced this wealth for me."

DEUTERONOMY 8:17

We have discussed materialism, the most common form assumed by the spirit of Mammon. But Mammon has some other disguises that also can deceive us. I remember watching a program about a top rock musician several years ago. He was in an exclusive antiques store in Las Vegas, and was selecting items for his home. As he walked about the showroom floor, trailed by the store manager, he pointed to first one item and then another, saying, "I'll take that." He added exquisite art objects and furniture to his purchases, worth hundreds of thousands of dollars, like you or I might add items to a grocery cart. He kept rapidly choosing more objects, but none of them seemed to be of any particular interest or value to him. He was simply collecting them. This is a perfect picture of the spirit of greed.

MAMMON HAS FRIENDS

The spirit of greed is financial or economic gluttony. It produces an overwhelming desire to have more of something than is actually needed or can even be used. The person consumes more than he or she needs but is never satisfied. He or she never has enough. It is the "shop 'til you drop" syndrome. Scripture records, "Whoever loves money never has money enough; whoever loves wealth is never satisfied with his income. This too is meaningless" (Eccles. 5:10). That rock star had a desire to possess more and more, with no saturation point in sight. That is the spirit of greed speaking.

Another manifestation of Mammon is the spirit of covetousness. Coveting always casts an envious eye to the other person. It is a strong desire to possess something that belongs to somebody else. The covetous person is always comparing himself to others to see if he is lacking or if someone else is "one up." No matter how much the covetous person has, he always finds that someone else has something he wants. With today's proliferation of credit cards, people can easily act out on their covetous desires. Credit cards allow us to be greedy, materialistic and covetous, and they can enslave us to poverty. We buy things we would never buy on a cash basis, because we would buy only what we have cash for. But credit cards allow us to extend ourselves well beyond our financial means.

A more subtle form of Mammon is the spirit of pride or self-reliance. This spirit deceives us into thinking that we are producing our wealth based on our efforts. Instead of looking to God for provision, we depend upon our boss or our job, our investments or business, other family members or even the government to meet our needs. Scripture makes it clear that God is our source, not anyone or anything else. "You may say to yourself, 'My power and the strength of my hands have produced this wealth for me.' But remember the LORD your God, for it is he who gives you the ability to produce wealth, and so confirms his covenant, which he swore to your forefathers, as it is today" (Deut. 8:17-18).

God taught me this lesson a few years ago. We had a multi-millionaire in our church who gave very generously. He would write checks for $100,000 to our church without blinking. One time he handed my wife a check for $500,000 to give to our building fund. And then he and his family left our church. At first I was really worried. My mind was filled with thoughts like, *How are we going to balance the budget without this man, who was unquestionably the biggest tither in our church?*

But the Lord spoke to my heart and said, "This man is not the provider of HRock Church; I am. Look to Me and never look to another as your provider." I repented and began to thank God for

sending this man for a season to our church. He left right before
the recession of 2008 started. Yet, during the recession, we didn't
lay off one staff member. In fact, we have given raises and bonuses
to our staff. We have actually hired more staff, because God is our
source. When you put your trust in Him and not in anyone else, including yourself, He truly will meet all your needs according to
His riches in Christ Jesus (see Phil. 4:19)!

A Very Different Face of Mammon

So far, all the forms of Mammon we have discussed focus on acquiring things and influencing people through amassing wealth.
The spirit of parsimony looks very different. People who are deceived by this spirit are very capable of acquiring and saving
money, but they are incapable of spending or using that money.
Parsimony is the inability to give or spend money, and it is expressed in miserliness and hoarding. These people may have
wealth, but they cannot let it go. Outwardly, they may actually
look poor. The stereotype is the person who dies with thousands
of dollars under his or her mattress.

The miserly person is often miserable and fearful. We read in
James 5:3, "Your gold and silver are corroded. Their corrosion will
testify against you in your flesh like fire. You have hoarded
wealth." In Ecclesiastes 5:13, we read, "I have seen a grievous evil
under the sun: wealth hoarded to the harm of its owner." The most
famous example of the spirit of parsimony is found in the character of Ebenezer Scrooge in Charles Dickens's classic story *A Christmas Carol*. Scrooge is wealthy, but he is entirely miserable, for he
hoards every penny. He lives an austere life and complains about
every expenditure. His inability to enjoy his prosperity is con-
trasted with his employee Bob Cratchit's ability to enjoy everything, despite his poverty.

Jesus warned us about the spirit of parsimony and the dangers
of hoarding in the following parable: "The ground of a certain rich
man produced a good crop. He thought to himself, 'What shall I
do? I have no place to store my crops.' Then he said, 'This is what I'll

do. I will tear down my barns and build bigger ones, and there I will store all my grain and my goods. And I'll say to myself, "You have plenty of good things laid up for many years. Take life easy; eat, drink and be merry."' But God said to him, 'You fool! This very night your life will be demanded from you. Then who will get what you've prepared for yourself?' This is how it will be with anyone who stores up things for himself but is not rich toward God" (Luke 12:16-21).

I was reminded of this parable when I saw a reality TV show on extreme couponing. For these people, the medium of exchange was not money, but grocery and cleaning items they were able to obtain by combining coupons and saving hundreds of dollars. They literally had their garage, or rooms in their houses, devoted to storing all the goods they had couponed. In most cases, they had enough stored away to supply them for a decade or more. All of them intended to keep on couponing and clearing out additional living space for storage.

THE PROSPERITY GOSPEL

Satan seldom deceives us by telling us blatant lies. Rather, he deceives by hiding an ounce of error in a pound of truth. God does want to prosper us, and His Word is full of promises to bless us abundantly. But there's a variant of this truth, often called the "prosperity gospel," that has strayed into some error. While asserting the truth that it's God's will to prosper us, they have lost touch with the true purpose for wealth. They say their luxurious lifestyles are simply a sign of God's favor in response to their claiming His prosperity promises. They are professing to serve God, but actually they want God to serve them. They will give, but they always expect to be repaid. They will help the needy, but it's to keep themselves blessed. If they apply the right prosperity promises, God will deliver the blessing. They have reduced their relationship with God to a formula.

God does want to meet our needs and give us abundance so that we can bless others. His main purpose for our prosperity, however, is to advance His kingdom, not to give us a lavish lifestyle. Repeatedly, Christ told us that we should be more concerned about the treasures we have laid up in heaven than about the material possessions we have gathered here on earth. Since we take nothing from earth when we die, it is clear that the treasures we have in heaven are people, not things. The primary purpose for our prosperity here is to bring people into God's kingdom, not to pursue a lifestyle of the rich and famous.

The Ultimate Purpose of Money

God places great emphasis on how we handle money. There are more than 2,000 verses in Scripture that deal with prosperity and wealth, and 16 of Christ's 38 parables focus on money. Christ explained why our attitudes and behavior with money are so important: "For where your treasure is, there will your heart be also" (Matt. 6:21; Luke 12:34). Do you notice a repetitive theme here? It all comes down to our hearts. Why is this so?

God's first and foremost intention is to form a Christlike character in us. Everything in our creation and daily preservation relates to this, and He will not cease until this is accomplished in us. We cannot become Christlike through our own efforts. God will do the work in each of us through His grace. So what is our part? We are to choose life, to say yes to the empowering work of His grace within us. We choose to align ourselves with His plan and purpose.

Ever since the Garden of Eden, we have been choosing to either trust and rely on Him or to be self-reliant. What we do with our finances makes our choice evident. The spirit of Mammon encourages us to trust ourselves and wealth. The problem is that self-reliance does not work, for we were created to be in a relationship with God as our provider. Originally, we lived in a trusting relationship with Him, and He provided our needs on a daily basis. We had no need to store excess.

When we decided to go our own way, we faced limitations for the first time. We experienced vulnerability and fear as we struggled for scarce resources. The reality of the fallen world is that it is divided into haves and have-nots. We spend much of our energy and time focused on storing up wealth and possessions to take care of ourselves, to have a reserve against the curse of poverty and lack. God's intention for us hasn't changed. Through Christ's redemption, He offers us the restoration of everything we lost in the Fall, including prosperity. He wants us to understand and use prosperity as He does, as a tool to bless others. When we amass wealth to feel secure or to aggrandize our identity, we are worshiping it, for we are looking to it to provide what only God can give us.

Father God knows that Mammon constantly tempts us to be self-reliant. He provides us with guidance and direction on how to take authority and dominion over wealth. It's our choice whether we will follow His counsel and accept His training to reign, or be deceived by Mammon and the many ways it seeks to seduce us and bring us into bondage. As Jesus plainly told us, it comes down to two choices, and we can only pick one: "No one can serve two masters. Either he will hate the one and love the other, or he will be devoted to the one and despise the other. You cannot serve both God and Money" (Matt. 6:24).

PUTTING IT ALL TOGETHER

Materialism is the primary manifestation of Mammon. Other forms are the spirits of greed, covetousness, pride and self-reliance. They all seek to amass wealth and accumulate possessions. The spirit of parsimony hoards money and can't release it, while the prosperity gospel is a misapplication of God's promise to bless us. Our attitudes and behavior with money demonstrate what our hearts truly treasure.

ASK YOURSELF

1. Do you see tendencies in yourself to be influenced by the spirits of greed, covetous, self-reliance, pride or parsimony? How are these tendencies manifested in your attitudes and behaviors?

2. When it comes to your finances, what makes you feel most secure? Do you trust this more than you trust God as your provider? Why?

3. Take a look at your checkbook or debit statement for the last month. What do your expenditures say about what you treasure?

LIVE IT!

Think about your current financial situation. Think of this situation as an opportunity to train for reigning in God's kingdom. How might this change in perspective influence the way you make decisions in your situation?

2 5

DISARMING THE
PROSPERITY ROBBERS

The weapons we fight with are not the weapons of the world. On the contrary, they have divine power to demolish strongholds. We demolish arguments and every pretense that sets itself up against the knowledge of God, and we take captive every thought to make it obedient to Christ.

2 CORINTHIANS 10:4-5

We've seen that God wants to prosper us, but most of us have a distorted image of God, and of ourselves, that prevents us from believing and receiving His blessings. Poverty and Mammon are both demonic spirits that seek to establish strongholds in our hearts to steal the authority and dominion God has restored to us. They kill our identity of being made in God's image, and destroy our trust in Father God by replacing Him with self-reliance in our ability to get wealth. They also reinforce strongholds already in our hearts caused by our orphan mentality, our heart wounds and years of cultural conditioning from family, society and media influences.

In order to disarm the control of these prosperity robbers, we need to understand our vulnerabilities by identifying the mental, emotional and spiritual roots of these strongholds. We all know that wherever there is garbage, you will find rats. In the same way, wherever mental and emotional garbage exists in our hearts, we will find demonic spirits attempting to oppress us with their deceptions.

To demolish these strongholds, we must clean up the garbage and exterminate the rats. Both are necessary, for if we only clean up the garbage, the rats are left and can still do damage. If we exterminate the rats, the garbage that remains will only attract more rats. This means that we need to go through a process of both inner healing to address the mental and emotional garbage in our hearts, and spiritual deliverance to break the power of demonic spirits. Both inner healing and spiritual deliverance are necessary to effectively demolish strongholds.

Too often, people focus on one thing—either inner healing or spiritual deliverance, assuming the stronghold is destroyed. Things may improve for a time, but they soon find themselves struggling again with the same distorted attitudes and behaviors, often feeling more hopeless and defeated than before.

In the next section, I have outlined a set of general principles I have found useful in helping others break the stronghold of Mammon and the curse of poverty in their lives. Inner healing and spiritual deliverance have been described in detail in other excellent resources. There are also ministries that provide each, and often it is helpful to work through these processes with additional assistance from others who are experienced.

Believe, Renounce and Receive

Deliverance, the process of tearing down demonic strongholds of oppression, consists of three major types of activities. It has some aspects in common with inner healing. However, deliverance addresses spiritual influences on our hearts, while inner healing deals with our distorted thoughts and emotions. We must look honestly at what we believe, and bring our thoughts in line with the truth of Father God's Word. We must renounce the demonic spirits that are oppressing us, and the mental and emotional garbage we have been storing in our hearts. We must receive God's Spirit and His healing.

Believe

It's important to take an honest look at yourself, especially your attitudes and behaviors toward wealth. What do you really believe? Who or what do you trust? Are you relying on God's provision, or do you look to the bottom line in your bank account for security?

Are you financially responsible, or does money "just run through your fingers"? Can you be content with what you have, or do you always need something more?

In order to identify some of your attitudes and behaviors to prosperity, you may want to look back at the results of the Prosperity Quotient self-assessment you completed in Section 3: You Prosper as Your Soul Prospers. People with a PQ of Poverty Piety or The Despondent are more likely to be influenced by the spirit of poverty, while The Emotional Spender, Prosperity Reliant and The Miser PQs are more likely to be influenced by the stronghold of Mammon.

Your motives are of special importance. Do you primarily see God's promises as a way to gain personal prosperity, or do you want to be transformed into a Christlike giver? Are you interested in advancing your own interests, or are you truly Kingdom minded? The condition of your heart is everything, and God regards your heart first and foremost. You can ask God to help you in this self-examination process: "Test me O LORD, and try me, examine my heart and my mind" (Ps. 26:2). He is willing to share His wisdom with you. As James states, "If any of you lacks wisdom, he should ask God, who gives generously to all without finding fault, and it will be given to him" (1:5).

Throughout this process, you need to align your thinking with Father God's Word. An important lesson from the parable of the Sower is having ears to hear; that is, seeking to hear and understand God's Word. You need to meditate on God's promises concerning prosperity and choose to agree with what the Holy Spirit reveals to you. As you spend time in this process, the divine seed of the Holy Spirit within you will grow, casting down lies and deceptions, and increasing your trust in God's truth.

RENOUNCE

You will need to renounce attitudes and behaviors toward prosperity that you know are not godly. It doesn't make any difference how you acquired them; you must turn from them, ask God to clear your heart and mind, and choose to embrace His Word. This is not something you do in your own strength; you come to God willing to receive His grace to accomplish it.

An important part of this process is releasing bitterness and judgments you may be carrying by forgiving your parents for the financial situation in which you were brought up. You also need to forgive others who may have hurt you financially, such as a boss who passed you over for promotion, or someone who may have cheated you in a financial dealing. Unforgiveness is a powerful form of self-pollution that you must renounce completely. It's important to remember that forgiveness is an act of your will, not an emotion that you feel. You choose to forgive out of love for your Father God and a desire to be like Him. You probably won't feel a change of emotion toward the person you forgive at the time, but as you continue to walk in forgiveness, your feelings will change.

Once you have identified and renounced your distorted attitudes, behaviors and unforgiveness, and have aligned your heart with God's Word, you have cleared your heart of the mental and emotional garbage stored there. With nothing left to feed on, the control exerted by the spirits of materialism, greed, covetousness, parsimony, pride and poverty can be broken and renounced.

Sometimes these spirits have generational roots that also must be renounced. Many people find it helpful to have someone assist them in this process, but the following is a prayer you can use on your own:

> *Heavenly Father, all the silver is Yours and all the gold is Yours. My heart is Yours also. I give You my whole heart, all that I have and all that I am. Jesus, You are the Lord of my life, and by Your grace I will follow You and obey You. In the name of Jesus, I repent of and renounce every stronghold of Mammon and the spirit of poverty in my life. Jesus, I make You my Lord and Savior. Keep my heart pure for Your glory. In Jesus' name. Amen.*

RECEIVE

Once you've emptied your heart of the mental and emotional garbage and demonic strongholds that were there, it is important that you replace them with the presence of God's Holy Spirit. Jesus warned us that evil spirits seek to return to influence us. "When an evil spirit comes out of a man, it goes through arid places seeking rest and does not find it. Then it says, 'I will return to the house I left.' When it arrives, it finds the house unoccupied, swept clean and put in order. Then it goes and takes with it seven other spirits more wicked than itself, and they go in and live there. And the final condition of that person is worse than the first" (Matt. 12:43-45).

Guard your heart by being filled with God's Holy Spirit. Being filled with God's Spirit at one point in time is not enough. Ask God to refill you daily with a fresh impartation of His Holy Spirit. If you have never received the infilling of the Holy Spirit, you can do so now. There's no correct way to pray; simply tell God that you desire to be filled with His Holy Spirit, and He will fill you. If you want, you can use this prayer:

> *Dear Father God, I come to You and acknowledge that I have rebelled and gone my own way. But I have repented of my rebellion and accepted Your gift of salvation in Jesus Christ. I give up going my own way. I want to follow You all the days of my life. I surrender to You, Father God. I believe You desire to give me the gift of Your Holy Spirit. I ask You right now to fill me with Your Holy Spirit. Grant me the power of the Holy Spirit to do Your work. Thank You, Father God, for Your love and for Your gift of the Holy Spirit to me. Amen.*

Make it a daily practice to till the soil of your heart by spending time with God in His Word. Doing so will keep you open and receptive to His truth and promises. Like the sower in the parable, you will be planting seed in good ground, and you can expect your heart to yield an abundant harvest of faith and trust in God's promises. Take time with the process of inner healing and spiritual deliverance, remembering that it is foundational for receiving everything else from Father God.

The great South African writer and pastor of the nineteenth century, Andrew Murray, beautifully described the process of tilling the soil of our hearts in his preface to the book *The Lord's Table*: "Spiritual, divine truth does not become our possession at once. Although I understand what I read, although I consent heartily to it, although I receive it, it may speedily fade away and be forgotten, unless by private meditation I give it time to become fixed and rooted in me, to become united and identified with me. Give yourself, give your Lord time to transfer His heavenly thoughts to your inner, spiritual life. When you have read a portion, set yourself in silence before God. Take time to remain before Him until He has made His word living and powerful in your soul. Then shall you understand what the Lord Jesus says: 'The words which I speak unto you, they are spirit and life.'"[1]

A final word: As you go through this process of breaking strongholds, never allow yourself to be condemned by what you find in your heart. Father God is not judging you; He only desires that you get set free from everything that hinders you in becoming who He created you to be. The process of renouncing and breaking free of strongholds is part of your training for reigning in God's kingdom. You are His beloved child, and you were born again to have your complete dominion and authority restored to you. You are destined to become Christlike in every way.

PUTTING IT ALL TOGETHER

Inner healing and spiritual deliverance are both necessary to effectively demolish strongholds. When only one process is addressed, there may be a temporary improvement, but you will soon find yourself struggling with the same distorted attitudes and behaviors. Deliverance involves believing God, renouncing the lies and deceptions of spiritual strongholds, and receiving God's Holy Spirit and heart healing.

ASK YOURSELF

1. What strongholds related to prosperity and wealth may currently exist in your heart?

2. How might your life change financially if the strongholds were destroyed?

3. How would being set free from your financial strongholds better equip you to advance God's kingdom?

LIVE IT!

Read the quote from Andrew Murray again. Using the meditation method he outlines there, spend time and meditate on Matthew 6:24-34. Let this passage become fixed and rooted in you. Record the thoughts God reveals to you.

Note
1. Andrew Murray, *The Lord's Table* (New York: Fleming H. Revell, 1897), p. 7.

THE UNIVERSAL
LAWS OF
PROSPERITY

Prosperity operates on basic universal laws of giving and receiving, called sowing and reaping. The laws of sowing and reaping work for everyone who employs them, without regard to gender, ethnicity, nationality or income level. Just ask any farmer. This section focuses on these universal laws, using both natural examples from farming, and biblical references.

Many books on giving begin with these laws, but if we do not understand the fundamental principles we've touched on thus far, such as . . .

- the heart of our Father God
- the state of our own orphan hearts
- the connection between our mind and heart
- God's desire to prosper us
- the oppression of the spirit of poverty and the stronghold of Mammon

. . . then the universal laws of prosperity will have minimal impact in our lives.

God knows one of the biggest challenges we face in life is how we handle finances, for it reveals where we really put our trust: in God or in wealth. He wants to provide a continuous supply of everything we need. The way to tap into His supply is to trust Him and sow abundantly by becoming a Christlike giver. Unless we sow this way, we will never reap.

God desires for us to go much deeper than wanting Him to prosper us. As we surrender to His love, He gives us His grace that becomes both the motivation and the inner power to transform our hearts into Christlike givers. He is inviting us to embrace Christlike giving, His giving, to bless others and advance His kingdom.

2 6

ASK ANY FARMER

As long as the earth endures, seedtime and harvest, cold and heat,
summer and winter, day and night will never cease.

GENESIS 8:22

Have you ever heard of Farmville? If you are familiar with Facebook, you probably have. Farmville is a real-time farm simulation game that allows members of Facebook to manage a virtual farm by planting, growing and harvesting virtual crops, trees and livestock. It is one of the most popular game applications on Facebook today with more than 75 million active users.

Whether we're a virtual farmer, an actual farmer, or we've never set foot on a farm, we are all subject to the laws of sowing and reaping in life. Before we look at how these principles apply to our prosperity, let's take a look at them in relation to farming. I need to make one disclaimer: I have no agricultural background. (The only thing I ever grew was marijuana, which of course was before I gave my life to Christ.) I do not have a green thumb, and you will never see me doing gardening. But the principles I'm about to share are so simple and so basic that it doesn't take a degree in agriculture to make sense of what God teaches in His Word.

THE LAY OF THE LAND

Jesus frequently referred to agricultural illustrations when speaking to His disciples. In fact, Jesus told *nine* agricultural parables. He understood the world of agriculture because He was surrounded by farming. In Galilee, agriculture was the major industry. Everywhere

Jesus went there were fields and farms growing figs, grapes, olives and various grains. So it was natural for Jesus to use farming examples in His teachings.

Any farmer can tell you that there are some universal laws when it comes to farming. The first one is that sowing and reaping are constants. There is no way to escape them. If you are farming, there is no other option. A wise farmer realizes that his responsibility is to sow. God will make the seed grow and provide the harvest, but only if the farmer sows. He is confident in this because everywhere he looks, he sees that increase is a basic principle of nature. All plants and animals reproduce and multiply.

In farming, timing is everything. Whether it's planting seeds, waiting for them to germinate and grow, or harvesting, every phase has its own time and season. There's really no downtime in farming. It's a 24/7 task, 52 weeks a year. Even in winter, the farmer keeps busy maintaining equipment and getting ready for spring planting.

In farming, the farmer is always looking ahead. Each year is a new year. Last year he may have had a bumper crop or a bust, but this is a new year, and he looks forward to what this year will bring. Farming is hard work, but he keeps on working, even when he feels like giving up, because he knows that his hard work will pay off. No matter what challenges the farmer faces, he always knows that it's too soon to quit.

One last word: Universal laws work for everyone. For example, the law of gravity works whether you're male or female, old or young, and regardless of your culture, ethnicity or nationality. Gravity works the same way for every person. It doesn't work better for males than it does for females, or for Americans than it does for Chinese. The same is true for the laws of sowing and reaping. They work equally well for every farmer who employs them.

THE LAWS OF SOWING AND REAPING

Let's look at these laws in relation to farming.

TAKE TIME TO PLOW!

A farmer can have the best seed in the world, but if he doesn't take time to prepare the soil, he's not going to get much of a harvest. The soil needs to be turned over, plowed and tilled. This is hard, sweaty, backbreaking work, and no one enjoys it, but it has to be done.

THE LAW OF CONSERVATION

Another way to say this is, "Don't eat your seed!" Every farmer understands that he cannot consume his entire crop. He must save some in order to have seed to plant the next year. Even if he is hungry, he will not eat the seed he dedicates for planting, because that is his future. Instead, he will first put aside a certain percentage of the current crop as seed for next year, before he begins to consume the rest of the harvest. He doesn't resent having to do this. He does it willingly, knowing that he is ensuring continuous harvesting in the future.

THE LAW OF RECIPROCITY

Every farmer knows that you reap what you sow. You don't plant corn and expect to harvest wheat. He understands that like produces like. This is the way God established it in the beginning. "Then God said, 'Let the land produce vegetation: seed-bearing plants and trees on the land that bear fruit with seed in it, according to their various kinds.' And it was so. The land produced vegetation: plants bearing seed according to their kinds and trees bearing fruit with seed in it according to their kinds. And God saw that it was good" (Gen. 1:11-12).

THE LAW OF SEASONS

Farmers understand that there is an order to sowing and reaping. You must plant seed before you can reap. How would you feel about a farmer who went out and stood in his field looking around for his crop, and when you asked him, "What did you plant?" he replied, "Nothing"? You would think that farmer was pretty stupid, for how could he expect to reap a crop when he hadn't sown any seed?

God established a universal order in sowing and reaping. He stated, in Genesis 8:22, "As long as the earth endures, seedtime and harvest, cold and heat, summer and winter, day and night will never cease." Ecclesiastes 3:1-2 echoes this reality: "There is a time for everything, and a season for every activity under heaven: a time to be born and a time to die, a time to plant and a time to uproot."

THE LAW OF EXPECTATION

A farmer expects the harvest. He believes that what he sows will produce a crop, for he trusts the universal law of sowing and reaping. He doesn't let temporary weather conditions influence his decisions. Circumstances or hardships don't prevent him from planting, because he expects that planting will result in harvest. If he did not believe this, he would be swayed by temporary events. As Ecclesiastes 11:4 says, "Whoever watches the wind will not plant; whoever looks at the clouds will not reap." Weather fluctuations and circumstances are temporary, but the law of sowing and reaping is universal and constant.

THE LAW OF PERSEVERANCE

The farmer realizes that there is a waiting period after he sows the seed. For a while the ground will not look any different. But he doesn't dig up his seed to see how it's doing. He understands the principle of patiently waiting. "The earth produces the crops on its own. First a blade pushes through, then the heads of wheat are formed, and finally the grain ripens" (Mark 4:28, NLT). He also waits until the crop is fully mature, knowing that he will not reap the best harvest if he becomes anxious and tries to gather it prematurely.

THE LAW OF PROPORTIONS

Every farmer expects to reap in proportion to what he has sown. If he has a 500-acre farm, and he plants 250 acres of corn, he does not expect to reap corn on all 500 acres. The limits he puts on the seed planted will limit the crop harvested. Scripture puts it this way: "Remember: A stingy planter gets a stingy crop; a lavish planter gets a lavish crop" (2 Cor. 9:6, THE MESSAGE).

THE LAW OF INCREASE

Crops multiply seed. A farmer doesn't sow a kernel of corn and expect to reap a kernel of corn. No, he plants two kernels of corn and expects to get a stalk that will have three to four ears of corn. Each ear will have about 400 kernels, so that stalk is yielding 1,200 to 1,600 kernels for the two kernels planted. This is the way it always is with sowing and reaping. You always reap more than you sow. Psalm 126:6 states, "He who goes out weeping, carrying seed to sow, will return with songs of joy, carrying sheaves with him."

The farmer knows that he will harvest more seed than he plants. After he has set aside the seed for next year's crop, he is free to enjoy the rest of his harvest. He has worked diligently, and he deserves to enjoy it. "Who plants a vineyard and does not eat of its grapes? Who tends a flock and does not drink the milk?" (1 Cor. 9:7).

FINAL CONDITIONS

This discussion would not be complete without mentioning two more important conditions for successful farming. The farmer continuously checks the soil to ensure that it is providing what the seed needs. He will make sure that it receives the right amount of water and the right fertilizer, and he will continue to monitor the soil throughout the growing season.

Every farmer keeps his combine in his own field at harvest time. He knows that he cannot reap his neighbor's harvest, only his own. He works his own field and is content with his own harvest. He rejoices when his neighbor has an abundant harvest, knowing that his turn will come.

These principles, when applied to farming, are simple and straightforward. You can easily understand them and readily agree with their logic. In the next entry, we will look at how they apply to our prosperity.

PUTTING IT ALL TOGETHER

The universal laws of sowing and reaping, when applied, work equally well for all farmers regardless of their ethnicity, nationality or income level. Understanding these laws as they apply to farming provides insights to us in how they will apply to our prosperity.

Ask Yourself

1. Which of the laws of sowing and reaping is the easiest for you to apply to prosperity? Which law is the most difficult for you to apply to prosperity?

2. Come up with at least five examples of how the laws of sowing and reaping work in everyday life. (Hint: To have a friend, be a friend; and so on.)

3. What might this mean: "If you don't like the crop you're reaping, consider the seed you are sowing"? Apply this saying to your life.

Live It!

Think of your finances. What are you sowing and what are you reaping? Do you want to make any changes to your current situation? If so, what change? How will you do it?

SOWING AND REAPING PROSPERITY: PART ONE

Do not be deceived: God cannot be mocked. A person reaps what he sows.

GALATIANS 6:7

In the last entry, we looked at the universal laws of sowing and reaping as they relate to farming. When applied in this way, these laws make sense and seem very straightforward. But sowing and reaping are not only universal laws in agriculture; they are also laws governing every aspect of our lives. For example, if you want to have friends, you need to be a friend. If you want others to respect you, you need to respect them. While these statements describe the way life works, perhaps you've never thought of them as statements about sowing and reaping, but they are.

The following popular folk story illustrates the operation of sowing and reaping in our lives. Fleming was a poor Scottish farmer. One day, he heard cries for help coming from a nearby bog. Running to the bog, he found a terrified boy screaming and struggling to free himself. Farmer Fleming saved the boy, and the next day, a fancy carriage pulled up to his humble cottage. The nobleman who stepped out was the boy's father, and he offered to repay Fleming for his favor. He spotted Fleming's son standing at the door and said, "Let me take him and give him a good education."

Farmer Fleming's son eventually graduated from St. Mary's Hospital Medical School in London, and went on to become known throughout the world as the noted Sir Alexander Fleming, the discoverer of penicillin. Years later, the nobleman's son was stricken with pneumonia. What saved him? Penicillin. The name

of the nobleman? Lord Randolph Churchill. His son's name? Sir
Winston Churchill.

While it is uncertain if this story is historically accurate, it
continues to be popular because it points to a reality we all readily acknowledge: there is a law of reciprocity in life. We do reap
what we sow.

The laws of sowing and reaping apply to our prosperity just
as they do to every other area of life. And just as these laws work
for everyone when applied in farming, they work for everyone
when applied to prosperity. It doesn't matter if you're rich or poor,
male or female, live in a highly developed economy or a third world
country, the laws of sowing and reaping prosperity, if applied, will
work for you.

In fact, it is impossible to escape the laws of sowing and reaping. Deciding not to sow is a decision not to reap. Sowing and
reaping are equally in force whether we are talking about positive
or negative results. God's Word tells us, "Do not be deceived: God
cannot be mocked. A man reaps what he sows. The one who sows
to please his sinful nature, from that nature will reap destruction;
the one who sows to please the Spirit, from the Spirit will reap
eternal life" (Gal. 6:7-8).

In other words, what I reap depends on what I sow. For example, if I drink and drive, I'm much more likely to be in an automo-
bile accident. If I run charges on my credit card up to the maximum
limit, I'm likely to get stuck paying very high interest rates. If I
spend time talking and playing with my children when they are
young, I am more likely to have good communication with them
when they are teenagers. If I decide to direct deposit a certain
amount of my income to savings each month, I will build up a nest
egg for the future. The point here is that sowing and reaping work
equally well in both positive and negative circumstances.

Sowing and Reaping Prosperity

Let's look at how the laws of sowing and reaping relate to prosperity.

A Matter of the Heart

Just as a farmer needs to take time and prepare the soil by plowing, so too we must consider the condition of our hearts. We have already spent considerable time in previous sections looking at the condition of our hearts and the possibility that we are harboring strongholds that can hinder our ability to receive Father God's good gifts. Hosea 10:12 reminds us, "Sow for yourselves righteousness, reap the fruit of unfailing love, and break up your unplowed ground; for it is time to seek the Lord, until he comes and showers righteousness on you."

The parable of the sower and the seed (see Matt. 13:3-9) demonstrates that the condition of our hearts (the soil) is of utmost importance, because the same seed, God's Word, was sown in each type of soil, but it only produced a harvest in the good soil. This is why we must focus on the condition of our hearts first, because it determines everything else. We will not be able to effectively employ the laws of sowing and reaping for prosperity if our hearts are full of emotional wounds and spiritual strongholds. We must open our hearts for God's grace to transform us into Christlike givers.

Sow Seed

This seems like an obvious statement, but when it comes to prosperity, people often don't see the logic. The farmer understands that he cannot consume his entire crop, so he sets aside a certain percentage of his current harvest as seed for next year. In the same way, we need to set aside some of our income to sow into God's kingdom as He directs. God promises, "Remember this: Whoever sows sparingly will also reap sparingly, and whoever sows generously will also reap generously. . . . Now he who supplies seed to the sower and bread for food will also supply and increase your store of seed and will enlarge the harvest of your righteousness" (2 Cor. 9:6,10).

God promises to bless and multiply our seed, but we must give Him something to work with! I meet people all the time who tell me they just can't give because they have so many bills. What they don't realize is that by not planting any financial seed, they are keeping themselves in a cycle of lack. If I can encourage them to begin to give on a consistent basis, they are surprised by how God supplies their need. So I encourage you, if you have a need, plant your seed!

You Reap What You Sow

A farmer who plants corn expects and wants to grow a corn crop. God makes it clear that the financially generous will prosper financially. Proverbs 11:24-25 states, "One man gives freely, yet gains even more; another withholds unduly, but comes to poverty. A generous man will prosper; and he who refreshes others will himself be refreshed."

Some people do not give to God financially on a regular basis, but they are quick to say, "I volunteer my time" or "I teach a Sunday School class." Clearly, these are important contributions, and there is a reward in doing them, but it is not financial. If you want to reap financially, you must sow financially; there is no other option.

Again, let's not get "super-spiritual." Think of it this way: You can't sow anger and reap peace. You can't sow harsh words and get soft answers in return. You can't sow hate and reap love. You can't sow laziness and reap a promotion. So why do we think we can sow something other than finances and reap finances? The same universal law of sowing and reaping applies. If you sow money, you will reap money.

Sow First, Then Reap

Again, this statement seems very straightforward, but you would be surprised how many people don't apply it when it comes to prosperity. Remember the farmer, who didn't plant, standing in his field while waiting for a crop to come up? We all can readily agree that would be a stupid thing to do, but that is what I see in the church all the time. It is a mentality that says, "When I really get some serious money, then I will start giving." You cannot reap before you sow. You have to first sow something. People have said, "It takes money to make money." This saying is true. God says to first sow into the kingdom of God (see Matt. 6:33). It doesn't take much, because He promises to multiply it. Whatever you sow, you will reap.

Trust God and Expect a Return

The farmer doesn't let weather or circumstances change his sowing and reaping. He expects that planting will result in harvest. In the same way, we need to keep our focus on God's promises regarding our prosperity and not on our circumstances or events around us. God promises us a return on our investment with Him, regardless of the state of the economy, our job situation, income level or the amount of bills we owe. God's words are true and changeless. They do not depend on external circumstances.

When economic times are difficult, it is easy to get caught up in bad news and begin to think in terms of limitations. But remember, God blessed Isaac abundantly even in a time of famine. In that culture, famine was the equivalent of a recession or even a depression. We read in Genesis 26, "Isaac planted crops in that land and the same year reaped a hundredfold, because the LORD blessed him. The man became rich, and his wealth continued to grow until he became very wealthy" (Gen. 26:12-13). God made Isaac wealthy in the midst of an economic downturn!

Remember Job? He ran into a streak of terrible misfortune and lost everything he had. In modern-day terms, we might say Job was busted and bankrupt. But God did not desert him. In fact the Lord restored everything and more to him: "The LORD blessed the latter part of Job's life more than the first. He had fourteen thousand sheep, six thousand camels, a thousand yoke of oxen and a thousand donkeys" (Job 42:12). Even in today's economy, that would be real wealth. In Job's time, it made him the richest man in the entire East. You can't get too down and out for God to restore you to prosperity again.

God's Word promises, "Honor the LORD with your wealth, with the firstfruits of all your crops; then your barns will be filled to overflowing, and your vats will brim over with new wine" (Prov. 3:9-10). Although stated in agricultural terms, God is telling us that if we invest our money in His kingdom, we will prosper abundantly.

So once again we have a choice. Do we trust our Father God, who is loving, generous and changeless, or do we trust our reason and our shifting circumstances? Whichever way we go, we will surely reap what we sow.

Let's stop here and consider what we have discussed so far. We will finish looking at the laws of sowing and reaping prosperity in the next entry.

Putting It All Together

The same laws of sowing and reaping that operate in farming apply to prosperity. We must sow financial seed to get a financial return. We must sow first to reap, and we must expect a return for our sowing. Above all, we must trust God and believe His promises to us.

Ask Yourself

1. Are you sowing financial seed on a regular basis into God's kingdom? Why or why not?

2. Are you giving to God in other ways (time, talent and more) and expecting to be blessed financially? Do you see why this cannot work?

3. Have you been waiting to get that raise or some extra money so you can start giving? Do you see why this cannot work?

Live It!

If you haven't been sowing financial seed regularly, why not start now? Ask God to help you trust Him as your Provider. Then ask Him for direction on how much to give. Do it faithfully and record changes you see in the following areas: your trust in God, your finances, and the ways He provides for you.

28

SOWING AND REAPING PROSPERITY: PART TWO

Give, and it will be given unto you.

LUKE 6:38

In the last entry, we looked at several laws of sowing and reaping and how they apply to prosperity. Let's consider several more.

GOOD THINGS COME TO THOSE WHO WAIT

After planting seed, the farmer waits for his crop to come up. Just because things don't immediately look different, he doesn't doubt the harvest. You will never hear a farmer say, "I tried planting that corn last week and it didn't work." I have heard some people complain that they have been faithful in their giving and still have not seen a breakthrough in their finances. There may be root heart issues why their breakthrough has not taken place, or the Lord may want them to learn how to persevere and contend for their financial breakthrough.

Sometimes people give, but afterwards they have second thoughts. They cannot wait for God's return on their seed, and they begin to grieve over the money they no longer have. We have had people give at a conference, and the next week they call the office and ask for the money back. I know they are digging up their seed, but we do give their money back to them, because we don't want people to give out of a grudging heart.

I learned a valuable lesson about perseverance and waiting for God's timing when Sue and I came to California in 1984. We

thought we would see revival because the Lord had given me a prophetic dream in 1982 to come to Los Angeles. He said that there
would be a great harvest and revival. Naturally, I thought the revival would break out the moment we got off the plane; but we
spent 10 years of sowing our prayers, tears and finances. Ten years
later, in January 1994, the revival broke out. I have no regrets over
the 10 years of persevering. I was not ready and didn't have the
character to handle what God wanted to do through the revival. I
learned the importance of persevering and the wisdom of waiting
on God's timetable.

The Lord promises good things to those who wait. "Let us not
become weary in doing good, for at the proper time we will reap a
harvest if we do not give up" (Gal. 6:9). Notice that this verse promises that we will reap "at the proper time" if we do not give up. Pa-
tient perseverance can be difficult, especially in the face of adverse
circumstances. But we must remember that God's words are the
truth, and what He promises, He will deliver. His timing is perfect,
and we must trust that if there seems to be a delay, it is for our
good and not for our detriment.

How You Sow Is How You Reap

No farmer expects to reap 500 acres of crops if he only planted 250
acres. The same is true for prosperity. God is completely just. The
measure with which we sow is the measure with which we reap. If
we give generously, we will reap generously. "Give generously [to
the needy person] and do so without a grudging heart; then because of this the LORD your God will bless you in all your work and
everything you put your hand to" (Deut. 15:10).

It is important to understand that God does not look at the
amount we give, but at the true cost to us that our gift represents.
Jesus made this clear when he was at the temple treasury with His
disciples. The rich were putting in large offerings with much fan-
fare, but that didn't impress Jesus. He saw a poor widow quietly
put in two mites, probably the equivalent of two pennies today.
He turned to His disciples and said that the widow had put in

more than all the others, because they gave their gifts out of their wealth; but out of her poverty, she put in everything she had (see Mark 12:41-44; Luke 21:1-4). In Jesus' eyes, that little widow was due the biggest return, for she made the biggest investment.

YOU REAP MORE THAN YOU SOW

If crops didn't multiply seed, a farmer would never get ahead. But seed is multiplied many times over in each crop. If a farmer plants an apple seed, he doesn't get an apple, but a whole apple tree that will produce bushels of apples for decades to come. That's quite a return for a small investment.

This same kind of return works with prosperity seed as well. "Now he who supplies seed to the sower and bread for food will also supply and increase your store of seed and will enlarge the harvest of your righteousness. You will be made rich in every way so that you can be generous on every occasion" (2 Cor. 9:10-11).

When Jesus described God's kingdom, He often used terms of increase or multiplication. For example, in Matthew 13:31-33 He said, "The kingdom of heaven is like a mustard seed, which a man took and planted in his field. Though it is the smallest of all your seeds, yet when it grows, it is the largest of garden plants and becomes a tree, so that the birds of the air come and perch in its branches. . . . The kingdom of heaven is like yeast that a woman took and mixed into a large amount of flour until it worked all through the dough." Jesus was indicating here that increase is the normal return in the kingdom of God.

In case that language is too symbolic for you, Peter asked Christ directly what he could expect in God's kingdom. When Peter said to Jesus, "We have left everything to follow you!" Jesus replied, "I tell you the truth . . . no one who has left home or brothers or sisters or mother or father or children or fields for me and the gospel will fail to receive a hundred times as much in this present age (homes, brothers, sisters, mothers, children and fields—and with them, persecutions) and then in the age to come, eternal life" (Mark 10:28-30).

FOCUS ON YOUR HARVEST

Just like the farmer keeps his combine in his own field at harvest time, so too we need to focus on the harvest God sends to us. The farmer knows that his harvest is not affected in any way by the abundance of his neighbors' harvest. His harvest is affected by the type of seed, the measure in which he sowed and the condition of his soil.

Often, in the world of finances, we have a mindset of limitation. That is, we think of money as a scarce commodity that is available only in a limited supply. Therefore, if our neighbor is prospering, we fear there may be less for us. This might be true in the human system of wealth, but God's kingdom does not work this way. It has no limitations. He can bless each of His children abundantly and never run out of resources. "[God] is able to do immeasurably more than all we ask or imagine, according to his power that is at work within us" (Eph. 3:20).

God wants us to trust Him and in His ability and desire to prosper us. He asks us to demonstrate our trust by sowing financial seed into His kingdom. If I say that when you respect others they will show respect back to you, you have no difficulty agreeing. Why? Because you fully trust and expect that the respect you have sown into the lives of others will be returned by them to you. What God is asking us to do with prosperity is no different. He is asking us to trust Him, His promises and the laws of sowing and reaping that He has established in the earth. When we sow finances into His kingdom, we will reap prosperity.

This principle is illustrated in the story of *The King and the Beggar*, a fable from India. An extremely poor beggar sat by the road one day, holding his one possession, a small bowl, which contained a little rice. While he was sitting there, the king came by. Falling to his knees, the beggar lifted his bowl, expecting the king to give him some coins. But to his surprise, the king held out his hand, expecting the beggar to make a contribution.

The beggar was very angry. He thought to himself, "Here I have almost nothing, and this king expects me to give him a contribution!" So he grudgingly took three grains of rice from his bowl and placed it in the king's hand. The king put the grains of rice in his tunic for a moment, and then replaced them in the beggars bowl and walked on. As the beggar looked down at his bowl, he was surprised to see three grains of solid gold rice. Immediately the beggar felt ashamed. "Why didn't I give all I had? I should've known that the generous king would always give me back more than I gave to him." The same is true for our Father God. We can never out-give Him. He asks us to sow, and to expect an abundant return.

Despite the fact that this analogy is clear on paper, it is often more difficult to grasp in our hearts. The way we handle finances and our attitude toward prosperity are extremely important to God. In the next entry, we will look at how He uses prosperity in our lives as a major way to develop the Christlike character in us as part of our training to reign in His kingdom.

PUTTING IT ALL TOGETHER

We will reap prosperity if we wait patiently for it. If we sow generously, we will reap generously. God gives the increase, so we reap more than we sow. When we see others' prosperity, we don't have to worry about lack, for God will supply our need abundantly.

ASK YOURSELF

1. Do you think it is possible to trust God in other areas if you don't trust God with your prosperity? Why or why not?

2. According to the laws of sowing and reaping for prosperity, are you able to see why you are not prospering as you would like? What are those reasons?

3. Has looking at the laws of sowing and reaping changed your view of prosperity in any way? If so, how?

LIVE IT!

If you truly trusted God as your provider, how would the way you currently give change? Write down these changes. Are you willing to implement them now? If yes, do so. If no, what is hindering you?

2 9

LET'S TALK FERTILIZER

For we are God's workmanship, created in Christ Jesus to do good works, which God prepared in advance for us to do.

EPHESIANS 2:10

THE WORST JOB IN THE GARDEN

I made the disclaimer earlier that I am not a gardener, and that is the truth. However, that does not mean that I escape every part of garden work. As a teenager, I was sent on errands to get supplies, and I can tell you the errand I dreaded was picking up fertilizer for my dad. Personally, I can't think of anything to commend fertilizer. It stinks. It smells. It is nasty, and I hate handling it. But I know that it provides protection for seeds, holds in moisture and provides nourishment to growing plants. Knowing the positives of fertilizer doesn't make me like it any better. I'd still like to avoid it if I could.

The challenges in our lives are like fertilizer. They are inevitable, but we see them as noxious, and we want to deal with as few of them as possible. Actually, challenges strengthen us in ways that nothing else can. They reveal and refine our character. Every athlete understands this principle and purposely challenges himself every time he works out, to do just a little better or go just a little further. But in everyday life, we try to dodge and avoid as many challenges as we possibly can.

I remember when our first child, Gabriel, was just starting to walk. It was such an exciting time, watching him try to work his wobbly, chubby little legs. He would teeter precariously, and I had

Ché Ahn

to stop myself from rescuing him unnecessarily. Of course, when he was in danger of really hurting himself, we did break his fall. But we had to allow him to take many falls on his own, for we knew this was the only way he would learn how to walk. If we constantly made it easy on him by picking him up and carrying him around, he would never learn to walk.

In much the same way, our Father God allows circumstances to challenge us, not to frustrate or discourage us, but to produce mastery by strengthening us and refining our character. He desires us to become Christlike givers and regain our original created identity. He wants to help us break free of the strongholds and the distorted thoughts and feelings that hinder us from walking in our identity in Christ. He exhorts us in Philippians 2:12-13, "Continue to work out your salvation with fear and trembling, for it is God who works in you to will and to act according to his good purpose." He knows that growing into the full stature of our created identity in Christ is a process that will involve many challenges over time, but He also promises to give us the grace to do it.

THE CHALLENGE OF MASTERING WEALTH

One of the biggest challenges each of us face in life is how we will handle wealth. Will we master it, or will it master us? Father God understands that money is a form of power, and it exposes the desires and motives of our hearts like almost nothing else can. In fact, prosperity is such a major area of challenge for us that God addresses it frequently in Scripture. There are more than 2,000 verses in the Bible that deal with money, compared to around 500 verses each relating to prayer and faith, and about 700 verses on love. Nearly half of all the parables Jesus told refer to our attitudes and handling of money.

Why is money so powerful in our lives? As we previously discussed, our attitudes and behavior with money reveal what or whom we regard as our source of provision and abundance. If we see ourselves as our source, we are aware of our limitations, and we fear lack. We focus on money to supply the security and provision that only God can give us. We value acquiring wealth and things, seeking to fill the void within. Wealth becomes our treasure, and it dominates our heart (see Matt. 6:21). But we do not need to fear lack and try to grasp all the wealth we can, for Father God promises there will always be an abundant supply for us (see Phil. 4:19).

Our Father God is a lover and a generous giver. In fact, the central dynamic of the Trinity is radical, self-giving love. We were created for intimacy and partnership with Father God, to be part of His dynamic of love. Our Father God is limitless. Everything is His, and He delights to be our Provider. We can never amass on our own what He wants to funnel to us and through us. He only wants us to trust Him and focus on His provision for us, rather than on our own efforts to gain wealth.

God's idea of provision is a continuous supply of everything we need. For instance, in the Garden of Eden, Adam and Eve didn't need to collect and hoard food; it was constantly available for the picking and eating. There was no need to save up for a rainy day. When God led Israel through the wilderness for 40 years, He daily supplied them with manna to eat. There was no need to gather and store extra manna. In fact, when people tried to store it, the manna became rotten and full of maggots (see Exod. 16:20). God definitely wanted His children to trust Him for their supply every day.

This emphasis on daily provision is reflected in the prayer our Lord Jesus taught His disciples when He said, "Give us this day our daily bread" (Matt. 6:11, NKJV). Again the emphasis is on receiving our daily supply from God, who willingly provides. Jesus elaborated on God's provision in the Sermon on the Mount: "Therefore I tell you, do not worry about your life, what you will eat or drink; or about your body, what you will wear. . . . Look at the birds of the air; they do not sow or reap or store away in barns, and yet your heavenly Father feeds them. Are you not much more valuable than they? . . . So do not worry, saying, 'What shall we eat?' or 'What shall we drink?' or 'What shall we wear?' For the pagans run after all these things, and your heavenly Father knows that you need them. But seek first his kingdom and his righteousness, and all these things will be given to you as well" (Matt. 6:25-26, 31-33).

Ché Ahn

Instead of a life dominated by the need to find safety and security in things and wealth, God invites us to be bold, cheerful, Christlike givers, generous and confident in Him as our provider. He longs to share His joy in giving and blessing others through us. He wants our motivation for accumulation to be for distribution to His kingdom and to those in need. If we truly believe that He wants to continually provide for us, and we trust in Him, we will become conduits of His provision to the world around us. By mastering wealth, we come into a place of authority and power over the abundance of God's kingdom, and able to tap into its true riches.

Fertilizer Never Smelled So Good!

We are re-created in God's image in Christ, but we still have the choice of going our own way or seeking His purpose, direction and destiny for our lives. He provides clear commandments on how to proceed, but He never coerces us. Instead, He regards the condition and motivation of our hearts, looking for us to allow Him to make us generous givers. We reveal our choice through our attitudes and behavior with our money.

This is the challenge that is constantly before us. Who do we trust more? Ourselves or our heavenly Father? When we assume the responsibility of providing for our own prosperity, we forfeit true freedom and enter a world of bondage. We become ensnared with money as a source and expect it to provide for us in ways it never can. We have lost the understanding of the true purpose of wealth; and without that vision, we lack the restraints that will provide and protect our true prosperity. We have separated ourselves from the wisdom of our Father God, and like a city without walls, we are open to the lies and delusions of the spirits of Mammon and poverty (see Prov. 25:28; 29:18).

How then do we proceed? We embrace the challenge and realize that the fertilizer never smelled so good! What am I saying? Let me illustrate with a story. A little girl, who lived in the country, wanted a pony. For years, every Christmas and birthday, when she was asked what she wanted, she would eagerly reply, "Just a pony, that's all I want." Her father patiently explained to her each time that there would be no pony, but she still persisted.

One day, she rushed in and embraced her father, shouting, "Oh, thank you, Daddy! Thank you!" Her father was confused as she went on and said, "Thank you so much for the pony!" She pulled her father out the front door where he saw a huge pile of fertilizer sitting in his driveway. Apparently, a neighbor down the road ordered a truckload of fertilizer, and it was delivered to the wrong address. But his little daughter was full of joy. She knew when she saw the poop that there just had to be a pony in there somewhere!

Does the idea of getting excited about fertilizer seem strange to you? James 1:2-4 instructs us, "Consider it pure joy, my brothers, whenever you face trials of many kinds, because you know that the testing of your faith develops perseverance. Perseverance must finish its work so that you may be mature and complete, not lacking anything." Actually, I like the way the *Amplified Version* translates verse 4: "But let endurance and steadfastness and patience have full play and do a thorough work, so that you may be [people] perfectly and fully developed [with no defects], lacking in nothing."

James is telling us that our challenges are not capricious—they serve a purpose in training us to reign in God's kingdom by perfecting the maturity of a Christlike character in us. "God, Who tests our hearts [expects them to be approved]" (1 Thess. 2:4, *AMP*). You see, our Father God knows that the challenge to master wealth will be difficult; but He expects us to master it. He has every confidence that we will rise to the occasion, and the Christlike character of our hearts will be perfected and approved (see Heb. 6:12). There really is a pony in all that poop!

BE A WORLD CHANGER!

God is offering us the most exciting, fulfilling, rewarding life we can possibly imagine. When we choose God's way, we become willing, generous, Christlike givers, open to His leading. We let Him work out His destiny and purpose in us, and we will harvest a crop of real life, abundant life. He promises us in Ephesians 2:10, "For we are God's [own] handiwork (His workmanship), recreated in Christ Jesus, [born anew] that we may do those good works which God predestined (planned beforehand) for us [taking paths which He prepared ahead of time], that we should walk in them [living the good life which He prearranged and made ready for us to live]" (*AMP*).

A few years ago, several hundred elderly people, 95 years and older, were asked, "If you could live your life over, what would you do differently?" The three most common replies were, "I would reflect more," "I would risk more," and "I would do more things that would live after me when I'm gone." A major regret was that their lives did not have more significance and impact on others.

We all want our life to have purpose, and to leave something of value for others. It's no accident that we desire this, because Father God created us to have authority and dominion, to be significant in our world. Not too long ago, I heard this story about Steve Jobs, the late CEO of Apple. Apparently, his superior sales abilities were evident early in life, and as a young man he was offered a lucrative starting position with a well-known soft drink manufacturer. He promptly declined, saying, "That's not enough for me." When asked how much more salary he would require, Jobs replied, "I don't want to spend the rest of my life selling flavored sugar water; I want to change the world."

God has issued an invitation to us to enter His world of prosperity and wealth management, by trusting Him to be our provider and following in His footsteps as generous givers. The choice is ours. Do we want to accumulate "stuff" (flavored sugar water), or do we want to change the world?

PUTTING IT ALL TOGETHER

All of us face the challenge of mastering wealth. We must decide who or what is our source, and what is the purpose of prosperity. God uses this challenge to reveal and mature our character so that we can walk in our true identity in Christ.

Ask Yourself

1. What financial challenge are you currently facing? In what way could it be an opportunity to gain more mastery over wealth?

2. Has this entry provided any clarification for you on Philippians 2:12: "Continue to work out your salvation with fear and trembling"? If so, in what way?

3. What prevents you from relying on Father God as your provider on a daily basis?

Live It!

Make the decision to become a world changer. Ask God to give you specific guidance on how to become a Christlike giver and learn to trust Him as your provider. Expect Him to give you direction. Write down His direction. Accept the challenge and do it!

3 0

THE RIGHT STUFF

*But love your enemies, do good to them, and lend to them without
expecting to get anything back. Then your reward will be great.*

LUKE 6:35

SELECTING ASTRONAUTS

Back in the late 1950s, when the United States made the commitment to enter the space race with Russia, no human being had
gone into space before. The task before NASA was to select the individuals who would be qualified to make those first flights.

President Eisenhower decided that the men should be military
officers with a proven record as test pilots. Additionally, all the
candidates had to be less than 40 years of age and possess a college
degree in engineering. The space capsule constraints required that
they be no taller than 5'11" and weigh less than 180 pounds.

Because little was known about the effects, physically and psy-
chologically, of being in space, potential candidates were put through
a series of extreme mental, physical and environmental tests as
well as an intensive battery of health examinations. They were also
subjected to various stress conditions and examined psychologi-
cally by two psychologists and two psychiatrists.

The result was the first astronauts, known as the Mercury 7,
who became national heroes. Their selection process and their missions in space were immortalized in 1979 by the author Tom Wolfe
in a book titled *The Right Stuff.*[1] They all had "the right stuff" and
performed up to the stringent standards set for them.

THE FULLY COMMITTED HEART

God is looking for His children to have "the right stuff." "For the eyes of the LORD range throughout the earth to strengthen those whose hearts are fully committed to him" (2 Chron. 16:9). What type of heart is a "fully committed" heart? It is a person who is seeking God's purpose, destiny and direction, a person committed to training to reign. These are people who are continually tilling the soil of their hearts and planting the seed of His Word so that they can bring forth an abundant harvest for God.

Father God describes them as being "willing and obedient" (Isa. 1:19) and states that they will inherit the good of the land, that is, they will prosper. How does a person become willing and obedient? "Do not let this Book of the Law depart from your mouth; meditate on it day and night, so that you may be careful to do everything written in it. Then you will be prosperous and successful" (Josh. 1:8).

Too often this passage from Joshua is interpreted only in the light of prosperity. We're told if we meditate on God's Word, we will prosper. But that is really not the focus of what God is saying. He is telling us that if we meditate continually on His Word, we will become willing and obedient to do what He says. This willing obedience is highly prized by God, and will result in prosperity.

At the risk of sounding like a broken record, it all comes down to the condition of our heart. Our heart motive is everything to God. He is not just looking for givers; He is looking for willing and obedient givers. There are those people who may give, and even give generously, but their motive is to get. They are still focused on wealth as their source and provision. God wants us to catch His vision of being a giver.

God rewards the motives of our hearts, not our gifts, no matter how large they may be. He is looking for children who want to conform their hearts and become givers like their Father God because they love Him. They are seeking His face, not a gift from His hand.

God dislikes legalism in any form, for He realizes that it is nothing but manipulation. In ancient Israel, the Lord upbraided the people for not wanting to know His Word. They wanted His blessing but were not interested in knowing His way. They went through the motions of worship, but it was only for the blessing they wanted to get. He told them, "These people come near to me with their mouth and honor me with their lips, but their hearts are far from me. Their worship of me is made up only of rules taught by men" (Isa. 29:13).

Christlike giving is not a formula for getting God to bless us with prosperity. Christlike giving is an opportunity to grow in conformity to our Father God's image, to become willing and joyful givers even as He is.

The Most Misquoted Verse on Giving

We have all had this verse quoted to us many times. It states a universal principle of giving: "Give, and it will be given to you. A good measure, pressed down, shaken together and running over, will be poured into your lap. For with the measure you use, it will be measured to you" (Luke 6:38). Taken out of context, as it frequently is, the verse appears to be a formula for prosperity. It seems to be saying that all we have to do is give and we will prosper, and the bigger the gift, the greater the prosperity.

But if we back up and read the passage, putting the verse in context, we get a different message:

> Give to everyone who asks you, and if anyone takes what belongs to you, do not demand it back. Do to others as you would have them do to you. If you love those who love you, what credit is that to you? Even "sinners" love those who love them. And if you do good to those who are good to you, what credit is that to you? Even "sinners" do that. And if you lend to those from whom you expect repayment, what credit is that to you? Even "sinners" lend to "sinners," expecting to be repaid in full. But love your enemies, do good to them, and lend to them without expecting to get anything back. Then your reward will be

great, and you will be sons of the Most High, because he is kind to the ungrateful and wicked. Be merciful, just as your Father is merciful. Do not judge, and you will not be judged. Do not condemn, and you will not be condemned. Forgive, and you will be forgiven. Give, and it will be given to you. A good measure, pressed down, shaken together and running over, will be poured into your lap. For with the measure you use, it will be measured to you (Luke 6:30-38).

The central message of this passage is that we are to be givers. God is inviting us into His kingdom, which operates in a totally different way from the world as we know it. In many ways, His kingdom is upside down from our world. He encourages us to give when others can't pay us back, to give love when people don't deserve it, and to give mercy to people who wrong us. We are to treat others as we would like them to treat us, before they do, and whether or not they ever reciprocate.

This is reckless giving that goes contrary to all the wisdom of the world. The world would tell us to pay back in kind, "an eye for an eye." The world would tell us the way to prosper is to grasp everything and hoard it, for if we give it away, we will have lost it. It's the philosophy "get all you can, can all you get and sit on the can." But God encourages us to give liberally, and He says that when we do, we are imitating Him.

In *The Blessed Life*, Robert Morris summarizes it this way: "In other words, God is saying, 'When you give just to give, I'm going to reward you by giving back to you in much greater measure.' The reward comes because we have allowed God to do a work in our hearts in the area of giving—not in the area of getting. It's our hearts the Lord is concerned about. And a properly focused heart is more excited about the giving part than the receiving part."[2]

Jesus also makes it clear that when we give this way, it will be given back to us. In other words, if we give without expecting anything in return, our reward will be great, for we will be acting like our Father God.

THE GRACE OF GIVING

Our willing obedience has transformational power. As we make the heart choice to become givers like our Father God, His grace is released in us through the indwelling power of His Holy Spirit. He does not expect us to become givers through our own effort, but only to make the choice to surrender in love to Him. In Philippians 2:13, Paul assures us, "It is God who works in you to will and to act according to his good purpose." This is an extraordinary verse, for it says He will not only perform the action in us, but if we allow Him, He will also give us the motivation to become givers.

God never asks us to do something that He does not give us the grace to perform. As we surrender and give ourselves to Him, He increasingly fills us with Himself, His abundance and His blessing. His love continues to grow within us and we become conduits of that love. We mature in Christlike character as givers and become increasingly like our Father God. Through our giving, we reveal His kingdom to the world (see 1 John 4:15-17). The grace of God has tremendous power to transform not only us but also the world around us as we allow Him to release His grace through us.

As the grace of giving is released within us, we reap the following benefits:

- We know God as our provider. We are assured of His provision and we're aware that everything comes from Him. We are only giving back what comes from His hand (see 1 Chron. 29:14).

- We overcome financial fear and worry. We are seeking God and His Kingdom first, and we experience His daily provision of all our needs (see Matt. 6:31-33).

- Giving brings order to our financial management. Our priorities are different. We're no longer consumed with accumulating things. We've been set free to be world changers (see Prov. 3:9-10)!

- We are able to cast down the strongholds of Mammon and resist the Spirit of poverty (see Luke 12:15; 1 Tim. 6:7-10).

- Our giving releases the transformational grace of God into the world around us. Our giving primes the pump. It not only releases the grace of giving within us, but it also releases the grace of giving in others (see Matt. 5:16; 1 Pet. 2:12).

We have very little appreciation for the transformational power of God's grace. Bill Johnson, the senior pastor of Bethel Church in Redding, California, and one of my covenant friends, shared an amazing testimony about the grace of giving. One of his church members was at a drive-through Starbucks coffee shop. He noticed that there were some church members behind his car, so when he drove up, he asked how much was the order for the car behind him. The Starbucks attendant told him the amount. He picked up that tab and moved on. When the next driver came up and found that his friend had picked up his coffee tab, he decided to do the same for the car behind him. This went on and on for the next four hours! Uninterrupted giving for four straight hours, and most of the people in that line were not church members. God's grace of giving, operating in one person, transformed the behavior of a whole group of people for four hours.

God always provides direction and guidance when we choose to follow His way. In the next section, we will look at His specific instructions to us that help us grow in the grace of giving.

Putting It All Together

God is looking for people with hearts fully committed to be willing and obedient givers. These people don't give to get a blessing; they give to become conformed to Father God's image, because they desire to be a liberal and joyful giver like Him. They are secure in His provision, and they surrender to His love, allowing His grace to transform their hearts and lives.

Ask Yourself

1. Reread Luke 6:38. Do you see this verse differently now? If so, explain how your understanding has changed.

2. Look at the list of benefits released through the grace of giving. Which one would you most like to be reaping in your life right now? Why?

3. When you imagine surrendering to God's love and becoming a liberal giver, what emotion do you feel? Joy? Excitement? Fear? Resentment? Overwhelmed? Some other feeling? What causes you to feel this way?

Live It!

What does your behavior with money indicate about your heart? Do you feel free to give liberally in willing obedience to God? Honestly evaluate your heart motives in relation to your giving.

Notes

1. Tom Wolfe, *The Right Stuff* (New York: Farrar, Straus and Giroux, 1979).
2. Robert Morris, *The Blessed Life* (Ventura, CA: Regal Books, 2002), p. 102.

BECOMING
A CHRISTLIKE
GIVER

God desires that we become Christlike in every way. He gives us His grace, but we must trust Him and open our hearts in order for grace to release its transformational power within us. God observes our hearts, for He knows that all the true issues of life proceed from the heart.

He entrusts the resources of His kingdom to us. They are ours to responsibly manage or waste. Our management of Kingdom resources is another opportunity we are given to train for reigning. God wants us to be Christlike givers. Through the grace of giving, He wants us to progressively learn what we possess in His kingdom, the purpose for which we possess it and how to use it.

God's grace is a free gift to us. It is unearned favor and the fountain from which our good works flow. As we surrender to God's grace, it becomes both the power and the motivation to live a Christlike life. Grace is an inward transformational process, while the Law was an external set of commands regarding behavior.

Therefore, grace calls us to a higher standard of life and action than the Law ever could. As Christlike givers, we are not bound and limited to a mandated tithe. We are free to give when, to whom, and how God directs. We are ready and willing to give in any season, regardless of any circumstances, and our giving flows in harmony with the laws of sowing and reaping. Christlike giving is generous, blessing others and advancing God's kingdom.

In this section, I share my responses to the most common questions on giving that I am asked as a pastor. The section concludes with an aspect of giving that is central to God's heart: our involvement in the care and provision for the poor.

3 1

JUST WHO IS LORD?

Now it is required that those who have been
given a trust must prove faithful.

1 CORINTHIANS 4:2

ESTABLISHING OWNERSHIP

Several years ago, I heard evangelist and pastor Greg Laurie tell the following story: There was an older lady who was determined to be prepared if she ever felt physically threatened. So she signed up for a training course on using handguns, and completed it. One day after shopping, she returned to her car and found four men inside it. She immediately dropped her shopping bags, drew out her handgun and screamed, "I have a gun, and I know how to use it! Get out of the car!" The four men quickly got out and ran away.

Somewhat shaken, the lady loaded her bags and got into the car. But she wasn't able to get her key into the ignition. It slowly dawned on her that her similar car was parked several spaces away. So she did what she had to do. She loaded her bags into her own car and drove to the police station to turn herself in.

The desk sergeant nearly fell off his chair laughing. He pointed to the other end of the counter, where four men were reporting a carjacking by an old woman with thick glasses and curly white hair, carrying a large handgun. No charges were filed.

Like the old lady in this story, we all have a tendency to want to keep and defend what we think is ours. When it comes to money, I have seen financial squabbles break up marriages, destroy

family ties and result in lawsuits, all because people were protect-
ing what they thought was rightfully "theirs."

If the old lady had realized that the first car was not hers, she
would never have gone to such extreme measures to recover it from
the four men. She could have spared herself the emotional upset,
calmly walked past that car to her own car and gone home. I think
we would all be better off if we would realize that everything we
think we possess actually belongs to the original and rightful
owner, Father God.

Now you may be thinking, *Wait a minute. I work hard for my income, and I earn every penny of it! What do you mean God owns it?* That's
a fair enough question, so let me establish God's ownership rights.

To begin with, God is the Creator. "In the beginning God created the heavens and the earth" (Gen. 1:1). God originally made
everything. There is not anything we have that didn't come from
something that God originally made. Psalm 24:1-2 spells it out
clearly: "The earth is the LORD's, and everything in it, the world,
and all who live in it; for he founded it upon the seas and established it upon the waters." First Chronicles 29 echoes the words
of the psalmist as it discusses the fact that everything in heaven
and earth is the Lord's, and wealth and honor come from Him, because He is the ruler of all things. In the New Testament, we read,
"All things were created by him and for him" (Col. 1:16).

Second, it is clear that we have limited control over what we
think we possess. I'm sure you've heard the story of the two men
who were discussing the death of a Texas millionaire. One man
asked the other, "Well, just how much wealth did ol' Tex leave?"
The other man replied, "He left it all." Ol' Tex didn't really "own"
anything, because he didn't take a thing with him. None of us will.

Solomon wisely stated, "Naked a man comes from his
mother's womb, and as he comes, so he departs. He takes nothing
from his labor that he can carry in his hand" (Eccles. 5:15). The
apostle Paul noted the same thing in exhorting his young disciple, Timothy, on the proper use and handling of money: "For we
brought nothing into the world, and we can take nothing out of
it" (1 Tim. 6:7).

Managing God's Wealth

Right about now you may be wondering, *If I don't own anything, where does that leave me?* It actually leaves you in a very good place. Instead of being owner of a few material possessions, as a child of God, you manage your Father God's wealth.

An excellent Old Testament example of wealth management is the story of Joseph. Even though he was a slave in an Egyptian household, his master, Potiphar, entrusted everything he owned into Joseph's care. "[Potiphar] left in Joseph's care everything he had; with Joseph in charge, he did not concern himself with anything except the food he ate" (Gen. 39:6). In managing Potiphar's wealth, Joseph was able to eat the finest foods and wear the best clothes. Joseph handled and controlled the wealth and resources of the entire estate, even though they ultimately belonged to his master and lord, Potiphar.

Joseph is not the first example of wealth management. From the beginning, it is clear that God intended that we would have the responsibility of managing all of creation. In the Garden of Eden, He established Adam and Eve as having dominion and authority over everything else in creation. They were managers, not owners, as God clearly demonstrated when He placed the tree of the knowledge of good and evil off limits. When Adam and Eve violated the limitation and ate the fruit of the tree, they were acting like owners. At that point, they were evicted from the garden, because God was the rightful owner. He was their Lord.

When we understand our responsibility as managers, and what is being entrusted to us, we will realize that God is actually preparing us to manage the incredible wealth of His kingdom. This is much more wealth than we could ever amass through our own effort. Father God assures us that He will supply wealth for us to manage. "You may say to yourself, 'My power and the strength of my hands have produced this wealth for me.' But remember the LORD your God, for it is he who gives you the ability to produce wealth, and so confirms his covenant" (Deut. 8:17-18).

Think of it this way: Under the new covenant, we are God's children. We are joint heirs with the Son, Jesus Christ, and the kingdom of God is our inheritance. We have been given the responsibility of managing the wealth of the family business—the kingdom of God—here on earth. Our Father God has given us His power of attorney to act on His behalf in all our management activities. We can responsibly manage the resources entrusted to us, or we can squander them.

Wealth Management
Is Training for Reigning

The responsibility of management affects every area of our lives—our time, our interests, our abilities and talents, as well as our finances. It reveals our spiritual maturity, for the people who recognize that they are to responsibly manage have already established their agreement with God and aligned themselves with His purpose and destiny for their lives. They realize just who is Lord. And when it comes to our management of finances, God watches us carefully, for He knows that our actions reveal the motives of our hearts.

Jesus referred to motive when He said, "So when you give to the needy, do not announce it with trumpets, as the hypocrites do in the synagogues and on the streets, to be honored by men. I tell you the truth, they have received their reward in full. But when you give to the needy, do not let your left hand know what your right hand is doing, so that your giving may be in secret. Then your Father, who sees what is done in secret, will reward you" (Matt. 6:2-4).

In this statement, Jesus made it clear that Father God is looking for those who have a giving heart of generosity, like His. As our hearts become more Christlike, we can give generously, immediately obeying what we hear Father God tell us. We become fearless, cheerful givers, knowing that more will come because we are children of Father God. We are releasing resources under our management into our Father's kingdom, "the family business." Do we feel loss? Of course not, because investing in the family business strengthens the position of everyone in the family. We can give our resources easily and thankfully. This is the heart motive and attitude God wants us to have with our finances.

Understanding our position as managers of Kingdom resources produces selflessness in us. We align our hearts with Father God's heart and understand giving His way. We see that every financial decision is a spiritual decision. And because we have the assurance of God's provision, we are free from the fear of lack and the burden of providing for ourselves. Our hope is in our Father God, and not in money.

Paul summarizes this understanding in the first letter to his disciple Timothy: "Command those who are rich in this present world not to be arrogant nor to put their hope in wealth, which is so uncertain, but to put their hope in God, who richly provides us with everything for our enjoyment. Command them to do good, to be rich in good deeds, and to be generous and willing to share. In this way they will lay up treasure for themselves as a firm foundation for the coming age, so that they may take hold of the life that is truly life" (1 Tim. 6:17-19).

As we learn to responsibly manage Kingdom wealth, we develop the qualities to reign in life as God intended us to do. In responsible management, we establish a divine order in our relationships, first between us and God, and then between us and all else. This alignment produces authority in us as we recognize our right relationship to Father God as His beloved children. Through the grace of giving, we progressively learn what we possess in His kingdom, the purpose for which we possess it and how to use it.

Stephen De Silva describes this process in his book *Money and the Prosperous Soul*: "Facing God, the source of abundance, drives away the fear, insecurity and powerlessness you previously felt as you watched good things pass you by. From this new view, you expect good things. You expect that every need will be met at the right time. You expect that nothing will be impossible. You know that everything in your Father's Kingdom is yours."[1]

Martin Luther wisely said, "I have held many things in my hands and I have lost them all. But whatever I have placed in God's hands, that I still possess." When Father God knows that He can get prosperity through us, He will send it to us. And He will see that we are well taken care of, for He is a generous, gracious, kindhearted and compassionate Father. He can take care of us much better than we could ever take care of ourselves.

Father God has established some guidelines and directions to help us grow in the grace of giving. We will look at those in the next entry.

PUTTING IT ALL TOGETHER

We must realize that Father God is Lord and owner of everything. We are His children and heirs of His kingdom. God wants to give us the great responsibility of managing His wealth to bless others and advance His kingdom. Our responsible management of His kingdom resources is another opportunity to train for reigning.

ASK YOURSELF

1. If God is the rightful owner of everything, and you are His child, what is yours?

2. Does knowing that you have been entrusted with managing resources in the kingdom of God make you feel more or less secure financially? If so, for what reasons?

3. What qualities for reigning in life does responsible wealth management produce in us? Which quality do you currently need most in your life?

LIVE IT!

How does the knowledge that you are a manager of Kingdom resources change the way you think about money and managing your finances?

Note

1. Stephen K. De Silva, *Money and the Prosperous Soul* (Grand Rapids, MI: Chosen Books, 2010), p. 158.

32

THE GRACE OF
CHRISTLIKE GIVING

God is able to make all grace abound to you, so that in all things at all
times, having all that you need, you will abound in every good work.

2 CORINTHIANS 9:8

THE TRUE FREE GIFT

We are confronted with it virtually every day. It comes in various
forms: "buy one get one free," "free trial offer," "sign up now and get
your free gift." It always sounds so good, so tempting, but we are
naturally suspicious, because we've been told since we were children, "You don't get something for nothing," and "If it sounds too
good to be true, it is." So we ask ourselves, "What's the catch?" We
look for the fine print, and almost always we find that appearances
are not what they seem, and that free gift is not so "free" after all.

So it's little wonder that when God offers us a "free gift," we
have difficulty receiving it. But His free gift is the only true free
gift out there, universally offered to all and spontaneously given.
It is the gift of His grace; and while we all know it is freely given
to us, many of us do not realize what the gift is. We are familiar
with Ephesians 2:8-9: "For by grace you have been saved through
faith, and that not of yourselves; it is the gift of God, not of
works, lest anyone should boast" (*NKJV*). But what really is this
"gift of grace"?

Most of us have heard grace translated as "unmerited favor,"
or "unmerited blessings." The Greek word for grace is *charis*. The

basic meaning is "non-meritorious or unearned favor, bestowed as a gift, freely, and never as a reward for work performed." The Hebrew word most commonly translated grace is *hesed*, which means lovingkindness or steadfast love. Actually the word contains the compound idea of strength, steadfastness and love combined. Grace describes a central characteristic of God, and it is best depicted in His covenantal love for Israel. God demonstrates His grace by doing, showing, and keeping His promises of love forever (see Deut. 5:10; 7:9; Exod. 20:6; Ps. 136).

God's grace affects every area of our lives. It is God's work on our behalf and encompasses everything we receive from Him. God's grace excludes any idea of our works for merit, our works done as a way to obtain divine blessing, or as a payment for what has been given to us. The apostle Paul makes this clear: "What does the Scripture say? 'Abraham believed God, and it was credited to him as righteousness.' Now when a man works, his wages are not credited to him as a gift, but as an obligation. However, to the man who does not work but trusts God who justifies the wicked, his faith is credited as righteousness" (Rom. 4:3-5).

God's grace is more than just the free gift of salvation. His grace is the fountain from which good works are to be produced in our lives as we appropriate it by faith. Grace gives us both the power and the motivation to live a Christlike life. "For it is God who works in you to will and to act according to His good purpose" (Phil. 2:13).

Walking in God's grace is the New Testament way of life. We still follow the imperatives that God has established for us to live by, not as a means to gain merit but because we have received His grace that gives us the ability to do so. "For the law of the Spirit of life in Christ Jesus has set you free from the law of sin and death. For what the Law could not do, weak as it was through the flesh, God did: sending His own Son in the likeness of sinful flesh and as an offering for sin, He condemned sin in the flesh, so that the requirement of the Law might be fulfilled in us, who do not walk according to the flesh but according to the Spirit" (Rom. 8:2-4, *NASB*).

GRACE: A HIGHER CALLING

Before Christ died and was resurrected from the dead, human beings did not have the indwelling power of the Holy Spirit. In Old
Testament times, the Holy Spirit "came upon" certain kings and
prophets but was not dwelling within them. In giving the Mosaic
Law, God focused on the external behaviors that were required,
but His desire was always that His law would be written on our
hearts (see Jer. 31:31-35; Heb. 8:10; 10:16). This is why Jesus rein-
terpreted the Law to His followers. He told them:

> You have heard that it was said to the people long ago, "Do
> not murder, and anyone who murders will be subject to
> judgment." But I tell you that anyone who is angry with
> his brother will be subject to judgment.... You have heard
> that it was said, "Do not commit adultery." But I tell you
> that anyone who looks at a woman lustfully has already
> committed adultery with her in his heart.... I tell you that
> unless your righteousness surpasses that of the Pharisees
> and the teachers of the law, you will certainly not enter the
> kingdom of heaven (Matt. 5:21-22,27-28,20).

Jesus was telling His disciples that righteousness is not simply
a matter of external behaviors; it is first and foremost an attitude
of our hearts. Proverbs 23:7 echoes this: "As [a person] thinks in his
heart, so is he" (*NKJV*). The Pharisees were rigid observers of the external requirements of the Law, but their hearts fell far short of the
true intent of God's righteousness. Jesus lets us know just how deep
righteousness really goes. If it does not penetrate to the core of our
hearts, it is not the righteousness that God requires.

So our new covenant of grace calls us to a higher standard of
righteousness than did the Mosaic Law. Obviously, none of us on
our own can measure up to this higher standard, but we are not expected to do so. Scripture makes it very clear that Jesus Christ has
become our righteousness (see 1 Cor. 1:30). We also have the grace
of the Holy Spirit who lives within us and gives us a heart of flesh
that seeks to have a Christlike character, replacing our old heart of

stone (see Ezek. 11:19; 36:26; Gal. 3:13-14). Under grace, we are called to a higher standard of living, not to obtain righteousness, but because we are already righteous in Jesus Christ.

Under the Mosaic Law, the people were commanded to give the tithe, a tenth of all their increase to the Lord every year. Other types of giving such as the festival tithe, the charity tithe, the thanksgiving and wave offerings were also specified in the Law. These were external observances explicitly stated, and God promised to bless the people when they complied. There are many sincere Christians today who faithfully give the tithe because they believe it is mandated in Scripture, and that mandate is still valid today. I know, for I used to be one of them.

I was taught to tithe from the time I first became a Christian as a teenager, and it never occurred to me to question the teaching. My wife and I have always given more than the tithe every year since we've been married. However, more recently I find that my position is changing, due to what I believe is a deeper understanding of God's grace and its operation in our lives.

As I currently understand the Scripture, while Jesus was born at a time when the Mosaic Law was still in effect, He made it clear that He had come to effect a transition to a new way of life. He told the Pharisees, "From the days of John the Baptist until now, the kingdom of heaven has been forcefully advancing, and forceful men lay hold of it. For all the Prophets and the Law prophesied until John. And if you are willing to accept it, he is the Elijah who was to come. He who has ears, let him hear" (Matt. 11:12-15).

The prophet Malachi, more than 400 years before the birth of Christ, wrote that the Messiah would come and would be preceded by one with the mantle, the anointing of the prophet Elijah. I believe that what Jesus was saying was revolutionary. First, by claiming that John the Baptist had the same anointing as Elijah, He was claiming that He was the Messiah. He also was telling them that the Law and Prophets were in force until John, but that John's ministry was the forerunner that ushered in a new era, the kingdom of heaven.

Jesus often talked about the kingdom of heaven and described it in many parables. He knew that He was asking His followers to make a major paradigm shift. He gave the following analogy to help them understand: "No one pours new wine into old wineskins. If he does, the wine will burst the skins, and both the wine and wineskins will be ruined. No, he pours new wine into new wineskins" (Mark 2:22; see also Matt. 9:17; Luke 5:35-39). Jesus was telling them that the new life He was bringing would require a new paradigm in their thinking. They were no longer going to be held to external observances of the Law, for Father God would write His laws on their hearts. God would also give them His Holy Spirit to teach and empower them to live to a higher standard than the Law could ever produce.

THE NEW WINESKIN OF CHRISTLIKE GIVING

If the grace of God calls us to a higher standard than the Mosaic Law, what type of giving do you think God desires from us? Instead of adherence to a fixed proportion of our income, like the tithe, I believe that Jesus calls us to a life of Christlike giving in order to develop a heart of generosity in us like our Father God. The tithe required obedience to an external standard. Christlike giving is a partnership of generosity with Father God at the inner prompting of the Holy Spirit. It flows out of an intimate relationship with our heavenly Father. I have met many Christians who don't believe in tithing, and they also avoid the discipline of Christlike giving. They seldom give generously. But I have never met a person, when he or she began giving regularly at God's direction, who did not discover the joy of becoming a generous giver.

Why is the way we give so important to Father God? We were created to find our fulfillment in intimate relationship with Him. He wants us to put Him first in our lives, trust His promises to us and look to Him as our provider. We must see that He is King and we are His children, managing His resources. In this alignment, we regain our authority and dominion and can advance His kingdom here on earth. This is the Lord's work, not ours, but we must surrender to Him and choose His will and plan for our destiny. Only then can the transformational power of His grace be released in us through the indwelling power of His Holy Spirit.

Christlike giving is the obedient giving of our time, our abilities and our material possessions, based on the conviction that these are a trust from Father God, to be used in His service for the benefit of His kingdom. It is a mindset and a way of living in which we acknowledge Father God as Senior Partner and owner of everything. We are His children, His trustees, and the managers of the family business, His kingdom here on earth.

God's grace calls us to a life of sanctification in response to the new covenant. Our Father God has entrusted to us everything we have in life, and we use these God-given resources to accomplish God-given tasks. Our checkbook reveals what we really practice in giving as it reflects our goals, priorities, convictions, relationships and use of time. Our actions reveal to us the depths of our heart, and the extent to which the grace of a Christlike character is being formed in us.

Christlike giving is not about money; it is about our hearts and our relationship with Father God. He wants us to willingly enter into giving whenever and however He directs, because our hearts are becoming generous and full of grace like His. From ancient times, God's desire was to see grace displayed in His people, rather than external observances like sacrifices (see Hos. 6:6; Mic. 6:8). As we prove ourselves trustworthy in managing little (the material possessions entrusted to us), He knows that He can trust us with the true riches of His kingdom (see Matt. 6:19-21; Luke 16:9-13). Christlike giving becomes a demonstration of our spiritual maturity and our readiness to be released into Kingdom authority and dominion.

We are called to partner with Him in the greatest work of all time, the establishing of His kingdom here on earth. Christlike giving is one of Father God's disciplines in training us to reign. I think that if we truly understood the purpose of Christlike giving, we would embrace it eagerly and with joy.

A FINAL WORD ABOUT THE TITHE

I know there are Christians who believe in and practice tithing as a sincere heart conviction, and I have the utmost respect for them.

However, I believe that under grace, the call to Christlike giving has replaced the observance of the tithe.

Today a prosperity gospel has taken hold in the church that is focused on getting wealth instead of having a transformed heart. This thinking approaches Scripture as if it were a formula or ritual whereby, when we perform "tithing," God must bless us materially, like a divine vending machine.

The Scripture most commonly used to support this view is Malachi 3:8-10: "Will a man rob God? Yet you rob me. But you ask, 'How do we rob you?' In tithes and offerings. You are under a curse—the whole nation of you—because you are robbing me. Bring the whole tithe into the storehouse, that there may be food in my house. Test me in this . . . and see if I will not throw open the floodgates of heaven and pour out so much blessing that you will not have room enough for it."

Unfortunately, this teaching on the tithe from Malachi 3 frequently intimidates people, inducing guilt by telling them that if they don't tithe, they are robbing God and are under a curse. The passage is also frequently quoted out of context. As we discussed at the beginning of this book, when we take a text out of context, we are opening ourselves to a "con."

In the book of Malachi, God addressed Israel with a number of ways they had turned from Him and rejected His truth and direction. He told them, "Ever since the time of your forefathers you have turned away from my decrees and have not kept them. Return to Me, and I will return to you, says the LORD Almighty" (Mal. 3:7).

God wants to restore relationship with His people. Why does He say they are robbing Him? It's not about the material tithe, but what the tithe represents: an evidence of their putting Him first and trusting Him for everything they need. God is longing for the restoration of that relationship with them.

Why are they under a curse? It is not because God is cursing them for not tithing. By failing to tithe, none of their substance is sacred and consecrated to God. Consequently, nothing is blessed. They are living outside the covering of God's blessing and therefore are open to the effects of the curse. God is simply pointing out this fact.

God so desires that His people return to a right relationship with Him that He challenges them to test Him. He is telling them, "Put Me first, trust Me and be obedient again. Bring your whole tithe to Me to be consecrated, and see if I don't bless you abundantly." God established the laws of sowing and reaping at creation. He knew if Israel would obediently tithe as He had instructed them to do, they would abundantly reap. It was inevitable. His Word is unchangeable truth and always accomplishes His purposes.

God is promising to flood them with blessings for returning to Him. Sound familiar? This is the heart of the prodigal Father, overflowing with love as He pleads to His wayward children to return home.

PUTTING IT ALL TOGETHER

The new covenant of grace calls us to a higher standard of living than the old covenant of the law. We now have the indwelling power of the Holy Spirit who writes God's laws on our hearts and creates a Christlike character within us. We are no longer limited or mandated to tithe, but we are called to become Christlike givers who are always ready to give what and when Father God directs. As we faithfully manage the resources entrusted to us, Father God knows He can trust us with the true riches of His kingdom.

ASK YOURSELF

1. Do you think that as a Christlike giver you may be called to give a greater amount than the tithe? Why or why not?

2. Have you ever felt defeated when you were faced by a challenge that was too big? If you really believed Philippians 2:13, how would it change this type of situation?

3. How does becoming a Christlike giver lead you to greater intimacy with Father God?

Live It!

What do you think are the possible benefits of becoming a Christlike giver? What do you think are the challenges of becoming a Christlike giver? How can you overcome these challenges?

THE GIVING HEART

*They gave as much as they were able, and even
beyond their ability. . . . And they did not do as we expected,
but they gave themselves first to the Lord.*

2 CORINTHIANS 8:3,5

A PORTRAIT OF CHRISTLIKE GIVING

Jesus told a parable, recorded in Matthew 25, to illustrate how God
views our giving under the new covenant: An owner was going on
a long journey, and he divided the management of his property
between three of his servants. He gave one servant five talents of
money, one servant two talents and the third servant one talent,
each according to his management ability. Then the master left
on his journey. The servant who was given five talents put the
money to work and gained five more. The servant with two talents
gained two more; but the servant who had received only one talent
went and dug a hole in the ground and buried it.

When the owner returned, he called the three servants in to
account for their management of his property. He was very pleased
with the two servants who had put his money to work and earned
more. When the servant who had received one talent came, he said,
"Master . . . I knew that you are a hard man, harvesting where you
have not sown and gathering where you have not scattered seed. So
I was afraid and went out and hid your talent in the ground. See,
here is what belongs to you" (Matt. 25:24-25).

The owner was not pleased. In fact, he was angered and told the
servant that if he truly believed that he, the owner, was a stingy, hard

man, he should have put the money on deposit in the bank so that it would have at least gathered interest. Then the owner took the talent from that servant and gave it to the servant who had 10 talents. Jesus concluded this parable by saying, "For everyone who has will be given more, and he will have an abundance. Whoever does not have, even what he has will be taken from him" (Matt. 25:29).

What was Jesus trying to teach His disciples with the story? This is one of several stories that Jesus told His disciple about the kingdom of heaven. I think Jesus was trying to tell His disciples some important principles about giving in His kingdom. Jesus makes it clear that we are entrusted with the management of Kingdom resources.

Two of the servants managed their resources well, investing and producing increase in the Kingdom. The owner was very pleased with what they had done. But the third servant took his resources and kept them. He didn't manage them well, but simply held on to them. He represents people who are more interested in their own safety and security, hoarding up resources for themselves, rather than using them to bless others and advance God's kingdom.

What the third servant said reveals the type of relationship he had with the owner. He was fearful and felt intimidated by the owner. So rather than risk any type of loss, he hid the money and returned it to the owner. He did nothing with the resources entrusted to him. This is not the picture of someone in an intimate relationship with Father God, someone who knows how loving and generous Father God is. This is a person who does not trust Father God as a provider, and therefore cannot release resources but must play it safe and hang on to them. This is the person whose focus is on material prosperity as his security.

The owner was displeased with the third servant's lack of trust and mismanagement of resources. He stripped that servant of what little he had and gave it to the first servant who managed resources well. Jesus is explaining that those of us who use well what we've been given will be entrusted with even more to manage, and will have abundance. Those of us who mismanage what we've been given will have even the little we've been given taken from us.

Through Christlike giving, we become partners with God in His kingdom. Father God invests something in each one of us. We need to be careful not to waste what we are given, but to manage it at His direction for the work of His kingdom. This is an incredible responsibility, but Jesus wants us to understand that Father God has confidence in us, and through His Holy Spirit, He provides us the grace to be givers after His heart.

The Lord richly blesses us when we use our resources wisely. We read in Proverbs 10:22, "The blessing of the LORD brings wealth, and he adds no trouble to it." God wants us to trust that He will liberally supply all of our needs. The apostle Paul warns us not to put our hope in worldly wealth, which is uncertain, but to "put [our] hope in God, who richly provides us with everything for our enjoyment" (1 Tim. 6:17). Christlike giving is not just about managing Kingdom resources; it's also about enjoying every good thing our Father God provides for us.

WHAT DOES CHRISTLIKE GIVING LOOK LIKE?

There is no formula for Christlike giving. It is our loving and willing response to Father God's direction and the prompting of the Holy Spirit. Let's look at a few examples from Scripture.

THE WORLD'S BIGGEST PICNIC

The first example is a familiar story found in John 6:5-13:

> When Jesus looked up and saw a great crowd coming toward him, he said to Philip, "Where shall we buy bread for these people to eat?" He asked this only to test him, for he already had in mind what he was going to do. Philip answered Him, "Eight months' wages would not buy enough bread for each one to have a bite!" Another of his disciples, Andrew, Simon Peter's brother, spoke up, "Here is a boy with five small barley loaves and two small fish, but how far will they go among so many?" Jesus said, "Have the people sit down." There was plenty of grass in that

place, and the men sat down, about five thousand of them. Jesus then took the loaves, gave thanks, and distributed to those who were seated as much as they wanted. He did the same with the fish. When they had all had enough to eat, he said to his disciples, "Gather the pieces that are left over. Let nothing be wasted." So they gathered them and filled twelve baskets with the pieces of the five barley loaves left over by those who had eaten.

We are not told the details of how the small boy and his lunch were identified. Perhaps one of the disciples saw him, or perhaps the boy overheard the conversation and offered his lunch. One thing we know for sure is that neither Jesus nor His disciples would have put any pressure on the child to give his lunch. He did that willingly, and the result was multiplication. When we sow with a willing heart, we will reap abundantly. It is a universal law of God, as well as His promise (see Luke 6:38). We are not told what was done with the 12 baskets that were left over. I think that some or even all of them were given to that little boy to take home.

The Church Birthed in Giving

A second example is that of the Early Church in Jerusalem. After the day of Pentecost, the Church grew rapidly, and those early Christians were deeply devoted to each other. We are told in Acts 2:43-47, "Everyone was filled with awe, and many wonders and miraculous signs were done by the apostles. All the believers were together and had everything in common. Selling their possessions and goods, they gave to anyone as he had need. Every day they continued to meet together in the temple courts. They broke bread in their homes and ate together with glad and sincere hearts, praising God and enjoying the favor of all the people. And the Lord added to their number daily those who were being saved."

There is no indication that an offering was collected, or even that people were told to give. There was such a deep fellowship in the Holy Spirit that this group of people gave extravagantly to their newfound faith. It sounds like they were quite joyful. They are described as fellowshipping daily with each other with glad hearts, praising God. That doesn't sound like a group of miserable, begrudging givers. Only surrender to God's grace and obedience to the prompting of the Holy Spirit could produce hearts full of this type of giving.

THE CHURCH OF THE EAGER GIVERS

A third account occurs in the apostle Paul's second letter to the Corinthian church. Paul had just completed two years in Ephesus, and he was writing this letter from Macedonia. Although times were difficult for them, Paul commended the Macedonians for their giving to the famine-stricken church in Jerusalem: "And now, brothers, we want you to know about the grace that God has given the Macedonian churches. Out of the most severe trial, their overflowing joy and their extreme poverty welled up in rich generosity. For I testify that they gave as much as they were able, and even beyond their ability. Entirely on their own, they urgently pleaded with us for the privilege of sharing in this service to the saints. And they did not do so as we expected, but they gave themselves first to the Lord and then to us in keeping with God's will" (2 Cor. 8:1-5).

Several things are noteworthy in this account. The Macedonian church was probably not much better off than the Jerusalem church at the time. Even though they were extremely poor, they gave so generously that the apostle Paul was astounded. He describes their generosity as a result of the grace of God that was given to them. And he makes it clear that they were under no pressure to give, for he states that "entirely on their own, they urgently pleaded with us for the privilege of sharing in this service to the saints."

Have you ever been in a church service where people urgently pleaded for the privilege of giving? What would make this poor group of people want to give so sacrificially, and with such enthusiasm? I think Paul supplies the answer when he says, "They gave themselves first to the Lord and then to us in keeping with God's will." These Macedonians sought God's will and direction first and foremost, and promptly obeyed without any regard to their own situation. They were not playing it safe. They joyfully surrendered everything they had to the Lord, and willingly obeyed what He told them to do.

These three examples provide a good description of Christlike givers. They give willingly, obediently and promptly at the guidance of the Holy Spirit. At times they may give sacrificially, even ignoring their own economic situation in their eagerness to respond with the same generosity of heart as their Father God. It is the grace of God operating in and through them that motivates them to give in this way. Giving brings them joy, for they know they are sharing in establishing God's kingdom. They can give without reservation, regardless of the economic conditions around them, because they trust Father God as their provider.

GOD REWARDS CHRISTLIKE GIVING

We have already seen in the parable of the three servants that God blesses with abundance those who manage their resources well. God is interested in building His kingdom. He prospers generous givers, those who give when and as He directs. God will not prosper someone who is irresponsible and doesn't know where his money is going, or refuses to follow the Lord's direction.

All the laws of sowing and reaping that we discussed previously apply to Christlike givers, who give bountifully and reap bountifully. Christlike givers always retain seed. They don't consume all their resources, so they always have something to give. They give willingly and they wait patiently for the return they know will come. They know that by giving as God prompts, they become partners with Him in building His kingdom, and He will continue to prosper them more and more. They sow as He directs, and they are confident that the harvest is in His hands.

Most important, as the transformational power of God's grace works in their hearts, they live in the deep satisfaction of knowing that they are imitating the Father God they love and honor. God makes His will to Christlike givers abundantly clear in 2 Corinthians 9:8: "God is able to make all grace abound toward you, that you, always having all sufficiency in all things, may have an abundance for every good work" (*NKJV*). They are continually blessed to be a blessing to others.

PUTTING IT ALL TOGETHER

Under the new covenant of grace, Father God is looking for Christlike givers who will invest their resources to produce increase in His kingdom. Three examples of Christlike giving are: the feeding of the 5,000 by Jesus; the sacrificial giving of the Early Church in the book of Acts; and the urgent pleading for the opportunity to give by the Macedonian church, cited by Paul in the book of Corinthians.

ASK YOURSELF

1. How do Christlike givers benefit from the laws of sowing and reaping?

2. How would Christlike giving prompt the Macedonian church to urgently plead for the privilege to give to the Jerusalem church when it was facing famine?

3. Think of an example of a Christlike giver from the Bible, a figure in history or someone you currently know. What are the characteristics you see that identify this person as a Christlike giver?

LIVE IT!

How would you describe yourself as a giver? Look back at your Prosperity Quotient (PQ) from Section 3. How might your attitudes about prosperity hinder you from becoming a Christlike giver?

3 4

THE MO OF THE CHRISTLIKE GIVER

Each man should give what he has decided in his heart to give,
not reluctantly or under compulsion, for God loves a cheerful giver.

2 CORINTHIANS 9:7

EARLY ROOTS RUN DEEP

Giving has always come easy for me. Not once while I was growing up did I ever wonder or worry about provision. My parents were good providers and worked hard to give us a financially stable and secure home environment. Even though my father was a minister, he maintained a business on the side as a dental technician, which supplemented his income. My mother used her culinary skills and business acumen to open a highly successful restaurant in the DC area.

We didn't get everything we wanted, but we could afford occasional little luxuries. For instance, I remember when Converse tennis shoes were "the shoe" to have. They were significantly more expensive than the Keds my mother had been buying for me up to that time. But when I informed her that I had to have a pair of Converse shoes, she bought them for me. Our parents also assumed the responsibility of paying for our college educations.

They were generous givers to their church and the community. I think my childhood experience with my parents contributed to my ability to become an obedient giver and trust God to meet my needs.

After Sue and I got married, we tithed faithfully because that's what our church taught, but we always gave more than the tithe.

We believed in the principles of sowing and reaping, and we trusted God to be our provider. In 39 years of walking with the Lord, I can recall only two times when I was concerned about our personal finances, and each time God came through for us and showed Himself faithful.

One time was when I first moved my family to Los Angeles in the early 1980s. We had been given seed money to establish a church plant in this area; but after nine months, we ran out of funds. Things were looking pretty bleak, and we were wondering where the next mortgage payment and grocery money would come from.

Sue and I took our need to the Lord and thanked Him for His provision. We had been sowing faithfully and were confident that He would provide. Things did not change immediately, but we continued to put our request before Him and thank Him daily. When we absolutely had to have some relief, we were given a check for $5,000. I can still remember the joy we felt as we opened it up and began dancing around the house. Our Father God had come through for us again!

Christlike Giving Is a
Work of Grace Within Us

The promises in God's Word are wonderful, and there is nothing quite as sweet as a firsthand experience of God's provision. It builds faith in you like nothing else can. Father God means for each one of us to directly experience His loving provision for us, but it is only possible as we give to Him. In trust, we must step out and give Him something to work with.

This is why I opened with my story of early exposure to parents who were givers. I realize that in the area of giving, I have good early roots that run deep, and that made it easier for me to receive God's grace in this area. But perhaps you are not so fortunate. Maybe your parents did not know how to handle their finances well; or maybe you were born into poverty. As we discussed in Section 3 on the mind-heart connection, heart wounds affect our attitudes and behaviors, and can make it more difficult to trust God and receive His promises. On top of this, we all are contending with spiritual strongholds like poverty and Mammon, which can distort our understanding of God's will to prosper us.

This is why addressing the wounds we carry in our hearts, and demolishing the spiritual strongholds that come against us, is so important. I know this is repetitive by now, but I cannot stress this strongly enough. If you find yourself struggling with recurring fears about Christlike giving, you need to go back, examine your heart, and get the inner healing and spiritual deliverance you may need. You will never be able to become a Christlike giver until you do. Your Father God wants to offer you so much, but your ability to receive it will stay limited until your heart receives major healing.

This is where so many Christians become discouraged and conclude that God's Word "doesn't work." They don't trust God, so they can't believe His promises and receive His blessings. Instead of surrendering to His grace, they see what He promises and what He asks us to do, and they try to perform up to His standard through their own human effort. Of course, this cannot and will not work. From the beginning, Father God always intended that we would have His nature and live in partnership with Him through the life and the grace of the Holy Spirit. Most Christians accept their salvation as a work of God's grace through faith, but then they begin trying to live a Christlike life through their own efforts.

The early Galatian church attempted this mixing of grace and law to their detriment. The apostle Paul wrote to them, "Are you so foolish? After beginning with the Spirit, are you now trying to attain your goal by human effort? Have you suffered so much for nothing—if it really was for nothing? Does God give you his Spirit and work miracles among you because you observe the law, or because you believe what you heard?" (Gal. 3:3-5).

As we look at the MO of the Christlike giver, please remember that these characteristics are produced by the grace of God working within us. We are to believe God's promises and receive them by surrendering in trust to our Father God. We know that His grace will give us both the motivation and the power to become progressively Christlike in character.

Ché Ahn

The MO of Christlike Givers

Give with the Right Motive

Christlike giving is supernatural giving. In speaking of the extravagant giving, "beyond their ability," of the Macedonian church, the apostle Paul challenged the Corinthians: "See that you also excel in this grace of giving" (2 Cor. 8:7). The primary motive of a Christlike giver's heart is to give everything to God, to honor and love Father God because he or she desires to be like Him. The Christlike giver values eternal treasure in heaven over temporal, material treasures here on earth. This type of desire is something that God plants within our hearts as we surrender to Him.

Christlike givers understand that they are children of God, and they understand the incredible responsibility given to them to manage the resources of His kingdom. They trust God's continuing provision for them and can release their resources to bless others and invest in and increase God's kingdom here on earth. Unlike people in the world who fear lack and selfishly try to hoard their resources to feel secure, Christlike givers know they can't lose, for the increase of God's kingdom will never cease (see Isa. 9:7).

In contrast, the current prosperity gospel so popular in the church teaches that Christians should be wealthy and thus appeals to the selfishness of their hearts. If we give in order to get, we forfeit the real eternal rewards God promised. When we are focused on material gain, we show that we are still trusting in wealth for our provision and security.

The apostle Paul gave the Corinthian church some explicit instructions on how they should give: "Remember this: Whoever sows sparingly will also reap sparingly, and whoever sows generously will also reap generously. Each man should give what he is decided in his heart to give, not reluctantly or under compulsion, for God loves a cheerful giver" (2 Cor. 9:6-7).

Give Generously

Several things are immediately apparent here. Paul reminds the Corinthian church of the laws of sowing and reaping, and he encourages them to give generously. God loves generous, extravagant givers, for their actions say that they trust Him as their provider, and their hearts are Christlike. They readily give beyond their ability without regard to circumstances. The Gospel of John relates the story of one extravagant giver:

> Six days before the Passover, Jesus arrived at Bethany, where Lazarus lived, whom Jesus had raised from the dead. Here a dinner was given in Jesus' honor. Martha served, while Lazarus was among those reclining at the table with him. Then Mary took about a pint of pure nard, an expensive perfume; she poured it on Jesus' feet and wiped his feet with her hair. And the house was filled with the fragrance of the perfume. But one of his disciples, Judas Iscariot, who was later to betray him, objected. "Why wasn't this perfume sold and the money given to the poor? It was worth a year's wages." He did not say this because he cared about the poor but because he was a thief; as keeper of the moneybag, he used to help himself to what was put into it. "Leave her alone," Jesus replied. "It was intended that she should save this perfume for the day of my burial. You always have the poor among you, but you will not always have me" (John 12:1-8).

This story illustrates several things about the generosity of Christlike givers. Often their generosity is criticized, because it exposes the selfish motives of others. Judas stated a true fact: the price of the nard was a year's wages. But he could only focus on its value materially. Jesus responded to the deep love in Mary that prompted her extravagant gift. In fact, He said that wherever His story was told, the generous act of Mary would be included. She was to be perpetually honored for her gift. Our Father God is an extravagantly generous giver, and He is drawn to this trait in His children, rewarding them abundantly when it is present.

The other story is a contemporary one, told by author Randy Alcorn. A number of years ago, Scott Lewis, a businessman, attended a conference where Bill Bright (evangelist and founder of

Campus Crusade for Christ) challenged people to give one million dollars to help fulfill the Great Commission. This amount was laughable to Scott—far beyond anything he could imagine, since his machinery business was generating an income of under $50,000 a year. Bill Bright asked Scott, "How much did you give last year?" Scott felt pretty good about his answer: "We gave $17,000; about 35 percent of our income."

Without blinking an eye, Bill responded, "Over the next year, why don't you make a goal of giving $50,000?" Scott thought Bill had not understood. That was more than he had made all year! But Scott and his wife decided to trust God with Bill's challenge and asked God to do the impossible. God provided in amazing ways. With a miraculous December 31 provision, Scott was able to give the $50,000. Scott wrote Randy a note saying that in 2001, they passed the one-million-dollar mark in their giving, and they weren't stopping. Now that's extravagant, generous giving!

Give Thoughtfully and Prayerfully
Note that the passage in 2 Corinthians 9:7 says that each man gives "what he has decided in his heart to give." It's a deliberate decision based on prayer and planning. Christlike givers think about it, pray about it with their spouse, and take their giving seriously. They are led by the Holy Spirit, and not by their emotions.

I believe, based on this text, that impulsive giving is immature giving. You don't give just because you were moved emotionally, or somebody manipulated you. You give because you thought it out and were led by the Spirit of God. It is doing what you see the Father doing (see John 5:19). You decide in your heart to be prayerfully led by the Holy Spirit. This means that you are walking in ongoing intimacy with Father God. You are open to giving whatever and whenever He directs.

Like piano playing, giving is a skill. With practice, we get better at it. We can learn to give more, give more often and give more strategically. We teach the pursuit of excellence in our vocations. Why not make giving something we study, discuss and sharpen, striving for excellence?

GIVE WILLINGLY

The text says that giving should not be done reluctantly. Circle that word. Christlike givers never give out of guilt. Nor do they give grudgingly, that is, with a "grin and bear it" attitude. That is legalistic giving, and Father God wants us to have no part in it. Have you ever heard ministers on the radio or TV who have a crisis every week? They say things like, "If you don't give, we're going to go under this week." It's an attempt to manipulate, pressure and lay guilt on the listener. God expressly tells us not to give that way.

You are the only one who can make a decision on how much you will give. It is between you and the Holy Spirit. There is no condemnation. No one has the right to judge your giving. Never give out of guilt, compulsion or from a grudging heart. Be aware that at times you will need to pray for a willing and eager spirit, just like we need to pray about any ministry or area of commitment in our life.

GIVE CHEERFULLY

I think this is the most important characteristic of all. The Greek word for "cheerful" is *hilaros*. We get the word "hilarious" from it. God loves a cheerful giver. The New Testament Christians loved to give. Unfortunately, today in most church services across the country, when you take the offering, it's the low point in the service. It's when everything comes to a standstill. God says that in the New Testament, they were hilarious givers. Do you know why happy people are giving people, and giving people are happy people?

The root word for "miserable" is "miser." Misers are miserable. If you don't learn to be generous and give cheerfully, if you are stingy and always worrying about what you have rather than giving it away, you will never be a Christlike giver. The world is out there thinking, "If I get more, and get more . . . I'm going to be happy." But God says that if I give more, the happier I will be. Jesus said that. He said that the way to happiness is not to amass personal wealth, but to give. It is more blessed to give than to receive (see Acts 20:35).

People who give consistently are happier and healthier. Karl Menninger, the dean of American psychiatry and founder of the world-famous Menninger Clinic, noted, "Giving is a criterion of mental health. Generous people are rarely mentally ill." I don't believe many Christians have that revelation. If they did, they would give more. The most generous people I know are the happiest people I know. We are so blessed when we give, and this includes being really happy.

God's primary interest in our giving is our heart attitude, not the size of our wallet. He is far more concerned with the quality of the giver than the quantity of the gift.

GIVE PROPHETICALLY
Christlike givers stay prayed up and are sensitive to the leading of the Holy Spirit. They find multiple occasions to give, some of which are outside the usual channels. Every year, Sue and I pray about two major offerings. One is for Harvest International Ministry (HIM), the apostolic network that God has given me the privilege to lead. We want to sow into missions, and we believe in leading by example.

One year, God spoke to us to give a faith promise offering for $25,000 to HIM. The next week, I received two checks totaling $25,000, including one check for $8,000 from a pastor who "was just led" by the Lord to send the check as a personal gift to Sue and me. The quick response to our prophetic faith promise assured me that this was an important commitment to God.

The second way that Sue and I are prophetically led is how much we should give each year beyond the tithe. You see, my wife and I have practiced graduated giving each year. We pray each year how much we are to sow into our local church, HRock, and to HIM. Since 2010, by God's grace, we finally reached our goal to give over 50 percent of what the Lord has financially blessed us with. We didn't start out giving 50 percent, but over the years, we kept on increasing our giving each year. I am happy where we are at, but Sue now has faith to give away 90 percent, and for us to live on 10 percent. I have to admit I am not there yet, but I thank God for a wonderful wife who is full of faith! And may I add that the 50 percent we do keep is absolutely amazing. You truly can't out-give God!

Finally, I always carry a few extra hundred-dollar bills in my bill-fold, asking God whom I can bless. Often, when I am at a restaurant and see some of our church members, I will pick up their bill, unless the Holy Spirit tells me otherwise. One Saturday afternoon, I saw the whole Little League baseball team come into a family restaurant. They were so excited that their coaches were taking them out for lunch to celebrate a game they won. I felt the Lord speak to me to pick up the whole tab, so I went to the manager and said, "I want the bill for the Little League group." He was totally shocked and asked if I wanted them to know who picked up the bill. I replied, "Just let them know that a local pastor picked up the tab for them."

I didn't preach or introduce myself. In fact, my daughter was with me, and we simply slipped out the door. Once we were outside, my daughter turned to me and said, "Dad, you are the most generous man that I know." Her compliment and the joy on the faces of those Little League players was worth the whole experience, and I felt totally blessed by doing that act of kindness.

CHRISTLIKE GIVING BRINGS BLESSINGS

Paul described to the Corinthians some very important blessings promised by God to Christlike givers. They are found in 2 Corinthians 9:6-14:

- "Having all that you need" (v. 8): Christlike givers are promised that their needs will be supplied.

- "You will abound in every good work . . . [God] will enlarge the harvest of your righteousness" (vv. 8,11): Christlike givers' ministry is multiplied. They are blessed to be a blessing.

- "[God] will also supply and increase your store of seed. . . . You will be made rich in every way so that you can be generous on every occasion" (vv. 10-11): Christlike givers will be blessed with abundance so that they can give more.

- "Your generosity will result in thanksgiving to God . . . supplying the needs of God's people" (vv. 11-12): Christlike giving brings praise to Father God.

- "Men will praise God for [your] obedience . . . and for your generosity in sharing with them and with everyone else" (v. 13): People will praise God for you, your obedience to God and your generosity.

- "In their prayers for you their hearts will go out to you, because of the surpassing grace God has given you" (v. 14): People will be praying for you and asking God to bless you.

How would you like to partner with Father God in creating this atmosphere of generosity, abundant supply, blessing and thanksgiving? Can you imagine living in such an atmosphere? The more we enter into Christlike giving, the more we change our personal atmosphere and the atmosphere of the world around us. This is operating in our authority and dominion in advancing God's kingdom here on earth. It's becoming who we were created to be, and fulfilling our purpose and destiny.

PUTTING IT ALL TOGETHER

Christlike giving is the work of God's grace within us, but our ability to receive it will stay limited if our heart is still carrying emotional wounds. We may need both inner healing and spiritual deliverance to get set free. Christlike giving is characterized in generosity, thoughtfulness, prayer, a willing heart and cheerfulness. Christlike giving brings blessings of abundance, supplied needs and thankfulness and praise to God.

ASK YOURSELF

1. Do you think you might be mixing grace and law in your current practice of giving? Why or why not? Identify specific attitudes and behaviors that support your answer.

2. What are the reasons you give to the Lord? Are they legalistic, motivated by the desire to get, or by the desire to love and honor Father God?

3. Do you think you have ever given because you felt pressured, guilty or emotionally manipulated? How might you prevent yourself from giving this way in the future?

LIVE IT!

Try giving prophetically. Carry some extra cash this week and ask God to point out an opportunity to give. Record the giving event. What was the experience like for you? How did the receiver respond?

3 5

GUIDELINES FOR GIVING

*You will be made rich in every way so that you can be
generous on every occasion, and through us your generosity will
result in thanksgiving to God.*

2 CORINTHIANS 9:11

Over the years as a pastor, I've been asked a number of questions
about giving. I'd like to look at a few of the most common questions with you, because they may reflect questions you have about
giving. I want to preface this discussion by saying that my answers
to these questions are based on my searching both the Scriptures
and my own heart before the Lord regarding His will. What I am
offering to you is my best understanding at the present time, based
on my own experience and the experiences of many others with
whom I have counseled.

Ultimately, each one of us must determine in our own heart
what the Lord is asking us to do in a given situation, and follow
His direction. So I ask you to prayerfully consider these questions
and answers, and seek Father God's face for your own understanding. Never fear making an error, for if you are truly seeking God's
wisdom, He will lovingly correct you promptly.

HOW MUCH SHOULD I GIVE?

There is no prescribed amount or formula for giving established
in the New Testament. But there are guidelines that I think can
be very helpful. While I do not believe that the tithe is a man-

dated form of giving under the new covenant, we can learn some important principles from the practice of tithing. First, it involved regular giving, and giving as a primary priority, not as an afterthought. The tithe was consecrated to God, and was not to be used for any other purpose. It was financial seed and was set aside for sowing.

Regular giving is also advocated under the new covenant by the apostle Paul in his letter to the Corinthians. They were taking up a collection for the church in Jerusalem, and Paul provides this guidance to them: "Now about the collection for God's people: Do what I told the Galatian churches to do. On the first day of every week, each one of you should set aside a sum of money in keeping with his income, saving it up, so that when I come no collections will have to be made" (1 Cor. 16:1-2). The *Amplified Version* translates verse 2 this way: "On the first [day] of each week, let each one of you [personally] put aside something and save it up as he has prospered [in proportion to what he is given], so that no collections will need to be taken after I come."

Although no proportion is stated, Paul does appear to advise them to take up the collection in advance by the method of proportionate giving. What is clear is that he advocates regular giving that is directly connected to their increase in income. It is also clear that giving is a universal activity of everyone in the church. They are to set aside money, which means they were not to spend everything that they brought in, but always to have some reserve to give out at the Lord's direction.

I also want to encourage you to practice graduating giving, something that I know many Christians are practicing around the world. While I do not presume to establish graduated giving as the new covenant way to give, I nonetheless encourage you to pray about employing it, for I know you will be richly blessed. No matter the size of your current level of giving, set a goal to increase it over time, and see if you are not blessed with more. Whatever you do, give regularly, constantly seeking God's direction in your giving, and always have something set aside so that you can give when the occasion arises.

WHERE SHOULD I GIVE?

As a local church pastor, I may be biased, but I personally believe that you give financially first to the local church where you go to worship and where you are fed from God's Word. You can give additional offerings to other ministries, but I believe you first should give to the place where you are spiritually covered and receive your pastoral care. I think this precedent was established from the very beginning in ancient Israel. "The first of the firstfruits of thy land thou shalt bring into the house of the LORD thy God" (Exod. 23:19, *KJV*). The instruction here doesn't say to bring our first financial gifts to a TV ministry or some world relief program, but to the house of the Lord.

Over the years, Sue and I have supported many different ministers and ministries, such as Focus on the Family, World Vision and the 700 Club. But none of those ministers ever pronounced the dedication of our children to the Lord, visited our family in the hospital or gave us pastoral counseling. The point is that a television evangelist is not going to stand with you in ongoing prayer when you have a crisis, or perform your marriage ceremony, or bury a loved one who goes home to be with the Lord. But the local church and its pastors will. When you eat at McDonald's, you don't pay at Burger King, you pay at McDonald's, because that's where you got the service. I believe your first financial gifts belong with the local church you attend.

The apostle Paul told the early Gentile churches that they should support those who ministered to them: "The elders who direct the affairs of the church well are worthy of double honor, especially those whose work is preaching and teaching. For the Scripture says, 'Do not muzzle the ox while it is treading out the grain,' and 'The worker deserves his wages'" (1 Tim. 5:17-18).

I love what Billy Graham wrote in his classic book *Peace with God*: "The Bible says that it was Christ's love for the church that caused Him to go to the cross. If Christ loved the church that much . . . I must love it too. I must pray for it, defend it, work in it, give my tithes to it, help to advance it, promote holiness in it, and make it the functional, witnessing body our Lord meant it to be."[1]

In giving to ministries other than the local church, I would strongly advise you to give to organizations that are both financially responsible and fiscally transparent. A reputable accounting firm should annually audit their record of contributions received and expenditures made. In addition, they should be registered with a national organization like the Evangelical Christian Financial Association (ECFA), which provides potential donors with information on each ministry's governance, financial oversight, compliance with laws and regulations, intended purpose, and overhead costs. A ministry that goes through the rigorous process of registering with the ECFA has its financial house in order.

A second major area of giving that is extremely important to the Lord is giving to the poor. This type of giving is so important that I want to devote an entire entry to it, so we will take it up at length later.

I Can't Afford to Give, So What Do I Do?

When people tell me they can't afford to give because they have too much debt or they are barely making ends meet each month, I tell them they can't afford not to give. Remember the laws of sowing and reaping. They have to give God something to work with! I know that people will find that God will provide for all their needs if they will only begin to give regularly, despite how dire their circumstances may seem. But they must make the choice to trust God and put Him first in order to discover this. This is an important step in spiritual maturity that only they can choose to make.

Sometimes people tell me that when they are making more money, then they will start giving. Jesus said that if we are faithful with a little, we will be faithful over much (see Luke 16:10). Christlike giving is a heart issue. Your heart is not going to magically change when you're making more money. If you are not giving now, you won't do it when you have more income. Often when people tell me this, I know that they are living beyond their means. They do not want to do whatever they have to do to make adjustments, like lowering their standard of living so that they can be regular givers. I know God will bless them if they do, but again this is a choice they must make first.

Occasionally, someone will tell me, "I make a lot of money, and if I give as God directs, I might be giving away an enormous amount of money." I want to reply, "Yes, and you will still have an enormous amount of money left, plus be abundantly blessed." Some people never have enough. They have not learned the power of contentment, and they are still placing their trust in wealth to fulfill them. It's a self-defeating strategy.

I CAN'T GIVE VERY MUCH
BECAUSE MY INCOME IS SMALL

Christlike giving is a matter of our faithfulness to seek God's direction and obey it, as well as to trust God and put Him first. It has nothing to do with the amount we give, but everything to do with our willing obedience. Again, it is a matter of our heart. Remember the poor widow who gave the two pennies? Jesus commented that she gave more than all the other wealthy people who were giving large amounts, because He saw that her sacrifice was much greater than theirs. Don't allow the small amount of your gift to make you doubt its worth. Give it and reap God's blessing.

I OWN MY OWN COMPANY,
SO SHOULD MY COMPANY BE GIVING?

Some people consider their business to be completely separate from their spiritual life. But the laws of sowing and reaping work for a company the same way they do for an individual. Do you want God's blessing on your company? That should settle the question. I think all companies owned by Christians, all churches and Christian organizations should be giving regularly. At our church, HRock, we give more than 10 percent of our offerings to missions, and we have seen our church grow and prosper even in the midst of an economic downturn. We also give more than 10 percent from HIM to ministries that are not part of our apostolic network. It is all about advancing God's kingdom.

What If My Spouse Is Opposed to Giving?

Unfortunately, this frequently happens in marriages between believers and nonbelievers. First, I think you need to learn how to pray and appeal to your spouse. You can put up the challenge, "Let's try giving for three months and see if God does bless us." I heard about a man who didn't believe in giving. When he was presented with this challenge by his wife, he agreed, thinking this would be the perfect way to prove to her that her faith was just fantasy. However, during the three months of giving, he received an unexpected promotion, a huge raise and a new company car. He knew it was not coincidence, and not only was he converted to Christ, but he also became a regular giver as well.

If you are earning a separate income from your spouse, hopefully you at least have the freedom to give of your income. But if you still have conflict, my pastoral recommendation is that you wait and pray, until both of you are on the same page.

Putting It All Together

There are many potential questions about giving. Most focus on how much to give, where our financial gifts should go, and what to do when we feel we cannot give or can only give a small amount. God is looking for those who have purposed in their hearts to become Christlike givers. They trust God's Word and His promise that He will provide their harvest and bless their life in multiple ways, if they only sow.

Ask Yourself

1. Do you agree that your first financial gifts should go to your local church? Why or why not?

2. Are you now giving, or have you ever given, regularly? What is/was your experience with giving? Would you recommend regular giving to others? Why or why not?

3. Have you ever had a situation where God provided for you financially in a moment of desperate need? Do you think His provision was connected in any way to your giving?

Live It!

I want to challenge you to try graduated giving. Look at what you are currently giving and set a goal to increase your level of giving over the next three months, and see what happens. Are you willing to do this? Why or why not?

Note
1. Billy Graham, *Peace with God* (New York: Pocket Books, 1975).

3 6

LENDING TO THE LORD

*He who is kind to the poor lends to the LORD, and he will
reward him for what he has done.*

PROVERBS 19:17

The Bible contains more than 2,000 verses about caring for the
poor, and Jesus went so far as to suggest that caring for the poor,
or neglecting to do so, was caring for or neglecting Him. Despite
this fact, compared to the tidal wave of teaching on tithing, giving
to ministries and reaping prosperity in the church today, there is
relatively little teaching focused on meeting the needs of the poor.

I must confess, in writing this book, I was surprised and hum-
bled to find that in all the years that I have been a pastor, I cannot
remember one message that I gave exclusively on helping the poor.
I have taught many times on breaking the spirit of poverty, but I
cannot recall one message on taking care of the poor. I've taught
it as a side note or secondary point, but I cannot find a whole sermon on this topic. I can only guess, but I think, with a fair amount
of accuracy, that the same is true for most of my evangelical brothers and sisters.

We know that we are called to become Christlike through trusting our Father God and surrendering to the power of His grace
working through the Holy Spirit within us. It is His grace—not
any human effort on our part—that accomplishes this transformation of our character. Our willing and obedient giving, and
responsible handling of Kingdom resources entrusted to us, demonstrates our growing spiritual maturity. As we mature, we increase
in our ability to handle authority and dominion in advancing

Father God's agenda here on earth. Our loving care of the poor is one more opportunity to train for reigning and to develop a heart like Father God's.

Obviously, if the poor are addressed in more than 2,000 verses in Scripture, they are very important to Father God. He loves and cares for the poor and is concerned for their welfare. He expects us to be and do the same. He gave a number of commands to ancient Israel to ensure that the poor would have provision and receive justice. Jesus had powerful things to say about caring for the poor, calling us to a higher standard of loving and giving under the new covenant of grace. Providing for the poor was a major focus and activity of the Early Church.

Let's look at some examples from both the Old and New Testaments to better understand God's continuing emphasis on how we are to love and care for the poor.

LENDING TO THE LORD

There are many references made today to the passage in Malachi 3:10 where the Lord invites Israel to obey His command to tithe: "'Test me in this,' says the LORD Almighty, 'and see if I will not throw open the floodgates of heaven and pour out so much blessing that you will not have room enough for it.'" That we are invited by God to test Him is indeed impressive, and occurs only once in Scripture. However, every promise of God is an implicit invitation to test Him. How do you know if any promise is true? You test it and see if it delivers. God wants us to believe and test every promise He has ever given us.

I think Proverbs 19:17 is actually more stunning than Malachi 3:10. Father God tells us in Proverbs that if we give to the poor, we are actually lending to Him, and He will repay. The word "lend" means to permit the use of something with the expectation of return of the same or an equivalent; to impart or contribute something; and to provide, especially in order to assist or support someone. This verse is rich in meaning, so let's take a moment and unpack it.

First, by using the term "lend," God is stating that we are giving what we own, not something we simply steward. You don't borrow something from someone and then lend it back to him or her again. No, you lend what you own to someone else. We have been given Kingdom resources, and they are ours to manage or squander. God respects our right of ownership, and like any prudent borrower, He promises to return the loan with interest.

God has everything and doesn't need our offerings and gifts. But when it comes to His love and care for the poor, He has put Himself in the position of needing our help. Think of it! The almighty, all-sufficient God of the universe is soliciting our partnership in ministering to the poor! He is entrusting the poor, who are so precious to Him, into our love and care. What an incredible act of trust on His part! What an incredible privilege on our part! We are actually providing support for our Father God.

GOD'S HEART FOR THE POOR

The following samples of Old Testament Scripture express God's heart for the poor:

> The unfortunate commits himself to You; You have been the helper of the orphan. . . . O LORD, You have heard the desire of the humble; You will strengthen their heart, You will incline your ear to vindicate the orphan and the oppressed (Ps. 10:14,17, *NASB*).

> For he will deliver the needy who cry out, the afflicted who have no one to help. He will take pity on the weak and the needy and save the needy from death (Ps. 72:12-13).

> He defends the cause of the fatherless and the widow, and loves the alien, giving him food and clothing (Deut. 10:18).

> A father to the fatherless, and a defender of widows, is God in his holy dwelling (Ps. 68:5).

Throughout the Old Testament, Father God gives instructions on how the poor are to be treated. He recognizes that calamity and disaster can befall anyone, and so He tells Israel, "If one of your countrymen becomes poor and is unable to support himself among you, help him as you would an alien or temporary resident, so he can continue to live among you" (Lev. 25:35).

We live in a culture that frequently views the poor as people who want to freeload and are "working the system." Of course, sometimes this is the case. But Father God respects the poor and doesn't view their poverty as an automatic indication they are lazy and unwilling to work. He commands that they be given work opportunity: "When you reap the harvest of your land, do not reap to the very edges of your field or gather the gleanings of your harvest. Leave them for the poor and the alien. I am the LORD your God" (Lev. 23:22).

Loving and caring for the poor are so important to God that He compares it to an act of consecration, like fasting: "Is not this the kind of fasting I have chosen: to loose the chains of injustice and untie the cords of the yoke, to set the oppressed free and break every yoke? Is it not to share your food with the hungry and to provide the poor wanderer with shelter—when you see the naked, to clothe him, and not to turn away from your own flesh and blood?" (Isa. 58:6-7).

These instructions are emphasized again in the New Testament:

> Religion that God our Father accepts as pure and faultless is this: to look after orphans and widows in their distress and to keep oneself from being polluted by the world (Jas. 1:27).

> Give proper recognition to those widows who are really in need (1 Tim. 5:3).

> If your enemy is hungry, feed him; if he is thirsty, give him something to drink (Rom. 12:20).

That last command in Romans takes giving to the poor to a whole new level beyond the commands of the Old Testament. We are to care not only for our own poor, or the deserving poor, but for the poor who may be our enemy as well. This is pure grace in action. This is Father God calling us to Christlike giving.

To Ignore the Poor Is Sin

Scripture makes it clear that caring for the poor is not an option and that if we shut our hearts and ignore the needs of the poor, we do so to our own hurt:

> He who oppresses the poor shows contempt for their Maker, but whoever is kind to the needy honors God (Prov. 14:31).

> If a man shuts his ears to the cry of the poor, he too will cry out and not be answered (Prov. 21:13).

> He who gives to the poor will lack nothing, but he who closes his eyes to them receives many curses (Prov. 28:27).

> Now this was the sin of your sister Sodom: She and her daughters were arrogant, overfed and unconcerned; they did not help the poor and needy (Ezek. 16:49).

A side note: Most people think the reason Sodom and Gomorrah were destroyed was for the sexual immorality that was rampant in them. However, Ezekiel indicates that a primary sin was their lack of concern and provision for the poor. The New Testament also emphasizes that we must not neglect the needs of the poor:

> [The Pharisees and teachers of the law] devour widows' houses and for a show make lengthy prayers. Such men will be punished most severely (Mark 12:40).

> If anyone has material possessions and sees his brother in need but has no pity on him, how can the love of God dwell in him? (1 John 3:17).

By implication, the passage from 1 John indicates that a Christlike giver will have compassion on a fellow believer in need, and provide what he can. This is not something we do to become a Christlike giver, but something we do because we are Christlike givers and God's love dwells in us.

THOSE WHO GIVE TO THE POOR ARE BLESSED

There are numerous references that we are blessed when we give to the poor throughout both the Old and New Testaments. Remember, we are lending to the Lord, and He will always repay us richly.

Blessed is he who is kind to the needy (Prov. 14:21).

A generous man will himself be blessed, for he shares his food with the poor (Prov. 22:9).

If you spend yourselves in behalf of the hungry and satisfy the needs of the oppressed, then your light will rise in the darkness, and your night will become like the noonday (Isa. 58:10).

Sell your possessions and give to the poor. Provide purses for yourselves that will not wear out, a treasure in heaven that will not be exhausted, where no thief comes near and no moth destroys (Luke 12:33).

God is able to make all grace abound to you, so that in all things at all times, having all that you need, you will abound in every good work. As it is written: "He has scattered abroad his gifts to the poor; his righteousness endures forever." Now he who supplies seed to the sower and bread for food will also supply and increase your store of seed and will enlarge the harvest of your righteousness. You will be made rich in every way so that you can be generous on every occasion, and through us your generosity will result in thanksgiving to God (2 Cor. 9:8-11).

Proverbs 28:27 states, "He who gives to the poor will lack nothing." God wants us to lend to Him by investing in the poor through our giving. He makes it clear that He considers this gift to be a personal loan and guarantees us a return. Investing in the poor is like investing in the best blue chip stocks, for we can't lose! We bless others and receive a blessing at the same time!

CHARITY BEGINS AT HOME

Throughout Scripture, we are told to take care of our own poor. Especially in the Old Testament, Israel was to take care of the poor within their borders. God never commanded them to take care of the poor in other countries, but He did require them to take care of the alien poor who dwelt among them. The care of the poor was not left to chance, but was built into the tithing system under which Israel operated. We are all familiar with the yearly tithe that was to be given to the Levites. But there was another tithe collected for the poor and given every three years: "When you have finished setting aside a tenth of all your produce in the third year, the year of the tithe, you shall give it to the Levite, the alien, the fatherless and the widow, so that they may eat in your towns and be satisfied" (Deut. 26:12).

The same emphasis is seen in the New Testament. We are first of all to take care of our own family members, which includes our extended family. The apostle Paul instructed Timothy, "If anyone does not provide for his relatives, and especially for his immediate family, he has denied the faith and is worse than an unbeliever" (1 Tim. 5:8).

Paul wrote these instructions to Timothy in the larger context of how to determine which persons were truly destitute and in need of the church's support. The Early Church was very committed to helping the poor within its ranks, especially widows and orphans. Under Jewish law, the oldest son assumed responsibility for caring for his mother when she was widowed. Women who had no sons, or whose sons were deceased, could become destitute and were dependent upon the church for their ongoing support. The Early Church addressed this support as a serious concern and was very committed to seeing that "true widows" received care. In the same passage, Paul told Timothy, "The widow who is really in need and left all alone puts her hope in God and continues night and day to pray and to ask God for help" (1 Tim. 5:5).

In fact, the Early Church was so involved in caring for its own poor that deacons were appointed to dispense such charity: "In those days when the number of disciples was increasing, the Grecian Jews among them complained against the Hebraic Jews because their widows were being overlooked in the daily distribution of food. So the Twelve gathered all the disciples together and said, 'It would not be right for us to neglect the ministry of the word of God in order to wait on tables. Brothers, choose seven men from among you who are known to be full of the Spirit and wisdom. We will turn this responsibility over to them and will give our attention to prayer and the ministry of the word'" (Acts 6:1-4).

Throughout the book of Acts and the epistles, we read about the efforts of the Early Church to provide for their poor. The Jerusalem church gave extravagantly to see that all their members were supported. "All the believers were together and had everything in common. Selling their possessions and goods, they gave to anyone as he had need. . . . All the believers were one in heart and mind. No one claimed that any of his possessions was his own, but they shared everything they had" (Acts 2:44-45; 4:32).

When the apostle Paul was officially recognized as an evangelist to the Gentiles, the apostles in Jerusalem urged him to remember the poor: "James, Peter and John, those reputed to be pillars, gave me and Barnabas the right hand of fellowship when they recognized the grace given to me. They agreed that we should go to the Gentiles, and they to the Jews. All they asked was that we should continue to remember the poor, the very thing I was eager to do" (Gal. 2:9-10).

CARING FOR THE LORD
BY CARING FOR THE POOR

We know that Jesus perfectly mirrors God, and He is stamped with God's nature (see Heb. 1:3). When we look at Jesus, we see Father

God who cannot be seen; and in Christ we find out who we are and what we live for. Jesus sets an example for us, that we should do even as He has done (see Col. 1:15; Eph. 1:11; John 13:15) Jesus taught His disciples that loving and caring for the poor was loving and caring for Him:

> Then the King will say to those on his right, "Come, you who are blessed by my Father; take your inheritance, the kingdom prepared for you since the creation of the world. For I was hungry and you gave me something to eat, I was thirsty and you gave me something to drink, I was a stranger and you invited me in, I needed clothes and you clothed me, I was sick and you looked after me, I was in prison and you came to visit me. . . . I tell you the truth, whatever you did for one of the least of these brothers of mine, you did for me" (Matt. 25:34-36,40).

Jesus goes on to describe these as the actions of the righteous and declares that they have an eternal reward. Their acts of kindness to the poor identify them as one of God's children, having a Christlike character.

Today, the church in the United States has largely abdicated caring for its own poor to government programs and social agencies. We may provide stopgap assistance to a family in need, run a soup kitchen, a food pantry or clothes closet. We often designate several world mission groups that the church contributes to, but seldom do we see our own poor as our ongoing responsibility. Families and churches are to be the example of Christlike character and, as "salt and light," care for the poor in their midst and in their communities.

The local church can provide what no government program or social agency can: individual care. Individual care is personal. It has a face that sees individual needs, ears that hear individual stories, and a heart of compassion that feels individual pain and suffering. This type of care is up close and personal and desperately needed by the poor. It says to them, "You are important as a person. You are valuable and worth my time and attention." It is much easier to throw a little money at a need and walk away. That allows us to feel good about ourselves and look the other way when we see a fellow believer in need.

I am reminded of a story that I heard years ago about a preaching class at Princeton seminary. The professor gave the task of preparing a sermon on Jesus' parable of the Good Samaritan. They were to come individually to Miller Chapel and preach their sermon to the professor, and he would evaluate their work. But unknown to the students, the professor had arranged for a man to portray a needy poor person who would approach each student on the way into the chapel and ask for help. Not one student in the preaching class stopped to help that needy man. Here they were on the way to preach about the Good Samaritan, and not one of them recognized the parable when it was presented to them in real life!

The grace of Christlike giving goes beyond being an obedient, willing and cheerful giver. It is an entire lifestyle in which we live with the desire to fulfill our Father God's will and purpose here on earth. We want to advance His kingdom by saying what He says, doing what He does and loving as He loves. This is not just a spiritual stance, it has practical implications for how we live in society and how we seek to transform and reform it.

PUTTING IT ALL TOGETHER

Father God cares for and loves the poor, and He expects us to do the same. He states that we are lending to Him when we give to the poor, and He will repay and bless us. We are never to ignore the needs of the poor. First and foremost, we are to provide for our own family and the poor in our local church.

ASK YOURSELF

1. Do you currently give to the poor? If so, to whom and how? If not, do you intend to begin? If yes, when, to whom and how will you give?

2. What might be some ways you could give the poor an opportunity to work? Would you ever actually do this?

3. In what ways do you routinely ignore the poor? How can you stop doing this?

LIVE IT!

Think of several ways you can help provide for the poor other than giving money. (Hint: offer them a ride, give clothing, or watch their children.) Look for an opportunity to implement one way you have identified this week. Record your experience.

THE TRANSFORMING
POWER OF GRACE

The first thing you may notice about this section is that there's only one entry. This is intentional because we have taken ourselves to the threshold of a new level of living in Christ. We have followed Christlike giving to its inevitable purpose: the reformation of society produced through the transformed children of God.

God's ultimate intention is a family full of sons and daughters with Christlike character who assert their authority and dominion to usher in their Father's kingdom on earth. They are to infiltrate every one of the seven mountains of culture (more detail on this to come) with the love and life of Father God. They are salt and light in the world, and they live lives so significantly different that they show themselves to be colonies of heaven thriving in a hostile world system.

God wants us to be involved in reformation at both the individual and systemic levels, because the power of God's transformational grace is required in both if His kingdom is to advance. In this last entry, we will look at how the process can operate in addressing poverty.

The call to personal transformation is always a call to become a reformer of society. The two can't be separated. As our character is transformed into the image of Christ, we become filled with God's love and become one with His plan and purpose. We fulfill His deepest desire of coming into unity with Him and each other. We step into our destiny, and the greatest privilege in human history: the opportunity to infuse the earth with God's kingdom and glory once again.

3 7

God's Fifth Column

Let your light shine before men, that they may see your
good deeds and praise your Father in heaven.

MATTHEW 5:16

At the end of the 1930s, the outbreak of World War II in Europe seemed inevitable. The rapid fall of France, in 1940, led many to blame a "fifth column," a group of strategically placed Nazi sympathizers within the French government, rather than credit German military superiority. Political factions in France faulted one another for the nation's defeat, and military officials blamed the civilian leadership. All of this increased anxieties in the United States about the possibility of betrayal by subversives from within. In June 1940, *Life* magazine ran a series of photos under the heading "Signs of Nazi Fifth Column Everywhere."

Emilio Mola, a nationalist General during the Spanish Civil War, originally coined the term "fifth column." He told a journalist in 1936 that as his four columns of troops approached Madrid, a "fifth column" of supporters inside the city would rise up, joining his forces, and undermine the Republican government from within. The term caught hold and became a descriptor for a group of people who clandestinely undermine a larger group, such as a nation from within. A key tactic of the fifth column is the secret introduction of supporters into the whole fabric of the nation or system under attack.

God's Fifth Column

God has a fifth column. It is the seed of His kingdom, and it is planted in every one of His children through His Holy Spirit who dwells within them. While Father God greatly loves the world and all its inhabitants, He is using His fifth column to dismantle the world system dominated by Satan. Jesus Christ completely defeated Satan when He died and rose from the dead and triumphed over death and the curse. "And having disarmed the [evil] powers and authorities, he made a public spectacle of them, triumphing over them by the cross" (Col. 2:15). Victory over the world system is certain, but we, as God's children, have been given the task of liberating and occupying this world until Christ returns.

God wants us to be salt and light in the world. He wants us to be a city set on a hill that broadcasts His life and His love to the world: "You are the light of the world. A city on a hill cannot be hidden. . . . In the same way, let your light shine before men, that they may see your good deeds and praise your Father in heaven" (Matt. 5:14,16). Our lives are to be lived in such a way that we exemplify our Father's loving actions. We are to live in ways that are so significantly different that we show that we are colonies of heaven within the world system. As we live out God's will and plan through the character of Christ formed within us, we release the transformational power of God's grace into the world around us.

Father God also intends that we infiltrate the power structures of the world system. If we are to be effective as salt and light, we must be in positions of influence where we can have an effect. Of course, God always had a plan for accomplishing this, but I believe that we began getting a deeper revelation of how to be a fifth column within the last few decades.

INFILTRATING THE MOUNTAINS OF CULTURE

In the 1970s, Bill Bright, president and founder of Campus Crusade for Christ Ministries, and Loren Cunningham, director of Youth With A Mission (YWAM), held a meeting of great spiritual significance. Each man felt he had received a fresh word from the Lord. As they shared information, they quickly discovered that independent of one another, each had received an identical word regarding the transformation of society. God revealed to both men

the same seven "mountains of culture," along with a clear mandate that the Church was to prevail in each of them. These mountains consist of the major influences that shape every culture:
family, business, government, religion, education, media, and arts
and entertainment.

God's will is for each of His children to develop to their full potential and to influence and shift the atmosphere of the particular mountain of culture to which they are called. This is taking our
inner transformation of heart and the renewing of our mind and
utilizing them to advance God's kingdom by infiltrating the culture of the world. Our inner transformation and renewal creates
Christlike character within us and gives us access to our authority
and dominion in God's kingdom. We are to use that authority and
dominion to transform our society.

Maybe it seems a stretch for you to believe that you can influence the world around you. But the Bible says, "The LORD will
make you the head, not the tail. If you pay attention to the commands of the LORD your God that I give you this day and carefully
follow them, you will always be at the top, never at the bottom"
(Deut. 28:13). We are to use our influence to bring transformation
to the mountain of culture we inhabit, not for our personal glory,
but for the glory of our Father God.

ERADICATING SYSTEMIC POVERTY

As God's children, conformed to the image of Christ, we are called
to address societal ills at both the individual and systemic levels.
Why is this so? It's because the transformational power of God's
grace is needed both individually and systemically. Let's take an
example by considering poverty.

As we discussed in the previous chapter, poverty has an individual face that requires individual care. But poverty is also a systemic evil that infects institutions and culture in general. For
example, every year 6.9 million children worldwide under the age
of five will die from malnutrition. Every few seconds one of us on
this planet dies of hunger.[1] A recent policy paper put out by the

Brookings Institution indicates that poverty reduction strategies such as micro-finance and relief organizations produce insignificant and relatively ineffective results in lasting reduction of poverty.

However, they did have some good news: "Poverty reduction is currently taking place in all regions of the world. The bulk of the fall in global poverty can be attributed to the two developing giants, India and China. They alone are responsible for three-quarters of the expected reduction of the world's poor."[2] So, worldwide extreme poverty is actually decreasing. This is not due to donations, micro-enterprise programs or child sponsorship, but rather to sheer economic growth. Both China and India have massive populations and have made a number of interrelated decisions to open their countries to globalization. This has led to remarkable economic performances in which the GDP growth rates generally have stayed above 6 percent since 2003. Best of all, this wealth is trickling down to the lowest economic strata of their societies. The lesson we learn from this is that systemic disorders require an approach at the systemic level.

God's Governmental Poverty Program

In Psalm 72, King Solomon reflects on his role as a head of state and asks God to help him rule: "Endow the King with your justice, O God, the royal son with your righteousness. . . . He will defend the afflicted among the people and save the children of the needy; he will crush the oppressor. . . . All kings will bow down to him and all nations will serve him. For he will deliver the needy who cry out, the afflicted who have no one to help. He will take pity on the weak and the needy and save the needy from death. He will rescue them from oppression and violence, for precious is their blood in his sight" (Ps. 72:1,4,11-14).

Like Jesus, Solomon saw the "weak and the needy" as precious. Solomon regarded special care for the needy—even special affection for the needy—as a characteristic of government blessed by God. Like Jesus, Solomon did not care for the needy because he feared punishment if he didn't. He cared because they were precious to him!

If God Himself designed an economy, what would it look like? According to Leviticus, God did just that in ancient Israel. The Jews were an agrarian society, so their livelihood and wealth came from the land. Once they crossed over Jordan and entered the Promised Land, God had them divide the land equally among tribes and families. He established ownership, inheritance and private property. However, as time went on some people inevitably gained much more wealth, while others lost what they had.

God did not want the spiraling gap between haves and have-nots to go on indefinitely. He established a remarkable practice to economically reset that society. Every 50 years, the land had to return to its original owners. Every 50 years, every family had equal access to the means of producing wealth all over again. Those who would gain much knew it was only for a time. Those who lost everything knew they'd get another try. No one stayed poor through this system! There would always be some poverty due to man's selfishness and sin, but each family would have relatively equal access to the means of producing wealth every 50 years.

Perhaps God's wisdom here is exactly what our partisan politics tend to forget. Both individual character (which the Right sees as the root cause of poverty and wealth) and cultural inequality (seen similarly by the Left) have to be addressed for poverty to be defeated. I believe God calls us to a view that is neither Right nor Left, but one that embraces a third way that combines the best of both the other options. One's hard work should bring rewards, but not to the extent of an elite group dominating the means of a society's production. One's tragedy or laziness brings loss, yet not an irretrievable loss to one's innocent children and grandchildren.

To eradicate poverty requires reformation in both individual character and social justice. Character, of course, is developed with God's Word within the family and church settings. Government's role would be to make certain that justice in the form of equal opportunity is extended to everyone.

When God established the year of Jubilee, He promised to bless Israel if they observed it. He told them they would lend to many nations and borrow from none. He promised they would rule over many nations, but no one would ever rule over them (see Deut. 15:6). Unfortunately, Israel never implemented the year of Jubilee, and suffered famine and conquest as a result.

God's Design for the Mountain of Government

God makes it clear that He intends to judge all governments on the quality of their care for the poor. In Psalm 9:7-9, we read, "The LORD reigns forever; he has established his throne for judgment. He will judge the world in righteousness; he will govern the peoples with justice. The LORD is a refuge for the oppressed, a stronghold in times of trouble." The same positive qualities that Solomon sought—justice and righteousness—become the yardstick by which God judges governments of the world.

The prophet Daniel knew that when a nation is just, God would prosper that nation. So he advised the king of Babylon, "Therefore, O king, be pleased to accept my advice: Renounce your sins by doing what is right, and your wickedness by being kind to the oppressed. It may be that then your prosperity will continue" (Dan. 4:27).

The accountability of all governments to God is also reflected in Paul's letter to the Romans: "There is no authority except that which God has established. The authorities that exist have been established by God" (Rom. 13:1). Governments are accountable to God for the way they manage the seven mountains of culture. The charge to every secular government is twofold: promote justice and penalize wrongdoing. Scripture makes it clear that God will establish governments that do these two things.

The Church and Poverty

What is the role of the Church in addressing the needs of the poor? We have already discussed in some depth the mandate of the Church to care and provide for the poor. Writing this book has heightened my desire that an ever greater percentage of my own church's annual budget will go to the poor in our neighborhood. At HRock Church, we have been giving more than 10 percent of our budget to the poor around the world through Harvest International Ministry, the international apostolic network that I am privileged to lead.

Nationwide, however, the fact is that giving through churches is on the decline and needs to rise dramatically if we are to be like Jesus in our provision for the poor, locally and globally. I would like to see our church membership become a stronger example of Christlikeness, not just in offering money, food and services, but also by helping the poor in our community get out of poverty permanently. One way we can do this is to support elected officials and the legislation that best seems to line up with the character of God we see revealed in Scripture. We can seek to have a presence at local city council meetings when issues related to poverty are being addressed.

As a fifth column in the mountain of government, we can advocate for justice and equal opportunity for the poor with our votes, and by holding offices in local and even state and federal governments. For some of us, it may mean the choice of legal or social advocacy vocations. For others, it might take the form of offering retraining opportunities in our businesses. In whatever way we are involved, we will carry the transformational grace of God into that mountain of culture.

Most of all, I believe that we can be salt and light to our community and society by living lives overflowing with the grace of Christlike giving. We can reach out and make sure that poor Christians don't fall through the cracks, regardless of how deserving or undeserving we think they may be. We can follow the good example of the Early Church, which asked much of its members but also gave much. Because those early Christians were expected to aid the less fortunate, they could expect to receive such aid if and when they needed it. This resulted in a community where everyone could feel greater security against bad times.

They were asked to nurse the sick and dying, but they knew that they also would receive such mercy if needed. They were asked to love others and in turn received love. The Early Church mitigated relations among the social classes at the very time the gap between rich and poor was growing. The Church did not preach that everyone could or should be socially or politically equal. It did insist that everyone was equal in the eyes of God, and that the more fortunate had a responsibility to help those in need.

God is a realist, and we need to be realists too. He hates poverty and yet realizes that as long as sin exists, there will be cycles of poverty created and re-created. He seeks to institute economics of grace in order to diffuse, or derail, those cycles of poverty, and He asks us to partner with Him in His concern for the poor. Having been recipients of grace, we now become conduits of His grace to the world around us. We become openhearted, openhanded and generous, giving others what they need, knowing that God will continuously provide as we do.

As God's fifth column, we are called to actively infiltrate the seven mountains of culture with God's love and the transformational power of His grace. We have the most brilliant and victorious Supreme Commander, who will supply all our needs, including the revelation of how to accomplish our mission. We have been given the greatest privilege in human history, the opportunity to infuse the earth with God's kingdom and glory once again.

PUTTING IT ALL TOGETHER

We are God's fifth column, and we are infiltrating every mountain of culture with the light of God's love. We carry the ability to transform not only our own character, but also the society we live in. That ability is produced by the kingdom of God, which has been planted in our hearts by the Holy Spirit who dwells within us. All of this is set in motion by the transformational grace of God that we received when we accepted Christ.

ASK YOURSELF

1. Which mountain of culture do you feel called to infiltrate as a fifth column? What can you begin doing now to be salt and light in this area? Be as specific as you can.

2. Have you ever been to your local city council meeting? Are you willing to attend? I encourage you to attend one, meet your council members and record your experience.

3. What do you think of God's economic system of Jubilee every 50 years? Is it fair and just? Why or why not? How would our society be different if we practiced the year of Jubilee today?

LIVE IT!

Implement your response to question number 1 in the "Ask Yourself" section for one month. Evaluate your experience. Were you able to exert any influence that surprised you? Did you experience any disappointment? What did you learn from this experience about being a fifth column in an intentional way?

Notes

1. "Progress Towards Millennium Development Goal 4: Key Facts and Figures," Unicef, 2012. http://www.childinfo.org/mortality.html.

2. Laurence Chandy and Geoffrey Gertz, "The Changing State of Global Poverty," Unicef, July 2011. https://docs.google.com/viewer?a=v&q=cache:7mJO0J44pfkJ:www.unicef.org/socialpolicy/files/ChildPovertyInsights_July2011.pdf+&hl=en&gl=us&pid=bl&srcid=ADGEESjB6C9r8D9DAFBhqigaxn-n_BovvVJ5vIH4kmF17FYLWR4MyJ3iH26yiS0ZqzuaAF1TtqVatmz73nS_3ZVlFGYbylBU-gvEgxBmMJ9t7SKXs1R2N_0KCSDMndEFMKb3VuFux2cR&sig=AHIEtbQcKyj5DylKq-4zep9pTK-2Qio5rg.

ABOUT THE AUTHOR

Ché Ahn and his wife, Sue, have served as the senior pastors of HRock Church in Pasadena since 1994. Ché is the founder and president of Harvest International Ministry, a worldwide apostolic network of churches in more than 60 nations, with the common vision of "Changing Lives, Transforming Cities, and Discipling Nations." He is also chancellor of the Wagner Leadership Institute, an international network of apostolic training centers established to equip the saints for kingdom ministry.

Ché received his M.Div. and D.Min. from Fuller Theological Seminary and has played a key role in many strategic local, national and international outreaches, including being president of The Call, a youth prayer movement. He has authored numerous books, including *Say Goodbye to Powerless Christianity; How to Pray for Healing;* and *The Grace of Giving.* He also hosts his own television program, "Holy Spirit Today with Ché Ahn," which is aired on God TV. He ministers extensively throughout the world, bringing apostolic wisdom with a Holy Spirit importation of revival, healing and evangelism. His greatest desire is to see society transformed through Christians who understand and fulfill their ordained purpose.

Ché and Sue have four adult children and two grandchildren. For more information about Ché Ahn, his ministries and his resource materials, visit www.hrockchurch.com, www.harvestim.org and www.wagnerleadership.org.